# STRESS

## SOURCES AND SOLUTIONS

# STRESS

## SOURCES AND SOLUTIONS

### GAIUS DAVIES

**CHRISTIAN FOCUS**

To Nest and for Catrin
in sure and certain hope

ISBN 1-84550-028-8

10 9 8 7 6 5 4 3 2 1

First published in 1988 and reprinted 1989, 1991, 1994, 1998 by
Kingsway Publications Ltd, Lottbridge Drove,
Eastborne, East Sussex, BN23 6NT

This edition published in 2005
by
Christian Focus Publications, Ltd.
Geanies House, Fearn, Ross-shire,
IV20 ITW, Scotland

www.christianfocus.com

Cover design by Alister MacInnes

Printed and bound by
Norhaven Paperback AS, Denmark

# Contents

# PART THREE
## Patterns of Breakdown

# PART FOUR
## Controverial Issues

# ACKNOWLEDGEMENTS

The question asked by the apostle Paul: 'What do you have that you did not receive?' (1 Cor. 4:7) is doubtless a rhetorical one. But in producing this book my answer is that I have received most of it from the good offices of others. Some may prefer not to be mentioned.

It was Miss Myra Chave-Jones who first persuaded me to speak for *Care and Counsel* on the Christian and emotional stress. She kindly suggested to a publisher that a book might be made out of it. The Rev Dr John Stott was kind enough to comment favourably on the tape-recording of the lecture, and encouraged me to proceed.

Dr Douglas Johnson asked me to review Dr William Sargant's view on conversion for the Christian Medical Fellowship's journal *In the Service of Medicine*. I am grateful to the editor for permission to use material published there, as well as material on demon possession which first appeared in that journal.

The London Medical Group asked for a lecture on faith healing, which appeared in the *Journal of Medical Ethics* as 'The Hands of the Healer: has faith a place?' I thank the editor for permission to use that material here.

My views on old age owe much to two years spent with Dr Felix Post, and in research on dementia and depression.

I am grateful for permission to quote from Dr D. Martyn Lloyd-Jones' lecture on 'The Doctor as Counsellor'. Dr Lloyd-Jones influenced me, as he did so many young doctors in training, and my debt to him is too great to assess: his influence, to the discerning eye, may be seen on many of the pages of this book.

I am grateful too for permission to quote from C. G. Jung's book *Psychological Types.*

Many friends have helped greatly at various stages. The Rev Emyr Roberts, my old editor in my salad days of journalistic forays in the Welsh *Cylchgrawn Efengylaidd*, has been an ever-ready source of advice and criticism. My colleague on the editorial board of that magazine, Dr Geraint Gruffydd, has read numerous draft chapters while they were being rewritten.

My eldest brother, Alun G. Davies, has helped frequently, not only by reading critically but by making suggestions for improvements. I am most grateful to him.

I am grateful to Mr Chris Porteous for reading and helping with a late draft.

Early drafts were typed by Mrs G. Hamblyn, and this thankless task was shared by colleagues at King's College Hospital.

I am particularly grateful to my wife, Nest, and my four children who have been prevailed upon to read numerous chapters and make critical suggestions.

Unsuspecting students and others who have had parts of chapters tried out on them deserve thanks for showing what was more interesting and for stimulating further thought and preparation on my part.

Those colleagues who advised me not to proceed will doubtless be glad to be proved right in their judgement that the task I tried was an impossible one. If, however, any Christian who reads it is helped to make use of all the resources available for coping with stress in a better way, then it will have served its purpose.

Dame Cicely Saunders and St Christopher's Hospice know that I and my family, like many others, owe a great debt for much help in time of need. The proceeds from the sale of this book go to St Christopher's as a way of thanking them, publicly, for so much good work that they do in helping families to cope with loss before, during and after it happens.

# FOREWORD

For more than a century following the momentous 1730s the dominant influence in British Christianity was that of the Evangelical Revival in its various forms. The teaching given – that of Whitefield, the Wesleys, Rowlands, Newton, Wilberforce, Simeon, Chalmers, McCheyne, Booth, Spurgeon, and even Pusey – had at its heart the 'three R's' of the gospel: ruin, redemption and regeneration. This teaching focused on grace rather than nature, and in its concentration on the need for personal conversion and a Christ-centred, self-denying, world-conquering piety it touched only lightly on the glories intrinsic to created things and on the Christian's task of redeeming this fallen world. This left culture in something of a vacuum, and by the end of the last century a British version of German liberalism, affirming man's natural goodness, passionate for social progress, and uninterested in individual conversion, had emerged to fill it. Evangelicals then drew battle lines, denouncing as devilish anything that reinforced the 'social gospel' and that played down the necessity of a new birth. As so often in Christian history, values were divided to the impoverishment of both sides. Evangelicals largely jettisoned community concern, and concentrated on the inner life with decreasing sensitivity to factors affecting that life from outside.

Against this background of tension, pressure, beleaguerment, and defiant self-sufficiency, it should not surprise us when the Freudian tidal wave swamped the West, Evangelicals, seeing Freud as an apparently sex-sodden Jewish atheist and Jung as an apostate Calvinist with seemingly Hindu leanings, did a Canute and forbade the whole movement of therapeutic psychology to come near them. They denounced it as a devilish ploy for distracting people who could not cope with life from facing their real need, namely to get right with God through being born again, and many in making this case painted themselves into the corner of claiming that no born-again believer should ever touch psychiatry with a barge-pole, since there is never any need to do so. Though we properly look to physicians to care for our bodies, have we not got Doctor Jesus to bring peace and poise to our souls? What more do we need? To turn to mind-doctors would show shameful lack of faith in Jesus' power, and we must not do it. Forty years ago, when I was a new believer cutting my Christian teeth, this was the common view: Christian psychiatrists, and Christians who consulted them, were felt to be an embarrassment, letting the side down by calling in question the adequacy of Christ, and American Christians were thought to be mildly mad, or at least deeply shallow, for not sharing British inhibitions at this point.

Today, things are different. The bearing of physical and relational factors on the state of the mind is better appreciated, Freudian psychotherapy and Jungian analytical psychology have been largely upstaged by 'medical-model' clinical psychiatry, depression has established itself as the commonest cause of visits to the doctors both sides of the Atlantic, and Christians who feel that their faith forbids them to see a psychiatrist are happily almost as rare as Christians who do not feel free to consult a physician. Yet an acrid haze of suspicion and uncertainty still hangs over psychiatry in many quarters, and efforts to dispel it are still needed. The way to dispel it is to show what, under God, psychiatry can actually do, and that is where books like this one come in.

Here Gaius Davies joins the ranks of John White, Richard Winter, Montague Barker, the late Martyn Lloyd-Jones, and other wise Christians with physician's training and pastor's instincts, who have taken time out to show where psychiatry and psychiatric counselling fit in. Dr Davies is coolly realistic about the temperamental and traumatic ills to which Christians, like others, fall victim, for he knows that Christians, like others, are psychological invalids at the best of times, the only difference being that by God's grace we are at the deepest level in the process of recovering, whereas strangers to grace are not. His treatment of stress and what the care of those under stress involves has about it a down-to-earth circumspection that may seem low-key but will be found very salutary. Overheated super-spirituality, fouling up the conscience by treating all psycho-physical strain as a symptom of sin, unbelief or demon-possession, still, alas, runs loose among us; this book, please God, will put salt on its tail – and none too soon. May these Christianly and professionally shrewd chapters find the ministry they merit.

J. I. PACKER

# INTRODUCTION

This book is not written for the wise and prudent – for them there are, already, dozens of books on stress. It is written to offer help to Christians in three ways. I would like to inform, to try to change attitudes, and to lead to some practical help in dealing with the burden of shame and guilt that many people have when it comes to admitting any kind of emotional disorder.

To many, a Christian writing about stress from the standpoint of psychiatry is a strange sight. I recall one of my teachers scorning the new kind of psychiatrist who had a Bible in one hand and some of Freud's works in the other. In the last twenty years, however, increasing numbers of committed Christians have been training in psychiatry and the allied caring professions.

The Association of Christians in Psychiatry is a sign of the developing interest in this area. Such Christians may have some of Freud's works in one hand, but they study them critically. Their interest in what Freud and others taught is balanced by their use of other modern therapeutic tools. They use medication where it is of use, and realise that total care means being aware of as many aspects of the person's needs as they can possibly deal with. For them psychotherapy includes newer, well-proven means of helping people through techniques which owe as much to learning theory as to psycho-analysis.

If medical and psychological means are one side of their interest, such Christians have, on the other hand, a wealth of belief and experience documented in their Bibles, in biography and in history. They belong to an honourable tradition of caring for those who sink under stresses of various kinds, and who need help.

They would wish for the same kind of motivation as that which drove Lord Shaftesbury to serve, for fifty years, as chairman of the British Commissioners in Lunacy. They, like him, would like to see reform and progress in the care of the emotionally and mentally disturbed today.

Why offer information? Because, just as wars are too important to be left to the generals, so caring cannot be left to the caring professions. Yet, to care for those with nervous breakdowns or chronic illnesses calls for some specialised knowledge. If we handle explosives without some basic information about dynamite, we may be hurt – and we may hurt others too.

Why change attitudes? Because some of the hostility expressed towards psychiatry and psychology is not justified. A handsome performer who had been described at a television recording in which we both took part as a pop-star turned evangelist, talked with me over coffee afterwards. I told him I was a Christian working in psychiatry. He responded at once with the remark: 'God does not want his people to see psychiatrists.' In vain I spoke of Martin Luther, John Bunyan, William Cowper and C. H. Spurgeon – all men who had been frank about the depression they had suffered. But he was adamant: no doctors of any kind were required, since God healed all his believing children directly and without any medical means being needed. Such an attitude of rejection of the need of human caring from doctors and others makes its special contribution to the load of shame and guilt which many feel about their own needs.

In my view, Christians are quite evidently not exempt from any of the common conflicts and problems which afflict all mankind. Indeed, Christians often experience extra stresses which may add to their sufferings as human beings. The Bible is plain: 'We must go through many hardships to enter the kingdom of God,' said the great leader of the early Christian church, the Apostle Paul (Acts 14:22). The many hardships and troubles included, for Paul, being harassed at every turn: 'conflicts on the outside, fears within' (2 Cor. 7:5).

Ignorance and prejudice may be essential parts of superstition, but they do not belong to a Christian religion worthy of the name. We should not judge and condemn those who suffer or break down under stress. Rather, we should seek to offer understanding and support. Our faith should work through love. When it does work we may be able to show, in many practical ways, that love and hope can be among the most powerful forms of help in giving courage to cope with stress.

Stress has been much studied: one vital conclusion concerns the importance of preserving a balance in our lives and in our minds if we are not to suffer harm.

It will be evident to anyone who reads this book that I am fanatically concerned to be moderate. I would like to do something to help to restore the Christian mind to its proper place in our lives as Christians. That mind, when it functions freely and strongly, enables us to look at what we do and feel, instead of letting us be pushed around by our experiences and our wayward emotions. The arguments I am trying to state in different ways in the following chapters are about helping ourselves, as Christians, to maintain a healthy balance, which in its turn makes it possible to cope in a better way with the many stresses which may come our way.

I believe there is such a thing as Christian sanity. It is possible to be a committed believer and to be normal and healthy in the way we cope with life's stresses. Perhaps the most unhelpful thing that modern psychology has done is to limit the idea of what is normal in a way that excludes many splendid people.

The wider our spectrum of normality, the more likely we are to understand our fellows, and to help them to cope successfully.

# PART ONE

## Stress and the Christian

# 1

## Emotional Stress and the Christian

In this world you will have trouble. But take heart!
I have overcome the world (John 16:33).

O the mind, mind has mountains; cliffs of fall
Frightful, sheer, no-man-fathomed. Hold them cheap
May who ne'er hung there.

Gerard Manley Hopkins

We are not, as Christian believers, exempt from any of the stresses that affect everyone else. Our faith is not a passport to freedom from pressures, either ancient or modern.

Elijah was not only 'a man of like passions' as ourselves, with the same nature as a modern man of faith, but also (it would seem) he had a typical depressive experience of going out and asking that he might die in the wilderness.

If we met Elijah under his juniper tree, or Jonah sitting under his gourd saying, 'It is better for me to die than to live,' would we recognise the plight of either of them? Their feeling of hopelessness and helplessness are seen in our modern day in different guises.

### The walking worried: are they being helped?

In the last world war it was customary to distinguish between those who were in need of hospital admission and those who were called 'the walking wounded'. A distinguished psychiatrist recently adapted this phrase to describe the 'walking worried': those who were in great need of help but who were not being actively treated or given proper care of any kind.

Many of us, as present-day Christians, do not know how to find care and counsel. When we feel intolerable pressures from anxiety or depression we sometimes long for someone to listen and to understand. At times, in seeking help in our Christian circles, we ask for bread and are given a stone. Our fellow believers sometimes make us feel that we should never have such difficulties.

The suggestion is sometimes made that our condition must be due to some secret sin. At other times we may be made to feel that we are not trusting God enough, and are letting the side down by feeling sad and anxious.

I think of one able young man who was depressed, and had a fear of being unable to stay in the room where lectures were given in his missionary training college. He went to see his family doctor with high hopes, since his GP was a Christian. He was disappointed that he was told to get up early and pray more: no proper diagnosis or treatment was offered. Later, proper treatment and time got him better, and he went happily to his work in Africa.

If friends and physicians fail us, it is a fact that many of us feel rather ashamed or guilty if the suggestion is made that we should see a psychiatrist. We may fear that our cherished faith might be attacked by a doctor or counsellor. We feel, rightly, that anyone who is not a Christian believer cannot begin to understand us. Early in my training I had a lesson which taught me some of the dangers of this approach.

A dear old lady was admitted to the ward with a mild

depressive illness. But the way she described her depression (which followed having a lump in the breast removed, a little earlier, in hospital) was to say she had lost her joy in the Lord, and that this must be her fault. I made the mistake of trying to help her by dealing first with her Christian experience. For instance, when she quoted some verse of Scripture or of a hymn, I would go on to a subsequent verse which would (as I hoped) reassure her and put her mind at rest. My best efforts as a rather amateur counsellor did not help. In her case there was a physical basis for her depression which needed to be treated first.

A good, non-Christian psychiatrist recognised her need for medication and treated her successfully. Her Christian minister was very helpful in persuading her to stay and accept treatment without any feeling of letting her church down. It was amusing but sad that because the minister had the same name as myself the lady was very suspicious of the possibility that he and I were in league to harm her.

A year later I met her at a follow-up clinic as I walked through the out-patients department. She talked to me, and gave me a gracious ticking-off for having tried to talk to her as a Christian!

I would nowadays be much more careful to stress that it is possible for us, by looking first and foremost at the Christian aspect of the problem, to miss the fact that someone we know may have physical and psychological problems that also need careful attention .

## Problems ancient and modern
Many Christians find it hard to accept that problems of extreme depression and anxiety can affect the most devout and disciplined of Christian believers. Because the problems go unrecognised, an illness may develop and breakdown may occur. The result may be an attempted suicide or, tragically, the patient may kill himself.

When I hear of a Christian who has attempted to harm himself, I ask myself: 'How long have the problems been concealed or untreated?' We know from careful studies from researchers that 93% of those who have committed suicide showed clear evidence of mental illness in the months before they killed themselves. We know also that such patients tell one or more of their contacts of their intention to kill themselves. But not all of those whom they meet are like the Samaritans, and many are unwilling to listen and offer help.

This is not a new problem: if we look back over two hundred years we may study the case of young William Cowper, who became sufficiently depressed to try and hang himself after taking morphia. He was thirty-two then, and his first attack may have been provoked by his fear of taking up a clerk's post in the House of Lords, as well as his frustrated love for his cousin. It was *after* his treatment for his first attack of illness that he became a Christian. But his faith did not prevent him from having four further attacks of depression before his death, aged sixty-nine, in 1800.

The writings of those two remarkable eighteenth-century friends, John Newton and William Cowper, illustrate the paradox that such an illness as Cowper's presents to many modern Christians. The parson who had been the captain of a slave-ship before he became ordained, and the sensitive, best-selling poet together wrote a volume of *Olney Hymns*. Many of these hymns are still sung today, and have helped millions of believers for two centuries. One of them, '*Amazing Grace*', is especially popular.

John Newton was no stranger to despair and anxiety in his own life. He was a great counsellor of others in his remarkable volumes of letters, such as *Cardiphonia*. Newton coped very well with his own problems, unlike Cowper. Newton could write such a clear statement of Christian experience as this:

The heirs of salvation,
I know from his word,
Through much tribulation
Must follow their Lord.

His love in times past
Forbids me to think
He'll leave me at last
In trouble to sink.

True enough: but how does this certainty of Newton's so admirably expressed, help us to understand Cowper's sense of sinking in unutterable despair and desolation?

Newton did much to help Cowper, and it is quite wrong to attribute, as some have done, the blame for Cowper's illnesses to his friend's theology or his pastoral care. The best care available at the time was given to Cowper by his friends. In spite of this loving and caring supervision, Cowper often felt that he was 'a stricken deer that left the herd long since': yet he never blamed the herd, or any of his friends in the church. But his last poem on the subject of a castaway recalls how a sailor had fallen overboard in the Atlantic. His companions tried to rescue him but finally the sailor drowned. Cowper muses on the story and finds that misery 'delights to trace its semblance in another's case'. In the last of eleven verses he writes:

No voice divine the storm allay'd
No light propitious shone;
When, snatch'd from all effectual aid
We perished, each alone:
But I beneath a rougher sea,
And 'whelmed in deeper gulphs than he.

I know few places where the false beliefs – the depressive delusions, as the clinical description calls them – are so movingly expressed.

Few of us, when we sing some of Cowper's hymns like 'God moves in a mysterious way,' recall the tragedy of the author's life. Yet his lasting achievements are undoubted. When we visit the Cowper museum in the village of Olney – only eight miles from the M1 motorway, and an hour or so from London – it is possible to sense, in the house where he spent many years of his life, the poignant succession of little joys and large sorrows that made up the life of William Cowper.

## What can modern medicine offer?

When I wandered around the village of Olney my mind turned to the question: What if modern medicine had been available to Cowper? Would he have suffered less, and produced more poems and hymns? Was Newton misguided in some of his views: too strict and limited in his approach?

The question, for me, was answered by the case of an old man of seventy who appeared in my consulting room, having been sent by his doctor, for help with a similar depressive illness to that of Cowper just before his death.

David, (for I got to know him well in the two years before he died) had an unusual complaint. He said: 'I can find no place of repentance.' I replied: 'Though you have sought it with tears.'

He seemed surprised that a psychiatrist should recognize his reference to the twelfth chapter of the letter to the Hebrews, but it established that we spoke the same language.

He believed he had committed the sin against the Holy Spirit. He argued that his local church had called him to be an elder and he had refused. He thought that in this case the voice of the people was the voice of God and therefore he was disobeying God – an unforgivable sin.

His wife had died the previous year after suffering, for a decade, from cancer, for which time he had cared for her. He was evidently in the throes of a grief reaction following bereavement, and was all alone in his home.

In addition, he had suffered a small heart attack and also, evidently, a slight stroke which had left him weak on his left side.

All this was confirmed during his period in hospital. He was given anti-depressants and his mood returned to normal and his beliefs about being damned and lost forever were replaced by his normal cautious optimism.

He remained well, though frail, for the next two years and felt his depression after his wife's death had led him to mis-interpret the Bible at important points.

First, in order to treat the whole person we must first listen to him. This means getting the facts, the history, set out systematically. Once David had given his story the diagnosis was obvious, and treatment followed with some success. A non-Christian doctor would have given the same basic care. Many do not receive this help because they are afraid to talk to a psychiatrist. They say: 'How can I talk to a non-Christian who does not share my faith and may in fact attack it?'

Secondly, a modern approach does not despise the role of medication and proper drug treatment. We are nowadays witnessing a massive reaction against medication with drugs. Much of this is welcome and we must all be glad if those who need other kinds of support are *not* just given tranquillisers simply to try and avoid the more thorough treatment and help which is needed. Nor should any patient feel ashamed of the need for medication, any more than a diabetic should feel guilty about needing insulin.

Thirdly, a team approach is usually needed for the full benefit to be felt by the patient. By this I mean that physical factors should be sought and treated in any emotional or mental illness. Social factors are often vital: David's stroke and his heart condition were better treated when his loneliness and his isolation were replaced by the warmth, kindness and the care given by his sister and her husband. Alas, much of this social support has to be arranged by social workers for other patients. Important in the caring team are the community nurses, the psychologists and others who make their contribution to each individual case as may be needed.

We must not, of course, say that modern psychological medicine is a cure-all or panacea. Far from it. But the team of workers in the field of mental health may do their part to offer a wide range of help. The old adage may be fulfilled in a modern setting: to cure, to comfort or to relieve.

## Must it be a Christian doctor?

In my experience the biggest single thing that stops a Christian believer from seeking help in his anxiety or depression is, quite simply, that he ( or, more often, she) will not see a non-Christian psychiatrist. Any therapist who is not a Christian is anathema to them. Why is this the case?

We need to go back to Sigmund Freud and his book on religion *The Future of an Illusion.* This work has recently been republished, although it obviously belongs to a period when Freud moved away from his proper field of study to write of civilization and its discontents. He saw religion as largely wish-fulfilment, and thought that it kept its adherents in a position of dependence more proper to infancy than to adult life.

The fact that many psychoanalysts were Jewish but had abandoned their faith has often been remarked upon. Critics from within psychiatry have been led to say that they have created a substitute faith which is not particularly scientific or in any sense demonstrably true.

In practice, some Freudian analysts have been very hostile to the Christian faith. But others, like E. H. Erikson, show a deep and sympathetic understanding of those, such as Martin Luther, who display both the virtues of faith and a struggle with depressive illness. The way some Freudian views on sex have been made popular have also led many to be suspicious of psychotherapy generally.

I believe clinical workers in psychological medicine can be different: they can respect the faith of their patient, *whatever it is*, and not feel impelled to criticise or attack it.

If there is an emergency, where urgent help is needed for acute anxiety, serious depression or behaviour that leads us to suspect some mental illness, then we may compare it to a surgical emergency. If I have an acute appendicitis, I want a competent surgeon and a surgical team, and I will consider his skill more important than whether he believes in God or not. Later on, if at the operation he has found something that is not appendicitis but is perhaps a form of cancer or a chronic colitis, the situation changes. I may need to talk to the surgeon about how I live my life or how I face death. Then his beliefs, his attitudes and what he expects to do for me will be more important than his skill in getting me through an emergency.

I would, therefore, urge those in need to accept emergency help. It can be life-saving, and it can also prevent much misery and distress. Medical help and psychological treatment *can* be offered in a way that does not affect the faith of the patient in a spiritual sense, though it may of course require that he has sufficient trust in his therapist to work with him in treatment.

A more difficult question concerns the faith of the counsellors. Are therapists as non-directive as they claim to be? Of course they are not. We will return to this subject in a chapter on counselling, but we must look at one point now: the doctor who seeks not to judge or condemn a patient may be sincere, but his own beliefs and values still greatly affect him. This is why, in training, a therapist is helped to look at himself very critically to try and know enough about himself (enough, that is, to *avoid* influencing his patient unwittingly). The person who tells me confidently, 'I counselled her about it,' frightens me because it sounds as though the person has been told off or reprimanded rather than understood or helped.

Dr D. M. Lloyd-Jones pointed out in a paper he gave to young doctors that it was the conscience of the patient that mattered, *not* the conscience of the counsellor. We must seek to understand what is troubling the patient's mind before we can help to bring relief. Advice and guidance should be used so sparingly as never to become habitual. It is the patient or client that has to come to a decision.

Christians working in psychiatry are still few, but their numbers are increasing. There are a number of Christian professors of psychiatry too, and their writings are as welcome as their opportunities for leadership. As old prejudices are overcome it is to be hoped that it will become easier to obtain care and counsel which is more acceptable to believers. But we must make one important proviso: if a Christian doctor is asked to collude in *not* looking at the problems brought to him *because* he shares the same beliefs then much good can be lost.

For it is possible to hold the faith in a childish and immature way, and not in a way which reflects growth in grace and development in belief and practice. If a therapist is asked to enter into an unspoken agreement to avoid looking at such matters, he must refuse and gently but firmly insist on being as open and honest as he can be about all aspects of the problems brought to him.

We have mentioned prejudices and the hostility to psychiatry that exists. It is worth while looking at how some of them have arisen and resulted in two opposing views, both of which seem to me unacceptable.

## Two equal and opposite errors

One group of leaders has tended to spiritualise everything, saying there are no problems of personality, no psychological factors to consider at all. This group will blame any problem that arises on lack of faith or on sin; alternatively, either God or the devil will be held responsible.

The opposite tendency showed by the other group is to psychologise everything without ever seeming to recognise that there are (and always have been) acute spiritual problems which have little to do with stress or personality problems. This group will seek to explain such things as conversion, prayer or any supernatural elements in religion by reducing them to psychological terms only.

*Dangers of psychologising*

An example of the second group, those who reduce all spiritual experience in the Christian faith to mere psychology, may be found in the way the new birth (described in John 3) is approached. There is a popular work offering a prescription for anxiety which appears to say that what we must do to be born again is to cut ourselves off from the dependent, immature relationship with our mothers, to sever the emotional umbilical cord. This is to substitute a Freudian view of the Oedipus complex for what our Lord clearly teaches. But it also evacuates the doctrine of the new birth of its content in the New Testament's rich teaching of it. There *are* immature folk, and perhaps we all need help with our problems in connection with our parents, but the classical teaching of the new creation in Christ and the new birth does not in any way help a man to resolve his difficulties with his mother. To mix up the two modes of thinking is wilfully to confuse and to mislead.

Many church leaders and writers of the last half-century have resembled weathercocks on church steeples: by their books and sermons you may tell which way the wind is blowing in popular psychology. They respond to the current fashions: the power of positive thinking, theories about birth trauma, bio-energetics – all is grist to their mills. And, alas, key Christian doctrines, words and beliefs become devalued and emptied of their original meaning as they are linked to unproved (and often unprovable) theories. It is as if each popular writer wishes to offer his own branded amalgam of Christianity and psychology. I consider that to try and offer a mixture of theology and psychiatry to people without proper training in either discipline has proved highly dangerous and misleading.

Anyone who has been through an adequate training will know how tentative and uncertain are most psychological theories: the more honest and scientific the study of them, the less dogmatic and sweeping will be the presentation of 'the assured results of modern psychological study.' One thinks of how two leading writers – Dr John Bowlby and Dr Benjamin Spock – have changed radically in their theories and teaching. No one should, in my view, attribute to any leader of psychological thought (Freud, Jung or Rank, let us say) the kind of authority which the Christian revelation claims. It is, of course, sadly true that followers of these leaders have revered their teaching as if they had discovered a new revelation of the truth about the human condition.

*Dangers of being too spiritual*

How are we to answer those who spiritualise everything? If someone tells me that doubt and despair are sinful, and that the absence of peace and joy means that I am not a true believer, I am tempted to ask them to read the book of Psalms, and then some biographies of Christians who have not been afraid to describe their 'bad' psychological experiences. I think of John Bunyan, Martin Luther and Charles Spurgeon. Have they not heard that a child of light may walk in darkness? There is clear Christian teaching that God permits trials and testings: any proper view of providence must account for the mysteries of suffering and affliction as sent or permitted by God.

My complaint about the spiritualisers is that they are not spiritual enough: their view of wholeness or holiness is inadequate, too narrow for the breadth of human life as the Bible sees it, and too superficial and glib for the deep mysteries which true Christians have, with pain and great distress, had to go through. I want to say to them with Gerard Manley Hopkins:

> O the mind, mind has mountains; cliffs of fall
> Frightful, sheer, no-man-fathomed. Hold them cheap
> May who ne'er hung there.

Perhaps those good and admirable friends who say much of saving grace should be more aware of other aspects of God's grace which have been traditionally much prized in Christian teaching. They should not abandon what is sometimes called God's general or common grace. They would then see that many things in life – such as law, order, education, medicine, the arts, science and such things as are conducive to an ordered family and social life – are in the light of common grace aspects of God's goodness.

It follows from such an understanding that to care for the mental and physical health of others (and of ourselves) is a necessary duty quite apart from sin and salvation. This wider view leads to things like a belief in our vocation, our secular calling, and being fully part of life as God's creatures.

To think highly of Christ and his gospel is, of course, a hallmark of the Christian believer. But we must never forget that 'we have this treasure in earthen vessels'. The churches have often been conspicuously lacking in their *care* for the earthen vessels. I hope it will be clear that it is my view that everyone has a certain duty to try to care – and that this duty can be urged on us simply as human beings, and much more so as believers.

For a number of reasons the earthly vessels do crack and break. The next section of this book therefore deals with some common patterns of breakdown, and some ways of coping with them and perhaps preventing them.

## 2

## WHY DO CHRISTIANS BREAK DOWN?

> Hast thou no scar?
> No hidden scar on foot, or side, or hand?
> ... can he have followed far
> Who has no wound or scar?
>
> Amy Carmichael, *Gold Cord*

No one is exempt from the bad effects of stress.

Some of us are more vulnerable than others. Many who seem, at first sight, to be able to cope with large issues and big problems may yet break down. What looks to others like a small failure or rejection may lead to profound depression and a nervous breakdown. The hero in one field of battle may have his Achilles heel. A small weakness, in a stress situation for which he is unprepared and unprotected, may be the point of entry for destructive strains which may hurt badly or even kill.

Success may also spoil or lead to disaster. When an ambition has been achieved, boredom may follow and risks may be taken. To take risks with money, sexual relationships, alcohol or other drugs has often been seen, after the crash, to have been an attempt to stave off the kind of depression that often follows successful achievement. Sometimes the hard work and the long haul have meant breaking the rules of health and of a balanced life. The 'workaholic', perhaps more than anyone, shows this point clearly. He is praised for his commitment to work, and no one notices that he is paying the price of avoiding leisure, recreation and proper rest.

The work ethic of some Christians does scant justice to the built-in human needs for a balanced life. I have to remind some Christians of the Sabbath principle, the need for rest – to come apart and rest awhile. Their Sundays are busier than their weekdays, and they wonder that tiredness and irritability are what their Monday-morning colleagues see instead of peace and joy in believing!

## Shared stresses

If there is no exemption afforded to Christians for their faith, no remission for good conduct, then we may look at any period of life and expect to find believers just as liable to break down as those without faith. In childhood, problems of separation and its accompanying anxieties frequently lead to symptoms of physical distress or to school phobia.

In adolescence, hormonal, social and emotional pressures may all contribute to a host of problems that may lead to breakdown. Anorexia nervosa is only one serious example of how stresses may combine to produce illness at this time. Sexual problems in courtship, marriage and having children all make for critical periods in our lives.

The middle years bring their own 'mid-life crises'. Problems that have been postponed from childhood and early life sometimes hit us with devastating effects at this time. Work and money, careers and relationships both in and out of home, may all lead to anxieties which end in breakdown. Personality problems may only emerge properly in these middle years. Facing up to them is often depressing and requires major changes. Going through a breakdown may be one way of making much-needed adjustments. Many biographies bear witness to this.

It is said that we get more like ourselves as we get older. The strains of ageing may lead to serious crises too, and these may call for urgent help. Some of these crises are described in later chapters.

We like to think of past saints and heroes as free of stress and more than conquerors. The facts are otherwise. Even in the gospels we read of disciples full of envy and jealousy, jostling for first place.

The letters to young churches show breakdowns in behaviour causing scandal. These New Testament accounts, like those in the Old Testament, show honestly the falls as much as the triumphs.

The lives of Christians of other ages are a fascinating study. They show, among many other things, that those who have gone before us were never wholly free from strain and stress. The breakdowns that the heroes of the faith have suffered result in honourable scars.

## Special stresses for Christians

I think it is clear that Christians are, in addition to all the stresses that they share throughout their lives with everyone else, subject to others peculiar to the Christian lifestyle. This, of course, is not the popular view.

Many hymns suggest that we should hope for undiluted joy and peace. Consider the words of a much-loved hymn by the Quaker, J. G. Whittier, which begins:

> Dear Lord and Father of mankind,
> Forgive our foolish ways.

Its crucial verse runs thus:

> Drop Thy still dews of quietness,
> Till all our strivings cease;
> Take from our souls the strain and stress,
> And let our ordered lives confess
> The beauty of thy peace.

Ordered lives may certainly be prayed for, but should we ever expect the conflict and striving which the Bible describes as part of the fight of faith (and indeed of life itself) to be taken from us? I think not, and I turn from Whittier's passive quiet hope to the teaching of the New Testament.

The healthier view – much more true to life – is given by the Apostles Paul and Barnabas at Antioch, the place where the disciples were first called Christians. They were told: 'We must go through many hardships to enter the kingdom of God' (Acts 14:22). Later Paul describes how he was harassed by 'conflicts on the outside, fears within' (2 Cor. 7:5).

What are these extra stresses which, far from being taken out of our lives, are put into them by the mere fact of our being Christians? They have been grouped, from the earliest Christian times, into three kinds of conflict: we promise to fight manfully against the world, the flesh and the devil when we become Christians. What do these terms mean today, and how do they add to the strain and stress of being a Christian in the modern world?

Each presents an aspect of the challenge of an 'impossible ethic'. We will consider each in turn.

*The world*

There was a time when to call a Christian 'worldly' was a severe criticism. Why? Basically the world is good – God's world – but 'the world' is also an expression of that whole human organization which, through sin, is against God and also against our own best interests. In this sense Jesus tells his disciples that they are not of the world and they will be hated by the world. We are called, as Christians, to be in the world but not of it.

The Christian, trying to be loyal to his new nature, finds himself in conflict with the world at every turn. Yet he must try not to become paranoid. Those who oppose and persecute the

Christian do so, often, because they are blind to the truths which matter most to him. It goes deeper than misunderstanding; the enmity is a deep spiritual one.

There are two strands in the history of worldliness. The first is separatist or Puritan. Such people as the Quakers argue, perhaps rightly, that Christians sometimes have to dress differently, or show in clear ways that fashions and 'the thing to do' do not control them. All Christian ascetics, of whatever tradition, share this view. There is a great deal to be said for being different, because we *are*, as Christians, different in essential respects and it is bound to show. We can all, however, think of ways that being separate has become a caricature rather than a true picture.

The other strand says that we must immerse ourselves in the world, however much evil there is in it. It remains God's world even though it is so affected by evil. We must be lights in it and we must be salt to inhibit the corruption in it. We cannot influence the world if we are hermetically sealed away from everything in it that we dislike.

Some of us, Puritan by either nature or grace, need to learn from those Christian friends who point out that we must play our full part in worldly affairs if we are to be effective witnesses. Those of us who have a cavalier attitude to the world may learn from the dissenting, separatist tradition that we should be careful without being scrupulous.

## The flesh

How easy it is to misunderstand this word, and miss the Christian meaning. It does not imply that our bodies are sinful, or that sex or other desires are wrong in themselves. That way lies heresy into which many, such as the young St Augustine, may easily fall. Flesh, in the special sense that we have to fight it, means those things in our human natures which are alien to our best interests. The works of the flesh, like its fruits, are clearly described by our Lord and by the Apostle Paul (Matt. 15:19 and Gal. 5:19-21).

Even those who never use such Christian language speak of our lower natures, and accept that there is a conflict between flesh and spirit in all of us to some degree. Christians believe that this conflict becomes sharper and more severe as we grow in spiritual awareness. Thus:

> And they who fain would serve Thee best
> Are conscious most of wrong within.
>
> *Henry Twells*

An aspect of this conflict, described so well by Paul in Romans 7, leads him to write: 'What a wretched man I am! Who will rescue me from this body of death?' (Rom. 7:24).

Many, many stresses arise from this awareness of our sinful nature. We struggle to deny its demands to live a better life, delighting in God's law and living it out. Paul describes this as dying daily and living a life empowered by Christ's own resurrection life – living in his Spirit. Such words may sound far-fetched to many, but a deeper understanding of what the struggle with the flesh is all about enables us first to make sense of much that is a problem in our lives. To cope with the flesh is to fight successfully against its demands. In that fight we often fall, though we should never be utterly cast down. Some casualties in the struggle may be wrongly thought to be having a nervous breakdown when, for them, some severe distress is a necessary part of their Christian warfare.

*The wiles of the devil*

We have seen a great resurgence of interest in the devil, and it is not all healthy, as films like *The Exorcist* and books of the same kind show. Yet earlier Christians were not ignorant of the devices of the devil, though they sensationalised them less perhaps.

I will try to show how illness can mimic demonic possession in a later chapter. I believe we must not oversimplify and reduce our spiritual warfare to demon hunting and exorcism. Nor must we put all the badness in ourselves 'out there' in some demonic agency which we cannot control. We should never abdicate our own responsibilities, but deal with what is in our power to deal with, relying at the same time on prayer and the power of the Spirit in all the underlying conflicts.

A middle aged lady was slowly getting better in hospital after a serious depression with suicidal and homicidal anxieties. She told me, with a triumphant air, that her church minister had told her it was all 'an attack of the enemy'. I knew that the same minister had asked me to treat her medically: it was our plain duty.

There was, of course, no clash in my mind between giving proper medical care on one hand, and recognising the profound spiritual crisis she was going through, on the other hand.

I am certain that we should not yield to ideas of the demonic which, in practice, mean turning away from sound knowledge. When we do lose our spiritual common sense, we may lose our power to help others in a practical way.

A young man was sent to me with a history of bad deprivation and disadvantage in early life. The Christian doctor who sent him knew all about it. I was distressed to learn that the local house church had decided to exorcise 'the demon of asthma' from him. I thought such conduct inexcusable. Not unexpectedly, the next chapter in his history was that he tried to cut his throat. A proper, sympathetic understanding had been given up by his Christian friends for what was little less than a return to magic, rather than a proper Christian compassion and insight.

I fear that such examples of confused thinking may be multiplied. It is vital to provide balanced and wise teaching about the wiles of the devil today. Discernment is a gift which should be coveted by us all to avoid becoming fashionably involved with a return to the darkness of the Middle Ages. We should not give up hard-won wisdom for slick slogans.

## Breakdowns

What is a nervous breakdown? We usually mean that a person is suffering from symptoms of anxiety, distress or depression. These are so severe that they cannot work, or even function at home, and they withdraw from the normal demands of life. All this may be so obvious that a doctor or counsellor or hospital may be sought to provide professional help.

The more serious breakdown, where contact with reality is lost, is usually a psychosis. Hearing voices and having strange beliefs or experiences are common features. The majority of breakdowns are less severe, but such neurotic breakdowns still cause great misery, which may well be hidden.

When a car breaks down, we trust the trained mechanic and the good garage. We dread the bill, but feel fairly sure things can be put right. The mechanic knows how the car is made, how it should run, and what goes wrong. He has a maker's manual, and may also have been to the factory where the car was built. His garage often has a diagnostic centre – hidden faults may be detected. The wise mechanic often bluntly tells us what we have been doing wrong as car owners, blaming us for the breakdown.

Of course, cars are not human, and doctors, psychologists and other health-care workers are not merely mechanics. But there are similarities. Doctors and psychologists do not simply see the ill or the insane, they also learn a lot about normal human functioning. That is, they are taught much of value about how our bodies and minds work, how to think straight, how our relationships matter, and how bonds form in human life. These all form a large verifiable body of knowledge. The best of it does not contradict the knowledge revealed in that other maker's manual – the Bible.

Doctors disagree, as do Christian expositors, but on many essential matters there is surprising agreement. All care workers have a clear aim: they want to help the person recover from his breakdown, and do everything to promote this. We want the person, like the car, to be back on the road again and going well.

But what is it to go well and to be normal? In this fallen world no one is 100% normal. I know of no satisfactory definition of 'normality', and believe we are wise to accept a broad spectrum of human experience as normal.

Most people call the sort of behaviour that they cannot understand, crazy. But I think we should try to understand as much as we can, and accept wide differences. The last thing we should do is describe a narrow stereotype as normal. That way lies the production of sausages, though they may be stamped as Christian sausages. They are all too familiar: people who try to conform, flatten out their quirks of character, and change their accents to be acceptable by their group. We should never forget that our essential individuality is given to us by God. To become ever more full *ourselves* is one of the most vital things that God's grace can enable us to achieve.

### Grace and personality

'But we have this treasure in jars of clay' (2 Cor. 4:7). This reminds us that we live our Christian life in a very ordinary human setting. A clay jar needs looking after, and I am amazed how often we neglect our physical and emotional needs which belong to the integrity of that clay jar. God's grace has made us 'new creations', but we must not neglect our common lot.

We all have to live our lives with what our parents and our upbringing have given us. We will look, in later chapters, at how depression runs in families – blue genes, as one wit called them. It is a *tendency* that we inherit most of the time, not a disease as such.

How hard it is, sometimes, to accept the basic data – what we have been *given* to work with in our lives. A child may grow to realize that a bad temper, or a certain moodiness, is something shared with an aunt or a grandfather. For a young adult facing life alone, the equipment he has to cope with in facing the stresses that will come his way is the raw material of what his parents and his educators have made him. At times, his background and its legacy of temperament can be used positively. At other times, rebellion and kicking over the traces is a proper thing to do. Many a girl has decided that the one thing she will not do is resemble her mother, and she will do anything she can to avoid it. God's grace, I believe, can use many such reactions for good. It is important to know that there is no blind necessity, no cruel fate, which determines our life's pattern. We can, I think, adopt and Christianise W. E. Henley's poem 'Invictus' which ends:

> I am the Master of my fate,
> I am the captain of my soul.

Grace enables us to be much more the masters of our fate and the captains of our souls. Grace, as Gerard Manley Hopkins put it, 'Keeps all his goings graces'.

## Achieving a balance

Breakdowns may sometimes best be seen as a temporary loss of emotional or mental balance. We walk along a very narrow path, and it is easy to slip off, and sometimes fall precipitously. Having come to terms with his family and upbringing, the young Christian finds himself a new member of God's family in the church. This opens up new pressures that may be very stressful. I think, especially, of problems that a group may present, made worse if the leader is legalistic and authoritarian. Trying to conform to a tight set of rules (some of the most important ones often unwritten) may cause much distress, and even breakdowns. People can be made to feel failures and that they are beyond the pale.

I once read a warning from an American psychologist to his students. Think, he said, of being attached as aptitude testers to an army base camp in the Sinai desert. A young man is brought in with a severe stammer, and he has a history of being a bit of a psychopath who covered up a killing which he once performed in a temper. The details of his birth and upbringing are uncertain, with stories of being found in a river and being brought up at court. He also reports strange sights in the desert: a burning bush and a voice speaking to him. Would the staff psychologist have recognized Moses, or failed him in all the tests?

Nearer to our own day, what would we have made of two young men in their early failures: John Wesley and Martin Luther? Luther, failing to find peace, crippled with obsessions, has a fit in the choir at his first mass. Yet he goes on to find a faith which sustained him through many serious nervous illnesses.

Was Wesley, sent back home from Georgia after failures to cope with his work as a missionary and his affair of the heart, suffering from a depression? Yet, as every Methodist knows, he found an experience in Aldersgate Street where Luther's *Preface to Romans* was being read which made him feel his heart strangely warmed. His assurance of salvation led to a long life of service to God and man.

Many such men are pressured by the system in which they have been brought up. They have to find out for themselves how Christ can provide a personal answer to their problems, and they have to discover a new relationship which makes their attitudes to the pressures of life quite different from what they were before.

The balance we need is not just in looking after our minds and bodies. We also need a balance in mind, heart and will. Of course, we cannot neglect knowing Christian doctrine, but belief must be held in tension with experience. If we trust in Christ, love him, and have peace in him we are bound to feel this. That is why some of our forebears spoke of a 'felt Christ'. But a proper balance is not possible without the will too. We trust in order to obey: faith has to become a matter of action.

So often, a neglect of obedience (or flagrant disobedience) leads to breakdown and despair. Where there are friends who supplement a Christian ministry that feeds the mind, warms the heart, and commands the will to obedience, it is possible to have a balanced spiritual life that makes coping with stress easier. Dry doctrine will not help in itself. Thrills and ecstasies alone may be just as dangerous. And morality tinged with emotion alone will not be enough to enable us to cope. Only a full and balanced spiritual life can really provide the resources we all need. With them, no tribulation or trial need prove finally insurmountable, however difficult the process of enduring it all may be.

# 3

## Why Worry?
## Some Patterns of Anxiety

Therefore I tell you, do not worry about your life,
what you will eat or drink; or about your body, what
you will wear .... Who of you by worrying can add a
single hour to his life? (Matt. 6: 25, 27).

Besides everything else, I face daily the pressure of
my concern for all the churches (2 Cor. 11:28).

'It's so wicked to worry, isn't it? Jesus said so in the Sermon on
the Mount, and I read it in a medical book too.' The old lady
who was telling me this was twisting her hands, and her face
was screwed up with worry. It is sad that this was her
conclusion after reading a book which was meant to set her
mind at ease. It is, alas, common for those with a religious faith
to blame themselves for being anxious for any reason.

It is important to be able to worry in a way that is useful, for
fear and anxiety can have a positive role. Worry is really about
being afraid and there are times when it is life-saving to be afraid.
None of us would survive life's dangers without some anxiety –
it is part of a built-in signalling system which alerts body and
mind to be thoroughly aroused to meet an emergency. If a car

driver notices the white line in the middle of the road, he will be anxious to stay on his own side of the road, or else he will be taking risks and courting disaster. A *proper* anxiety about the elements of life, such as water and fire, might have averted many tragedies.

No kind of breakdown need follow normal anxiety, but the question is: When is it all right to worry? I would answer that worry is right when it is relevant to the circumstances and leads to appropriate action by the anxious person. It then fulfils its function, and though it may cause symptoms such as a thumping of the heart, these symptoms are not unpleasant and they meet a need for extra performance of some kind.

## Anxiety symptoms

Morbid anxiety – the 'wicked worry' of which my patient spoke – is simply normal anxiety that has got out of hand. The physical symptoms, the behaviour and the thoughts and feelings of an anxiety state may be impossible to distinguish from what anyone may feel in an 'emergency situation'.

Our bodies tell us that we are anxious by any of the following symptoms: tension headache, thumping heart, sweating, feeling sick, a churning stomach, a dry mouth, a weaker voice. Tension may cause frowning, backache, weak legs, clenched jaw and hands, hunched shoulders and stiff neck. Trembling, fidgeting, some problems with swallowing or breathing may all be other physical effects of anxiety.

All these symptoms may be welcomed by an athlete at the beginning of a race, because he knows that as the adrenalin flows he will run faster. Indeed, I have heard good athletes say that they conjure up in their minds a picture of a car crashing with their family in it, in order to produce this alarm/arousal reaction which they find improves their performance. An actress who does not have any butterflies may find she doesn't perform so well. But in a difficult interview, or an oral examination, a candidate who is made to feel anxious will find his mind going blank in addition to some of the other bodily symptoms.

It is a law, almost, that without a little anxiety no task is done that requires effort and is worth while. The same anxiety rises like a parabolic curve to an optimum where performance is at its best because the anxiety is manageable. The same curve descends (like an inverted 'U' shape) with further increase in anxiety, until with really high anxiety levels nothing can be done.

If this curve linking anxiety to performance is borne in mind, then the important thing is to keep worry within limits that enable us to perform at our best level. Anxiety, thus, as Henry V put it in his speech before Agincourt, enables us when required to:

> Imitate the action of the tiger;
> Stiffen the sinews, summon up the blood.

But if you have to feel like that before you can get into the supermarket, then you may have agoraphobia! Before a battle of any kind you need the anxiety, but you must try to get rid of it if it causes you to run away from a situation or a thing that you fear, or leads you to constantly avoiding it.

## Coping with anxiety

If anxiety cannot be handled it may lead to five kinds of problems: phobias, obsessions, hysterical symptoms, withdrawal into oneself, or frank depression. These will be looked at in turn and coping strategies will be described. But first it is worth describing ways in which *any* anxiety may be coped with in the hope that the complications may thus be prevented.

### *Special phobias*

Phobic anxiety may be one of the most disabling forms of the disorders which morbid anxiety brings in its train. At least some of the phobic responses seem to be inborn in the human infant:

certain shapes, noises, heights. But most phobias are learnt fears: they may be of animals (snakes, spiders, dogs), of situations (agoraphobia, claustrophobia), and of illness (hypochondria).

A spider phobia in a young wife prevented her from going on exciting geological expeditions with her husband, since these required her to sleep in a tent in countries where large spiders might appear. In this published case her treatment simply consisted of graded, prolonged exposure over ten hour-long sessions. During these the doctor would first talk of spiders, then bring a spider in a perspex case, and in later sessions allow the spider on the desk. The woman's anxiety was gradually lowered until she was able to handle the spiders with only slight anxiety during the last few sessions.

This method is sometimes called flooding or implosion, since high levels of anxiety are encouraged and experienced by the patient. The treatment (when it works) seems to result in the patient's anxiety response being extinguished; or perhaps the patient gets used to it, inured by a process of habituation.

A woman may be housebound due to agoraphobia. After a proper assessment of the condition much help may be derived by the flooding procedure: ninety minutes on several occasions with a therapist in a department store, for instance. While moving around in the crowd many of the physical symptoms (like sweating, faintness, palpitations) will be severe and then wear off as the patient becomes accustomed to the situation. But, of course, such a phobia is not as simple to cure as, for example, an animal phobia. There are frequent complications in the family, marital, social and sexual life of such sufferers. They have to be patiently disentangled with a team of medical, psychological and social work experts doing their part, with the additional help of nurse therapists.

A particular case may illustrate the complications of a phobic anxiety state of long standing. After twenty years of suffering a patient described to me recently how successful his treatment had been. In his case he had been unable to drive his car without a pill box in his pocket containing sedatives and tranquillisers. He had found two drugs which eased his anxiety – barbiturates and alcohol. He had known the horrors of being dependent on both. Yet his panic attacks still came. With much help in talking over his problems, and the kind of behaviour therapy described already, exposing himself gradually to more and more situations that were fraught with anxiety, he improved. Medication of an intensive kind was needed, both for his depression and his anxiety. Now he could look back over a year and feel pleased that he needed no pills or alcohol and no visits to the doctor or psychologist to live as he wished. He had driven abroad for the first time in twenty years and his married life was back to normal.

Had we but world enough and time, there are many such cases of phobias complicated by depression and affecting many lives adversely which might be helped. But lack of interest as well as of motivation (and perhaps ignorance and impatience) leave many thousands whose lives are as Macbeth says, 'cabin'd, cribb'd, confined, bound in to saucy doubts and fears'. It is no wonder that many form themselves into self-help groups like the Open Door association for agoraphobics.

*On becoming hysterical*

Hysterics today are not what they were. Women seldom have the vapours, and men do not have the equivalent of shell-shock. For a substantial number of sufferers, anxiety does not lead to panic and running away as in the phobic response to stress. The hysterical response to stress is, instead of avoidance, twofold: (a) anxiety may be removed from awareness and changed into a physical symptom; or (b) awareness may become split up by a process of dissociation of consciousness. The forms that these two varieties of hysterical symptoms may take are legion.

You do not have to be a hysterical personality to have a hysterical symptom, though it may make it easier if you are. The personality structure is described later on: here the point of importance is that a sufficient stress may lead to loss of power in a limb, as in a soldier who is terrified of leaving the shelter of his dug-out. Any part of the body may be involved in the 'mysterious leap from mind to body'. Blindness, loss of voice, pain of all sorts, loss of memory or loss of feeling in hand or leg, all may have a hysterical basis. Why does it happen? Is it done for gain? Yes, usually the patient is getting some substantial pay-off of which he is not, normally, fully aware. He is obtaining through his symptom, attention and affection which we all, surely, need and seek – though by less elaborate means. Dr Andrew Smith put it elegantly when he said that Robinson Crusoe was not likely to develop hysterical symptoms on his desert island, at least not until Man Friday appeared. There is no clinic or hospital which has not seen stress resulting in hysterical symptoms, and it takes great skill and ingenuity at times to prove, for instance, that a fit is hysterical and not epileptic.

But this should not be equated with malingering because the hysterical symptom is unconsciously determined and the malingerer, on the contrary, is fully, deliberately and consciously aware that he is pretending to be ill when he is not. It is wiser to agree that most of us make our appearance on a continuous line of 'illness-experience' that has hysterics at one end and feigning illness at the other. Which of us has not, from childhood to late life, exaggerated or protracted a symptom to escape school or duty? But the so-called Munchausen patient who presents himself in hospital seeking attention for feigned symptoms is surely an example where both elements have flowered in a most unusual form of personality problem.

The second type of hysterical response leads to the so-called split personality. R. L. Stevenson described a fictional form in

*Dr Jekyll and Mr Hyde*. Earlier Dr Morton Prince had described a woman with three apparently distinct personalities: what happens is that a part of the self becomes split off from the rest and appears to act differently. It is a theme which is historically of the greatest interest. Many trance states occur under stresses which are often socially sanctioned, as in religious rites. Everyone has, to some degree, the capacity to live their lives in different compartments: he may be a saint abroad and a devil at home. Or, contrariwise, a man may live one kind of life in business and may assume an entirely different personality upon turning his front-door key. What are we to say of the Mafia godfather who loves his family with devotion and kills without scruple?

There are, undoubtedly, forms of possession in religious experience which are examples of hysterical dissociation: the person in a state of trance assumes a different voice and character. It may be that some cult priests become 'professional hysterics' in the service of their society and its rites. Some such capacity to split up one's mind, its thinking and feeling, may lead to ecstatic experiences of 'possession'. I have often wondered what St Paul meant in this connection by 'the spirits of the prophet are subject to the prophets': it is clearly linked to his statement that peace, not confusion, should result from such prophetic possession.

*Epidemic hysteria*
At times hysterical responses take on epidemic forms. Beatle-mania and other pop-group hysteria is well known. It seems that other epidemics occur in small communities such as school, where a strong personality may show an illness which weaker and more suggestible people imitate. In the Middle Ages a bishop would isolate a monastery or convent where hysterical illnesses were found, to prevent the infectious and contagious symptoms running riot. A well-documented account of

epidemic hysteria (with both possession of a dissociative kind any many physical symptoms also) was in the case of the witches of Salem in the Bay of Massachusetts in 1692. The story has been recounted in Miller's play *The Crucible*. Those who wish to study a good account of how this witch-hunting epidemic came about should read it in Professor J. K. Wing's book *Reasoning about Madness*. Two recent studies of the parish documents of the time reveal a sad tragedy of nineteen 'witches' hanged and one hundred suspects jailed before the governor called a halt. The tragedy is played out against a background of quarrels between two influential families and a church struggle between an independent covenanted church and other churches. The four young women who were 'possessed' first were linked: a negro servant, the daughter of the parish minister and her cousin, and the twelve-year-old daughter of a wealthy family which had not lost its former influence. In some ways the most tragic event may have been when the perplexed local doctor handed the afflicted girls over to the local church minister. The women involved acquired great power, with excitement and attention as reward for their performances.

It is important to learn about the relevance of hysteria to such cases of possession. Sadly, tragedies are not limited to 1692. A few years ago a man killed his wife in Yorkshire after an all-night exorcising service. In 1980 in London, a woman died when two men with more zeal than knowledge used excessive force in, as they thought, exorcising her of demonic forces which they described (at their trial for manslaughter) as appearing in a black shape from the dying woman's body. These things ought not so to be, and it seems to me that increased knowledge of the peculiar religious stresses to which some are ignorantly subject might avert further tragedies. Firm guidance unequivocably given might stop the epidemic spread of hysterical symptoms through excessive religious enthusiasms.

*Obsessional anxiety*
While hysterical symptoms appear to be due to loss of control under stress, with consequent striking symptoms, the obsessional response to stress is very different. Here concern with control dominates the picture. Obsessional states may occur in anyone under severe stress, and in childhood it is normal to feel enormous control of things, for example, by not stepping on cracks in the pavement. Dr Johnson, of dictionary fame, had long-lasting symptoms like having to touch railings as he walked around London. He also had, until his 'late conversion', a long-lasting obsessional fear of death.

Some obsessional states occur because of brain disease and others because of underlying depressive illness. Obsessive-compulsive neurosis merits a brief description because of its great interest. It is the most severe kind of obsessional state.

A young adult or adolescent may develop an intense fear of dirt (associated sometimes with sexual problems) or an acute anxiety about aggressive feelings. One mild civil servant of almost forty had, twenty years earlier, been frightened by his urge to drop his baby brother head first on the floor when his mother had asked him to hold him for her. He began in the next months to check his hair and his clothes repeatedly and to wash in a ritualistic repetitive way. After a long history he responded to treatment which involved flooding his life with the kind of dirt-fears he most hated and then preventing him from carrying out his rituals.

An obsessional thought is a common problem, as for young Luther who wanted to blaspheme in the sanctuary. Any such thought is felt to be alien or silly, yet though resisted it cannot be kept out of the person's mind. It is often associated with a compulsive act, similarly resisted and then yielded to by the sufferer. The thoughts are often of a religious kind or about the meaning of life or God's will for them. The intense inner anxiety is often made less by pursuing a repetitive ritual of a kind which makes the level of inner stress bearable by transferring it to an outside procedure. We are not, here, considering the person who is punctual, very careful with money and scrupulously clean – such a person may be rigid and yet, within limits, may be free of symptoms. The behaviour and symptoms are different from the apparently similar obsessional personality, mainly because the former is happy with his lifestyle while the neurotic is far from happy.

The two remaining reactions to stressful anxiety are the withdrawn behaviour (sometimes called schizoid) and the depressive reaction. Both of these call for separate chapters.

For the successful treatment of most forms of anxiety, to understand how it affects each one of us is a big step to learning to cope with it. Learning is the essence of modern treatment.

# PART TWO

# EVERYDAY
# PROBLEMS

# 4

## STRESS AND DISTRESS: HOW TO HELP YOURSELF

I have learned the secret of being content in any and every situation (Phil. 4:12).

In this chapter we will look at ways in which stress becomes harmful to us. We may, by learning which organs are most susceptible to negative effects of stress, do much to help ourselves. We will see ways of looking at life's threatening effects to help in this process. We will also look at some ways of relaxing and meditating, as well as the importance of active methods, like being assertive, in the coping process.

### Good and bad stress

Stress is made up of any pressure from the outside world that can cause us to feel an inward sense of strain. One man's stress may be great fun for him, but it may kill another man. Think of the surf-rider and how much he enjoys coming in on those huge waves. With skill and pleasure he pits himself against the elemental forces driving the water. Another man, not even trying to take such risks, may be drowned by the same water, and sometimes by the same tide.

There has never been an age without stress, although we like to imagine a bygone age as idyllic. Today in our modern world the sheer pace of life means that we pass through many rapid changes. New kinds of epidemic, such as some heart diseases, result from the new social and economic pressures upon us. There are many such stress-related disorders.

The most interesting question in some ways is: Why don't we all develop a stress illness? For not everyone under pressure gets ill, or has a breakdown in his family or married life. Large numbers, in fact, never have a breakdown in health, in spite of all the stresses and strains. At the other extreme, a few of us develop a sense of strain which is out of all proportion to the small stress which, we feel, may have caused it.

How can we explain it all? Let us examine why some information about stress may help us to take a detailed look at our lives. We may find out that we can correct some things that may have been going wrong with the way we manage life's stresses.

## Shock and delayed shock

Once upon a time we spoke of how we might receive 'a shock to the system'. First-aid books taught us how to treat for shock. This was a way of saying that a disaster – or simply news of a disaster – might produce marked physical effects. Shock might cause a fainting fit, a dry mouth, a fast pulse, or a pounding heart. Being sick with fear might cause us to vomit, or lose control of other bodily functions. Sometimes shock results in a feeling that everything is going to pieces, and calls for immediate help.

*Delayed shock* used to be the way we spoke of the strange fact that many of us develop such serious symptoms as these, not immediately, but days or weeks after the news that shocked us was received. A delayed reaction of a physical or nervous collapse is common. Even without such a collapse, there may often be a period of inability to do those things at home and work which would usually be done without effort.

## Fight and flight

One of the first steps in making these matters clear was the discovery of adrenaline. Two tiny glands above the kidneys – the adrenals – were shown to be part of a complex process. When danger threatens, this fact is signalled via the brain and the pituitary gland to the adrenals. They produce more adrenaline, which enters the bloodstream immediately, thus helping the body's forces to be quickly mobilised to respond urgently.

Our body's internal environment – a kind of micro-climate, vital to our well-being – will undergo a disturbance with any storm or threat of one. If a danger to our safety appears, the bodily changes enable us either to stand our ground and fight, or else get away from the danger. The aim of these responses is to help us to restore, as quickly as we can, our previous state of body and mind, and to regain for ourselves a harmonious balance.

## Stress: 1953 Selye type

It was in Montreal in 1953 that Dr Hans Selye began to publish news of his many studies into what he called *le stresse*. He has gone on (and hundreds of researchers after him) to show that stress is a much more complicated matter than it had ever been thought to be. Consider an all too common example: a man in a good job who loses both his employment and the security that went with it.

John has spent fifteen years working in a firm that makes shirts. He has been promoted regularly and is now in a good position in middle management. With the economic recession he hears of cut-backs. He notices falling sales figures, workers being laid off, and then learns that a friend in a similar position has been made redundant.

He gets worried, loses sleep, and gets thinner. He is irritable with his wife and children and at work urges his salesmen to do better. He thinks of looking for another job but realizes many in his sort of job will also be doing the same. He thinks of the house and mortgage, the car and its expense. Will his wife have to work? Can she find work? Will the children suffer?

Then a letter arrives telling him he has to go, and he is told how little redundancy payments will be in his case. The anxiety he has been just about managing to control becomes worse. He suffers more stomach pains from the indigestion which often troubles him. He goes to his doctor, and investigations show that he has a peptic ulcer.

Dr Selye would distinguish three stages by which stress may lead to illness or breakdown. These are:

1. A stage of *alarm*: the signals were obvious that John's job was at risk, and he registered these with alarm.
2. A stage of *resistance*: he mobilises his resources to try and solve the problem that losing his job will pose for him and his family.
3. A stage of *exhaustion*: the threat arrives and is worse than he expected. For the time being he cannot cope and his physical health collapses.

**The target organ**
Selye has described his view, for which there is much good evidence, that each of us has a target organ where stress hits us, or where the strain is shown. The notion is as old as the story of Achilles' heel. The myth was that his mother held the infant Achilles by his heel while dipping him into the river which was meant to confer full protection upon him. The great warrior was thus vulnerable to attacks on his heel.

The stomach with its peptic ulcers was once a favourite choice as an example of a target organ. Now ulcers of this kind are better understood and may be treated earlier. But any part of the body may be affected. We may suffer physical infections easier under stress: a tonsillitis or streptococcal throat is an example. In the chest, bronchial asthma may be linked to stress; any number of stomach upsets may be similarly linked, and headaches may be due to tension just as many other aches and pains may be stress-related.

Attractive as the notion of a target organ may be, it is again safe to say that stress is more complex than this simple picture suggests. The physical and emotional pressures which are linked to their onset are only a part of the story.

## Being prepared for stress effects

If we compare Dr Hans Selye's views with those of the present day, it is like seeing the differences between the model T Ford car and the space shuttle. We know far more about what happens in the chemistry of our bodies under stress. It is not only a matter of a faster pulse, higher blood pressure, or mobilising blood sugar. It is also a matter of complex hormone changes, amines that are in the brain and nervous system, and the free fatty acids so important for our heart and arteries. It now requires a lot of basic knowledge to follow the descriptions that the text-books give us.

But what most of us want to know is: How can we be prepared for the effects of stress in our lives? And can we then do something to prevent the damage they may cause?

A good attempt has been made to measure stress. It is possible to look at a modern scale such as we reproduce here, to measure the impact in our lives. Two doctors called Holmes and Rahe developed the first version of this scale. They reckoned that what was important in stress was the amount of change it produced in our lives. They devised a method of measuring stress in Life Change Units. This method started with asking the persons being studied to assign 100 Life Change Units to the most important life event, which was thought to be the death of one's husband, wife or child. Then other events were rated by comparison with this event in its effects. Thus: marital separation rated 65 units; marriage, 50; gaining a new child, 39; obtaining a house mortgage or losing it, 30 units.

*The Social Readjustment Rating Scale[1]*

| Life events | Life change units | Life events | Life change units |
|---|---|---|---|
| Death of spouse | 100 | Change in responsibility at work | 29 |
| Divorce | 73 | Son or daughter leaving home | 29 |
| Marital separation | 65 | Trouble with in-laws | 29 |
| Jail term | 63 | Outstanding personal achievement | 28 |
| Death of close family member | 63 | Wife begins or stops work | 26 |
| Personal injury or illness | 53 | Children begin or end school | 26 |
| Marriage | 50 | Change in living conditions | 25 |
| Fired at work | 47 | Revision of personal habits | 24 |
| Marital reconciliation | 45 | Trouble with boss | 23 |
| Retirement | 45 | Change in work hours or conditions | 20 |
| Change in health of family member | 44 | Change in residence | 20 |
| Pregnancy | 40 | Change in schools | 20 |
| Sex difficulties | 39 | Change in recreation patterns | 19 |
| Gain of new family member | 39 | Change in social activities | 18 |
| Business readjustment | 39 | Taking on a small mortgage or loan | 17 |
| Change in financial state | 38 | Change in sleeping habits | 16 |
| Death of a close friend | 37 | Change in number of family get-togethers | 15 |
| Change to a different line of work | 36 | Change in eating habits | 15 |
| Change in number of arguments with spouse | 35 | Holiday | 13 |
| Taking on a large mortgage | 31 | Christmas | 12 |
| Foreclosure of mortgage or loan | 30 | Minor violations of the law | 11 |

It is possible for each of us to use such a scale to measure the recent changes in our lives, and to add up how many of these Life Change Units we have acquired in the previous six or twelve months. The point of Holmes and Rahe's studies was to show that we may then predict the likelihood of illness affecting us during the subsequent period of twelve months after the life

1. Richard Rahe and Thomas Holmes, quoted in Thomas Trauer, *Coping with Stress* (London, Salamander, 1986).

events have occurred. It is vital to bear in mind this delay in the effects of stressful life events being manifested. A case study shows this clearly.

A fine Christian lady in her thirties came to see me with a recurrent attack of depression. The huge anxieties and repeated, intrusive obsessional thoughts bothered her greatly. They filled her work and spiritual life with difficulty. Her good Christian friends had expected that buying a flat, moving in, and finding a new flat-mate should combine to make her feel better. On the contrary, the point being missed by her friends was that a change of home, fresh financial commitment to a mortgage and life insurance and all the uncertainties of moving in London were major events, with a promise of new risks to her health later on in the year.

She should therefore be seen to need more loving and caring support, not less. By extra care, a breakdown in health could be avoided.

There are many such examples of the way in which apparently small events can add up to a big source of stress which then puts us at risk. They all point to the fact that, since stress puts us at risk of emotional and physical distress and breakdown, we must learn for ourselves how to control and manage stress better in our daily lives.

## What can we do about stress?

We need not be flotsam and jetsam carried down on a tide of life events, whether they be adverse events such as a death in the family or positive, pleasant events like promotion, marriage or having children. Those who divide such things into exit and entrance events may seem to take a fatalistic view, but they should not be thought to be saying that there is nothing we can do about possible adverse consequences. A wealth of information is available about what we can do to help ourselves. We can describe some important aspects of coping under four headings.

*Perception of events*

The way we see and perceive life events matters as much as (or sometimes more than) the events themselves. We may all need to learn new ways to assess and appraise an event. Is it a threat or a challenge? We shall look at this part of coping more fully in the next chapter. It may be a long, slow and difficult learning process. It enables us to look at what is happening to us in the light of the aims and the values which govern our lives. Christians have sometimes spoken of looking at things that happen to us 'in the light of eternity'. This age-old principle means, I think, that we must learn to apply our faith to the way we think about stress.

*Rest and Relaxation*

Those of us brought up in a tradition that we should always be up and doing, or on the frankly muscular Christianity of some schools, may find it hard to see that we must come apart and rest awhile to get stresses into proportion. Some are fearful of any medication of any sort. They dislike the modern emphasis on relaxation. This aspect of resting has both good and bad possibilities, and relaxation can mean many things.

*Assertive skills*

These are a part of those active, social skills which are just as important as the passive, restful ones. There are positive ways of responding to stress, and we will try and see the differences between being assertive (which is usually good and useful) and being aggressive (which may be bad).

*Learning to adapt to changes*

Some of us are flexible, while others are more rigid. It may help us to see adapting as part of growth and development. Change is of the essence of any process of spiritual maturity. Those of us who are more rigid are prone to cry, 'Compromise!' when asked to adapt. But it is not always a principle that is at stake, but simply an adjustment to a way of doing something. To adapt, then, need not mean any threat or harm – it may be both useful and necessary as part of our progress.

## Relaxing and meditating

Some Christians express a fear that the links between some Eastern religions and meditation may make it harmful and to be avoided. I think this is an extreme and unnecessary fear. Consider what is involved in both relaxing and meditating.

Relaxation has four basic elements:

1. Many people, to begin with, repeat a phrase or a word to help to free the mind from ordered thinking for a time.
2. By shutting out active thought in this way we seek to become passive for a period of time.
3. We may practice muscle relaxation in a comfortable setting, sometimes with a special emphasis on control of our breathing.
4. We may do these three things in a quiet place, with our eyes closed.

This is only a modern version of an ancient practice of meditation. Here, for instance, is a fourteenth-century description written by Gregory of Sinai in a Greek monastery:

> Sit down alone and in silence. Lower you head, shut your eyes, breathe out gently and imagine yourself looking into your own heart. Carry your mind, that is your thoughts, from your head to your heart. As you breathe out, say 'Lord Jesus Christ have mercy on me.' Say it, moving your lips gently; or simply say it in your mind. Try to put all other thought aside. Be calm, be patient and repeat the process very frequently.[2]

It is a vexed question whether relaxation needs to be linked

---

2. R. M. French, *The Way of a Pilgrim* (New York, Seabury Press 1968).

to any religious belief to be effective. It is a fact that some centres of the Jewish faith teach similar methods. In Islam, there are Muslims of the Sufi persuasions who rely heavily on meditation. Perhaps the best known link is between yoga and meditation. The movement known as Transcendental Meditation is a relative newcomer and has caused many problems. It should therefore be avoided since there are more reliable ways of learning to relax. Many tapes by professional psychologists teach a proper method of how to relax.

I think that the technique of relaxation can be separated from any religious belief and still be helpful. Its aim is not to make us lose control (as many fear), but rather to help us achieve more control of ourselves. It is a small but significant help for many in seeking to achieve more mastery over strain and stress.

A recent clear description of how we should try to learn to relax gives the following simple instructions:

- Sit quietly in a comfortable position.
- Close your eyes.
- Deeply relax all your muscles, beginning at your feet and progressing up to your face. Keep them deeply relaxed.
- Breathe through your nose and become aware of your breathing.
- As you breathe out, say the word 'one' silently to yourself: breathe in, out, 'one'; in, out, 'one' and so forth.
- Continue for twenty minutes. You may open your eyes to check the time, but do not use an alarm. When you finish, sit quietly for several minutes at first with eyes closed, and later with eyes open.
- Do not worry if you are successful in achieving a deep level of relaxation or not.

*Problems about meditating*

Does relaxation work? Does it have dangers? What about the peculiar links with some kinds of meditation?

To learn to relax physically is surely good. There is no doubt about the benefits that accrue from it. Perhaps we should learn to link mental and emotional relaxation to the physical process. To do this, one method is to try and conjure up from our memories a peaceful scene. It may be lying on a quiet beach that we recall, or sitting by a river, in a field or a park. It helps greatly if we have this capacity to visualize such a picture in our minds while relaxing.

One kind of meditation has become a growth industry, with great wealth, a university and a crusade for world peace. It even claims to teach some people to fly without mechanical aid! Its claims are best rejected and its methods best avoided. Vehement statements are made by some Christians that yoga is of the devil. But the physical process of relaxing that may be taught in yoga classes does not usually have any religious content. Indeed, hatha yoga is an entirely separate discipline.

It seems to me that meditation as it is described in many parts of the Bible is a different and more active process than what we usually mean by relaxing and meditating.

In the Psalms, for instance, meditating is an active process where the mind seems to be fully engaged in thinking about God's truth as shown in his law or his works. It is quite the opposite of any process which disengages the mind and puts it, as it were, in neutral gear. There is everything to be said for learning more about stretching the sinews of our minds in reflection on all the deepest truths of our faith. But it is different from the relaxing-meditating that we have been describing.

Provisos about relaxation that are important include: learning about it in a supportive setting; from a skilled, experienced person or tape of instructions; preferably with a group of like-minded believers. With such provisos met, only good can come of learning to be able to switch off and rest, properly, for a regular time daily.

## Standing up for ourselves

Many of us are too polite and self-effacing in situations where these attitudes are not appropriate. We may use these as a kind of mask to try and hide the strain caused by frequent hurts. We may have a sense of inferiority almost amounting to feeling worthless. We may all benefit from learning to be assertive. It is worth looking again at assertiveness training. What is it all about?

Since the 1960s two tendencies came together in AT, as assertiveness training is known. The first was a willingness to let each one of us develop his own lifestyle, away from a rigid social straitjacket. This tendency may have gone too far, but it was one of the more acceptable faces of the swinging Sixties.

The second tendency arose from the swing (in counselling and psychology generally) away from Freudian styles of psychotherapy to a more active behaviour therapy. This led to an emphasis on what we can do to help to change our lives here and now. After a quarter of a century of practising assertive therapy, what is there of a permanent worth for us in it?

### Assertion not aggression

When we begin to think about it, most of us confuse assertion and aggression. A recent training manual states the differences between these two things clearly:

Assertion means standing up and expressing ourselves in direct, honest and appropriate ways. We are trying to say: 'This is how I see it; this is what I think; this is how I feel.' Being assertive is to relate to another person in this way without wishing to dominate, humiliate or degrade the other person involved. We seek to respect our own rights and those of the other person in a mutual way.[3]

This may be a simple and effective way of improving our

social skills and increasing our repertoire of responses. Some of us find it hard to say, in talking to others, 'Please let me finish,' or 'Let me think it over,' or 'No, it's not a good time for me.'

Being non-assertive, from this viewpoint, means to be dishonest about our feelings, indirect and inhibited, and self-denying in a bad sense. If we do not learn to be properly assertive, we will be left feeling hurt, anxious and angry. The person towards whom we are being non-assertive will also be left with bad feelings: these will include feelings of guilt, irritation and disgust.

*Aggressive* behaviour differs from being assertive, because then the directness is expressed at the expense of the other person, who is usually hurt or humiliated. In turn he is angry with us. In being aggressive we do not succeed in either making our feelings clear or in getting what we want. We may feel very self-righteous at the time, but that brief feeling of false superiority only makes us feel bad and guilty later on, when we reflect on our aggressive behaviour.

*Rights and duties: a Christian view*
I am left with nagging doubts about totally accepting the assertive philosophy (as opposed to any technique for assertiveness training). Here is a statement of that view:

'Assertive rights are often described as 'human rights' which suggests that all human beings inherently possess them. There should be no limitations imposed by anyone's culture. However, our view of legitimate assertive rights does, at least partially, reflect an American system of values.'[4]

Precisely! This is an understatement, since assertive rights are clearly linked to a philosophy of self-enhancement and self-fulfilment.

---

3. A. Lange and P. Jakukowski, *Responsible Assertive Behaviour* (Champaign, III., Researth Press, 1976), p. 7.
4. Ibid., p. 57.

Tom Wolfe called the 70s 'the me-decade'. All the counselling which has flourished since that time is in danger of being labelled the 'let's talk about me' method. This approach raises many problems for Christians. Here are some of them.

Where does a sense of duty, obligation and responsibility fit into all the talk of human rights? We must surely balance rights with duties. I accept that we need to be willing to look at the way we think and express our feelings in order to assert our rights in a better and more constructive way. But we have to bear in mind that all this must be done within a wider context of the constraints we have undertaken to accept and live by.

An example from the New Testament may help to make this clearer.

A member of a Jewish minority group (Saul of Tarsus) was brought up to be partly assimilated as a citizen of the Roman imperial state. Such a person might be expected, after his Christian conversion, to have difficulties in asserting his rights. Yet we may remember how that distinguished Hebrew of the Hebrews, the Apostle Paul, reacted. It is described in Acts 22:25. He was facing the combined aggression of a lynch-mob and of the Roman soldiers who wished to flog him. His assertive response was to say that he was a Roman citizen. It was a statement with wide implications. It led to Paul's release, to a transfer of his trials, and ultimately to his journey to Rome.

As Christians we are urged, even when speaking up for our faith, to do so with gentleness and respect (1 Pet 3:15). This version of the Apostle Peter's advice may be taken as an example of quiet assertiveness. It is very much the point, coming as it does from the same Simon Peter who is recorded in the gospels as being so quick tempered as to cut off someone's ear!

# 5

## How Do We Cope?
## A Christian View

Cope: To be or prove oneself a match for, contend successfully with (Shorter Oxford English Dictionary).

Watch ye, stand fast in the faith, quit you like men, be strong (1 Cor. 16:13, AV).

No, in all these things we are more than conquerors through him who loved us (Rom. 8:37).

What does coping mean? The word often seems to carry a rather negative meaning: 'Oh, I coped,' implies just managing somehow to avoid being defeated by a situation. It seems to have come to be used as the very opposite of a process of overcoming our problems.

### Coping and fighting
A dictionary will give us some eight different meanings of the word, but only one of them concerns us in this book.

'Cope' comes from an old French word, coup, meaning to strike in the course of a fight. It is a term that comes from the world of battle and struggle. It is concerned with facing difficulties and encountering obstacles. Coping is about being in a contest on terms which are equal. The combat it describes carries a suggestion that it may lead to success and triumph.

Far from implying that we should 'just cope as best we can' in a defeatist way, coping is about engaging more effectively in warfare. In this sense it fits more easily into a Christian vocabulary about the fight of faith, than if it is given the more usual meaning of trying to survive somehow.

The process of coping has three aspects: thought, feelings and actions. Some writers have concentrated exclusively on what we have to do: on solving the problem by appropriate actions. Others have, over many years, written about how hard it is to cope with the feelings of anxiety and sadness that are aroused by stress. In the last ten years there has been an increasing emphasis on the need to use our minds and to think our way through stresses and strains.

Every person who faces any serious change in his life feels stressed, and the way in which *thinking* about it can help is relevant to us all. It is perhaps more relevant to Christians than anyone else. We are told that God's grace and Christ's strength are available to us. Yet we can easily forget that we have to apply this grace to our lives and work out our salvation. It is easy for Christians to forget that God has given us minds and that we must use them in coping with our stresses.

## Don't pray: think!
When we feel threatened by any serious event, the first thing many of us as Christians feel we should do is to pray about it – whether alone or with others. Of course this reaction is right – prayer about anything is as vital to a Christian as breathing – yet at times we have to heed the advice: don't just pray, think! Prayer cannot be a substitute for thinking things out for ourselves, although it may influence the outcome greatly.

This chapter will be largely taken up with how processes of thinking are part of coping with stress. It will reflect the 'thinking revolution' among those who have worked with stress problems in the last ten years or so. It used to be said that to cope was simply to handle our upset feelings well. We will look at that aspect more closely in the next chapter on the stresses that follow loss. Again, we must not deny that the other aspects of problem solving are important: we need to learn all the skills we can, and use all the help from others that we can, in finding solutions to the problems that stresses bring. But before feeling and doing, comes the thinking.

By thinking I mean the process of seeing and perceiving life-events and changes in a clearer way. It is a process of appraisal and assessment. It is an attempt to achieve a sense of perspective. To see things in a Christian framework is often half the battle in coping with stress.

We could borrow and alter a slogan from British Rail and say that we must learn to let the brain take the strain. Our brains are immensely more powerful than the biggest bank of computers. We must learn to use them. Sadly, many Christians do not give their minds a high priority. As we enter churches for worship it has been said that we can easily leave our minds, like hats and umbrellas, outside.

## The double-take
When we hear about something that threatens to change our lives we make an instant response and later a more considered assessment. Our primary appraisal should never dictate our actions; it must never form the final decision. We must always do a double-take: we go on from the first shock reaction to looking at what is threatening us in a larger framework which includes our values and our beliefs.

This double-take is nothing new, of course. William Cowper put it memorably:

Ye fearful saints, fresh courage take,
The clouds ye so much dread
Are big with mercy, and will break
In blessings on your head.

But few of us can view threatening, dreaded clouds like that
without some effort. The second part of the appraisal makes us
ask, in effect, whether we can cope with the possible outcomes
of the threat we have received. We are forced to look at our
resources both in ourselves and in our friends, our family, our
faith, and other spiritual resources.

Consider the case of the threat that may be posed by an
illness or by apparently trivial pains. A child may complain of
abdominal pain for which no cause can be found. It persists
and doctors raise the question: Could it be serious? It must be
investigated in hospital. Parents and family may have a long
and anxious wait. Then the full impact of the disaster hits them:
the child has cancer and the outlook is hopeless. How can they
cope with the months of care and the inevitable death of the
child?

Reactions to such a real, personal disaster as this have been
divided into three stages: anticipation; impact; and what
happens after the impact. Dread may be the main feeling when
we wait (and who has not waited?) for possible news that a
terrible thing has happened. Questions flood into the mind
which often centre around the problem of losing control. Can I
prevent the disaster? Can I make the damaging effects any less?
Will I be able to endure it? Can I postpone it?

Waiting for bad news may be the worst strain of all. We
may distance ourselves from it in our minds. Some of us are able
to shut it off in a different compartment of our minds. We may
acknowledge that a disaster is likely to happen, but we also
avoid thinking about it. We may, that is, *deny* its implications for
us and those near to us.

Even while waiting with dread we may begin a reappraisal. For this more information – especially from others who have been through similar experiences – may help. We ourselves may cast our minds back to similar unhappy crises, and derive comfort and strength from remembering that we have lived through them.

Then the events may hit us, like a hurricane or a tornado. In this stage of impact, all our energies are taken up with actions that may have to be carried out. We may feel we are too busy to think. Yet even while the events we have dreaded are unfolding themselves, we may think: 'This is not quite as bad as I expected,' or 'So *that* is what it's like to live through a day like this.' Almost without realising it, we are *redefining* what the situation means to us, just as we are also constantly re-appraising what is happening.

This can lead to more constructive actions which we had not considered before the event hit us. And after the impact, what then? Mopping-up operations have to be conducted both in practical ways and in deep areas of thought and feeling. What has it all meant to us and what does it signify? Will things ever be the same again? If not, what are the new demands, and are they threats, or rather challenges, that we have to face?

**The Christian framework**
What does the Christian belief have to do with having a sense of perspective? And can it help us not to panic in our first reaction to any stress or strain? Do our beliefs and our experience as Christians affect the way we cope with any disaster, be it large or small?

Some areas of Christian teaching and belief are neglected and considered old fashioned by many people today. There is, in the Bible and in the faith of our fathers, a comprehensive view of the providence of God. This always reminds us of his fatherly care for us as his children. If we forget such teaching then a kind of dualism, a thinking in black and white, creeps back into our thinking.

Gordon Rupp tells the story of meeting an old farmer who complained bitterly about the bad weather and its effects on the crop that year. The farmer said: 'That Providence has got a lot to answer for, but there is One up there that will teach him his business.'

We may smile at the thought of such a simple approach: fancy splitting up the one God into two – one that is good and kind, and the other capricious and cruel. We can all slide imperceptibly into such thinking if we do not make a positive effort to hold on to the clear truths about God's love for us. Yet, when we forget that God has, as the negro spiritual puts it, 'the whole world in his hands', we slip into a way of thinking in black and white about God and Satan.

One example of this way of thinking is the recent case of a famous Christian healer who died of cancer. He died in spite of many promises that 'his sickness would not be unto death' which his friends passionately believed. One of the other healers whose ministrations had failed to save his life declared publicly that 'Satan had killed him.' Surely this is not the balanced Christian truth?

In such circumstances, when an evidently devout man cannot accept that the death of a much-loved Christian minister was part of God's will for him, I am reminded of the story of Job. Job's wife tells him, 'Curse God and die!' and he replies, 'Shall we accept good from God, and not trouble?'

An ancient dualism tries to supplant this basic truth of the Christian revelation that God's will is supreme and that all things work together for good to them that love him, as Paul tells his Roman readers. To quote again from William Cowper's hymn: 'Behind a frowning Providence he hides a smiling face' – and it is a Father's face.

Instead of attempting a comprehensive account of the

Christian teaching on suffering and God's love, let us seek to apply it to some common automatic reactions to strains and stresses as they occur in many minds.

1. *We are never abandoned*
An automatic way of thinking that many of us experience is that when we meet a stressful experience we are alone – either because no one can care for us as we would wish, or because we feel rejected by someone whose love we want, or because we feel unloveable and not good enough to be loved.

To counter these thoughts the Christian has to argue with himself, to pull himself up sharply, and even try to talk or preach to himself. We must remind ourselves that God loves us and that, as Deuteronomy 33:27 puts it 'underneath are the everlasting arms'. It may be difficult to feel that we are not abandoned, but we will never feel it if we do not remind ourselves of the truth of it.

Our Christian friends and the local group or church are the ones who may, in a stressful crisis, show us how we are loved. In many practical ways it is the ordinary believer who is a Christian friend who may help us to hold on to the basic fact that we are not rejected or deserted but still loved and wanted. It is such a relationship that has helped many to survive. There is a deep and repeated tendency in many of us to feel that we are not worth loving, that we are at the bottom of the pile, that we should in fact be rejected. Many feel this more at times of remorse about some unworthy behaviour or some sin that has been committed.

The Christian truth is that God loved us while we were his enemies and gave his Son to die for us. There is the powerful argument that if he did this, then nothing can separate us from his love. At times of stress, to hold on to this is hard without the help of friends and the solidarity of the 'household of faith'. It is vital that the tendency for feelings of rejection and abandonment are countered in our minds by constant recourse to the truths about God's love and the practical demonstration of this in his church.

## 2. *We are not hopeless*

It is so easy to feel that all hope is useless when some disaster strikes or threatens us. This leads quickly in vulnerable folk to a serious depression which may be fatal, either because the person kills himself or ceases to care for himself.

Christians have always made much of hope, but it easy to forget this when the strains threaten to break us. All of us can feel that catastrophe threatens. In the catastrophic reaction we amplify and exaggerate our fears, sometimes because the new strain reminds us of earlier ones (in childhood perhaps) when we felt really hopeless about our state.

It is interesting to recall an example of this from ancient times. In Psalms 42 and 43 the writer describes his sense of hopelessness leading to the state where he says: 'My tears have been my food day and night, while men say to me all day long, "Where is your God?"' He uses the past to increase his sense of perspective of what is in the foreground. He remembers his former joy in joining the crowds in thanksgiving. Then he argues with himself again: 'Why are you downcast, O my soul? Why so disturbed within me? Put your hope in God, for I will yet praise him, My Saviour and my God.'

I am not arguing that profound feelings of depression can be suddenly removed by such discussions with ourselves. But I do think that at an earlier stage when depression may threaten like a black cloud, we may talk ourselves out of it and rekindle hope. This hope is ultimately, for the Christian, in Christ himself. And it is felt in the sharing of his peace and by grace in the church which is his body. In practical ways many Christian traditions have developed weekly meetings (like the Methodist Societies) or house groups where daily problems can be shared in discussion. With a wise leader it is often possible to find real hope in a situation full of potential strain and despair.

### 3. *We are not helpless*

So often children and adults alike have been made to feel that they can do nothing in their lives to change for the better. They have felt helpless, without any proper response possible to them. It is a feeling that can produce, not a black cloud, but rather being in a deep black pit with no way out.

Such a feeling is very common and to counter it we must remind ourselves of how active the Christian is asked to be. He is expected to fight and to quit himself well, to be strong. He may *feel* helpless, but he is in contact with all the love and grace that Christ and his people offer him. But he must put his faith into practice, he must *act it* (not as a hypocrite 'acts', but in the sense of turning words into action).

This may be a small step of turning away from almost enjoying the darkness and despair to the first act of moving towards where it is light and warm. A book may enable us to do it. Or a friend's help may prompt the first reaction of doing something to change our own situation by our own wills being engaged.

### 4. *We ourselves can do something to change*

When the strain goes past a certain point there follows a 'paralysis of the will'. We feel we can do nothing. But every time we think or act in a positive Christian way it makes us not only feel better, it proves to us that we can affect what is apparently a hopeless and helpless state of affairs.

In other words, it helps us to feel we are in control and that we are not in a black hole with a black cloud on top of it. Mastering strain and stress is the most important thing to learn. This may be spoken of as a process which makes us feel better about ourselves and increases our self-esteem. What seems essential is to learn for ourselves at first hand that we can work out our own salvation, even though it is with fear and trembling. Every learning experience builds up the confidence of our hope.

## Learning from experience

It seems that learning to handle strain with this sense of perspective comes from looking back on many situations in our own lives, watching others do it, and from reading biographies and history.

We do not look at our past from a sufficiently Christian perspective. I think of John Newton's lines in an Olney hymn quoted earlier:

> His love in times past
> Forbids me to think
> He'll leave me at last
> In trouble to sink.

Or we may think of Toplady, putting it differently:

> The work which his goodness began
> The arm of His strength will complete.

Reflecting on and arguing from the past is basic to much of the Bible's arguments about personal coping with strain.

Biographies can show us how others have come through similar trials, and reading about Christians from a different age can throw light on our problem.

I remember a young minister who was considered to be depressed by his doctor and myself. It gradually emerged that his constant self-condemnation was connected with his own high standards and over-conscientiousness. We talked about it. He said how in a shop, if one of his small children damaged anything like the needles on an artificial Christmas tree, he felt compelled to tell the assistant in the department store about it. He worried endlessly about every small detail. His spiritual life was deeply affected by this.

What had helped him most in the whole twenty-five years of his reading was a biography of Martin Luther (*Young Man Luther* by E. H. Erikson). He saw how Luther found justification by faith and receiving the righteousness of Christ as the only way to prevent him from being driven to compulsions and obsessions as a young monk. Many have had a crucial learning experience through reading good, honest Christian biographies.

### In the light of eternity

There are some areas and countries which are suffused with a quality of light which enables artists to paint better and to see ordinary life in a different way. The Bible is such a country. In its pages a whole universe of grace can be glimpsed by those whose eyes are open to see it. In the New Testament this light may shine out suddenly through a passage of great clarity and beauty.

Consider Paul's words to the Corinthians:

> Therefore we do not lose heart. Though outwardly we are wasting away, yet inwardly we are being renewed day by day. For our light and momentary troubles are achieving for us an eternal glory that far outweighs them all. So we fix our eyes not on what is seen, but on what is unseen. For what is seen is temporary, but what is unseen is eternal (2 Cor. 4:16).

This is what Christian thinkers for centuries have meant by seeing things in the perspective and in the light of eternity.

Some modern clerics have no time for this. I recall one famous Methodist from the House of Lords saying on television: 'I prefer not pie in the sky, but jam where I am.' What a travesty of Christian truth! Of course we are grateful for our daily bread and for all the delights of God's creation which we can richly enjoy. But it is fatal to forget that all we have (as well as all the strains we may suffer) are to be seen in the light of eternity.

That is the ultimate perspective, allowing us to make sense of the situations we encounter. If we are to learn to cope better we must, in whatever stressful situation we find ourselves, keep this Christian perspective by actively placing the changing scenes of life into the Christian framework.

# 6

## COPING WITH THE STRESSES OF LOSS

No one ever told me that grief felt so like fear ... and no one ever told me about the laziness of grief ... I loathe the slightest effort

C. S. Lewis, *A Grief Observed.*

Brothers, we do not want you to be ignorant about those who fall asleep, or to grieve like the rest of men, who have no hope (1 Thess. 4:13).

When we lose someone we love, particularly if that person dies, there are severe stresses – perhaps the worst we ever face in our lives. If the death is sudden, there is no time to prepare for it. The grief that follows may last longer, and wreak far greater havoc, than if we had known about the possible loss and had been prepared for it.

A young mother telephoned her husband to say that their youngest son, who suffered from epilepsy, did not seem well. She asked him to come at once, and the husband replied that he would leave immediately on his motor-cycle. The mother and son waited for him on the pavement, and saw him arrive and signal that he was turning towards them.

To their horror, a large lorry came hurtling along the road, hitting the motor-cycle and running over the husband. Before the ambulance could get him to hospital he was dead.

Five years later, the widow is still suffering from the effects of the loss, and attending the hospital. The son, too, sought medical help for years after he lost his father.

## Breaking the bonds

Bonds of affection are broken when two people who love each other part. They are not simply bonds of love, though this may be the most important element in bonds of attachment. They give a shared security, a common concern, and a meeting of needs. They provide both persons who share the bond with a sense of worth, value and meaning. That is why, when a bond is broken, the person is so greatly missed. In our first case, the boy whose father died suffered from the loss of guidance and discipline just as much as the loss of love and care.

Human bonds differ greatly in their qualities. A mother's bond to her child is not the same as the one she has to her own parents.

Two adults who love each other will form a bond that depends for its true nature on the way their love has grown, and what experiences they have shared and for how long. This relationship will not only consist of good feelings, such as shared love, shared pleasure and the joy and happiness they have felt together. There will also, inevitably, be bad feelings. And when such bad feelings are examined they will be found to consist, at the very least, of disliking things in each other and being angry about them. There may well be hatred also, with painful memories of hurting and being hurt.

When we lose someone we love, therefore, it is tempting to think only of the pleasant things and to forget the less happy parts of the life we shared together. It seems to many who have worked with the bereaved that this process of idealising the lost person and denying the 'mixed feelings' is part of the problem of grief taking a wrong turn and making the mourner suffer more.

Christians are not exempt from any of the pains of loss. I am surprised how often believers feel guilty about their sadness and grief. They sometimes quote, as a justification for always keeping a smile on their faces, the words of St Paul in his very first letter to the early Christians (1 Thess. 4:13) saying that those of his readers who had lost loved ones should not sorrow and lament like the rest of the world as if they had no hope. My response is to point out that although the Christian does have a different hope, he shares the same problem of enduring sorrow as those who may have no belief in a future life after death.

When, in the gospel story, we are told that Mary and her friends were weeping because Lazarus had died, we are also told that Jesus wept. It may be argued that he wept because of the unbelief of the Jews, but we cannot forget that these same Jews also remarked, 'See how he loved him.' Feelings of sorrow, whatever their full causes may be, should not be a reason for feeling bad. An earlier generation of Christians spoke of the gift of tears, recognising that weeping was entirely proper at times and could be a release for which we should be thankful. Indeed, I often think that we need to learn to express our sadness, and that to cry and weep is a good and healthy way of meeting some of the strains of loss.

## The normal reactions to loss

If we think of what happens when we lose a loved one, we may then apply this knowledge to other losses. Losing a pet, such as when a favourite cat is killed or a much-loved dog dies, may at first sight seem to be trivial. Yet many can be profoundly upset by this kind of loss.

A woman lost her kitten. Neighbours were quite certain it had been killed – one man had seen it dead. But the woman would not believe it. She advertised on television offering a reward to find it. Her distress was evident, and she was much more upset about the kitten than about her teenage son whom she had 'lost' to the drug scene. It was easy to imagine that the kitten had been an object of affection in the way that her son had not been – he had been a most difficult person to love.

The loss of a loved one often follows four stages, as described by John Bowlby in his studies. First there is a kind of numbness, a shocked absence of any feeling. It is as if it was all happening to someone else. In this stage it is common to deny that the death has occurred. It is felt that there must be some mistake. It has to be someone else in reality that has died. Secondly, there are painful pangs of grief which affect the bereaved person physically. The throat and chest tightens. These are pains of separation felt in bodily form.

A third stage involves a yearning for the lost person and a searching for him. It involves tricks of the mind – we may think we have seen him in a crowd, and when the person turns and is obviously not the one we loved, there is the disappointment. We may hear the voice or feel the presence of the person we have lost. It is important to know that these normal feelings and perceptions in grief do not mean that we are going out of our minds or being ill. The fourth stage of normal grief and mourning involves the gradual acceptance of our loss, facing the new realities of life after it, and making new beginnings and new relationships.

When Jesus said in the Sermon on the Mount, 'Blessed are those who mourn, for they will be comforted,' he implied many kinds of mourning. But it is not fanciful to apply his words to the kind of loss we have been discussing. For only by going through a dark tunnel of grief can we come through to the light and comfort on the other side. If we refuse to mourn, and many do, we cannot obtain the comfort and consolation that is possible.

In most societies there are rites of mourning which involve behaviour before, at and after the funeral of the loved one. At their best, such rituals may provide real emotional support, and focus the care of friends, relatives and the community on the needs of the bereaved. Without the real and genuine expressions of personal care, as well as the clear statements of faith and hope which the religious services contain, such rites of passage may become somewhat sickly and sentimental. The meetings of old friends which can happen at funerals may help greatly in achieving the true ends of mourning by offering help and establishing the conditions which will make recovery from the loss easier.

**How can we tell if something is going wrong with grieving?**
Clearly, not everyone goes through grief without special help. While many do not suffer unduly and only need family and friends to support them, others need a doctor or counsellor. Twenty-five years ago I was starting to settle into a country medical practice when a recently widowed woman of sixty came to see me from a nearby village. She asked for a bereavement bottle. I had no idea what she meant, and asked the senior partner for advice. He explained that I should prescribe some suitable gentle sedative that would last for two weeks or so. I was not to think of it as a prescription of drugs for bereavement, but as a simple ritual which enabled the otherwise shy patient to come and talk about her loss and the problems of surviving without her husband.

No one had taught me, in medical school, about helping acute grief. But this country area had built up this habit, with many others, which ensured that care in a crisis would be provided. Thus the minister of religion would call and talk with the bereaved. The nurse in the community would do the same. The lawyer dealing with the financial affairs would do his part in supporting the bereaved woman by his efforts. Above all, friends who might be skilled at listening and being with the distressed family would call frequently at her home.

In spite of such help in what is now called 'crisis

intervention', more specialist help may be needed. Certain folk bottle up their feelings and grief becomes too intense or goes on too long because of their failure to mourn. In fact what seems to happen is that, instead of the feelings of depression and despair being a normal reaction to the loss, the grief seems to lead, in some cases, to a depressive illness which requires specialist help.

A woman had moved a few miles to a new house after living in the old one for twenty-seven years (all her married life). She gradually became unable to cope, had taken to her bed, and had become angry with her husband and withdrawn from her two children. She was miserable and despairing. My surprise was evident as I learned that as a young girl she had only just survived Belsen and the horrors of concentration-camp life. Why had she managed to survive all those trials, and yet become depressed after just moving a few miles?

One fact was that the date of her house removal was the date when she and her sister had walked from their first camp to Flossenburg and the cattle trucks which would take them to Belsen and apparently certain death. All except eight were dead in the truck by the time they arrived at Belsen. The anniversary had triggered off what was evidently a mixture of losses, including the death of her parents in Auschwitz and the recent death of a surviving aunt which also increased her sense of loss.

If the suffering and symptoms caused by the loss do not begin to get better after some six months then it is important to consider specialist help. Some may need such help earlier, while others may hide their real distress for much longer than six months.

It is no disgrace to require help. It may be that an earlier loss of a parent or brother in childhood has made us more vulnerable to the present loss. It should not be seen as a failure simply because we have called a doctor to help. Counselling from a specialist is usually needed, but this requires highly developed skills.

## Can we help ourselves?

There are many folk who seem to believe that the person who has lost a loved one is deliberately refusing to help himself, and that he hugs his grief to his heart, unwilling to let anyone else either share it or help him to cope with it. In one way the answer to the question of whether we can help ourselves is to say that we cannot help ourselves alone, but that we can do a great deal to help ourselves if we let others take some part in doing that.

There has been a remarkable growth in self-help organisations in the last twenty years, particularly for grief. Their very existence is evidence that it is only by approaching others that we can help ourselves. This may be illustrated by the organisation CRUSE which is for widows. It consists of groups of widows who invite anyone who has lost a husband to join them. It seems that by attending regular weekly meetings the new member learns how other widows have coped and survived their loss with all the changes in their social roles, the financial pressures, and the need to adapt to new possibilities. As the new widow sees what others have been through successfully, she begins to understand that she can do it for herself as well. Another organisation, *Compassionate Friends*, is a self-help group for parents who have lost children. In different countries there are many other groups which essentially rely on those who have experienced the strain of loss meeting together and helping each other. The role of any professional such as a doctor or a therapist is simply to provide back-up for such a group and not to take an active part in it. It seems that such groups function on at least three levels. First, they provide practical help and advice on adjustment in the months and years after bereavement. Secondly, they provide a general support of an emotional and social kind. Thirdly, they provide that special sharing which derives from the fact that each member feels that they have been through something similar. Therefore the sympathy is of a special sort which they cannot expect from someone who has not been through an actual experience of loss. This may be true even of a therapist who has no experience of this kind of suffering.

Some self-help groups have sought to extend their role to prevention. In Canada groups of widows have been trained to offer help to women whose husbands are either terminally ill or have recently died. The work of such groups has been intensively studied. I believe many Christian churches could benefit from carefully setting up such groups.

Parents who have lost a child from cancer, liver disease or multiple sclerosis have set up funds for research and for helping fellow sufferers. Instead of an unhealthy and inward-looking concern over their own plight, they have found that in helping others they helped themselves. Their efforts resulted in a new organisation for self-help and unexpected publicity for a needy cause.

## Difficulties in accepting help

A note of caution must be sounded: there are dangers in trying to help oneself entirely on one's own, without the support of others.

Grief has always been a private matter. It has a very malignant tendency to isolate the sufferer, to cut him off from his fellows. This may be a basic animal instinct. The wounded animal sometimes goes off on his own 'to lick his wounds', and does not return to the group until he has recovered. This method of coping with loss may make the bereaved person withdraw and turn in on himself. It will have damaging effects on his marriage, family or close friendships. Important relationships may thus be sacrificed, mainly because the grieving person feels bound to devote his energies entirely to the lost loved one.

If such a response to loss proceeds, the person involved may come to feel that there is no sorrow like his, and his feelings become exaggerated. It is then only a small step to come to feel that no one really understands him, and that those seeking to help him should be shut off and prevented from doing so. This is shown by the next case study.

Towards the end of an hour's interview with a father who a few years earlier had lost a child with leukaemia, we had traced six years of suffering that he had endured. His wife had confirmed to me during the interview how different her husband had become, and how this had imposed an almost intolerable strain on their marriage and on his capacity to work. I was about to offer some practical advice about treatment when the man said to me, 'Of course you cannot possibly understand any of this because you have never lost a daughter.' I had carefully concealed from the patient during the hour's interview that I had in fact lost a daughter who had died of cancer, because I considered it largely irrelevant to whether he would tell me his story frankly or not. I also thought that it would have made it more difficult for him to tell me. His remark showed that he had now become certain in his own mind that no one else could share the degree of grief which he had known and which had had such bad effects on his life. The next step for him would have been to share his grief, and to be able to come to terms with it in a way which he had, up till now, refused to do.

The man was in some sense seeking to preserve the bonds which had linked him to his ten-year-old daughter. Although by her death it appeared that the bonds had all been cruelly and finally severed, in his own heart and mind the reality of the bonds which linked him to her were as vivid as the day she had fallen ill. In the view of most of us who have worked with such people it is important to help them gently and gradually to unpick the knots which still bind them in memory to the person they have lost. Such knots consist of many strands and each one may need to be looked at in turn. In a successful period of mourning, the grieving person will be able – with great reluctance – to loosen the strands which are tied so tightly, to let go of the one they have lost, and to accept the new reality of life without them.

Another way of thinking about the same problem is to consider one's feelings about the person that has been lost, using the picture of money being kept either in the bank or being used in day-to-day transactions. In a case where grief has gone wrong, the person wants to keep all the emotions safely invested in a bank which is represented by the lost person. He feels that the feelings are safe in that bank, and does not notice that while this state of affairs continues his own emotional life is becoming impoverished, and the feelings which he ought to be expressing towards others in his life are simply not being allowed to find their proper place. In particular, it often seems that new relationships are not allowed to be formed because of a strong emotional loyalty and allegiance to the memory of the lost loved one. It is often a great discovery for such a person to find that the feelings he thought were safe in the dark vaults at the back of his mind, can be brought back into circulation and enjoyed without any sense of betrayal.

An example of this is the general feeling that where most people have had happy relationships in marriage or friendship before their loss, they are likely eventually to make new relationships of a similar kind and quality. In his study *Mourning and Melancholia* Freud pointed out that when a person's grief did not abate or become manageable, progress could often be made by realising how closely one had become part of the lost loved person. The difficult and painful step has then to be taken of realising that it is a part of oneself that one has lost and has to relinquish, and that the tie which was so important has to be dissolved, and new ties and investments made in new relationships.

## How can we help others with their strains of loss?
If we try to bring together the ways in which we can help those who have lost someone or something that has been dear to them and which were important because of the ties of love that existed between them, we may usefully think of three modes of

help which have been recognised for many years: to comfort, to console, and to counsel. There is a great deal of overlap between these three areas of caring, but it is worth considering them separately.

*Comfort*
The first instinct when we get to know that someone has lost a relative or friend is a comforting response. Often this is very much a physical matter, like touching, holding and hugging. To weep with those who weep, as the Bible exhorts us to do, is something which women and children may find easier. Men need to abandon some of their false views about virility and manliness, and learn more of the importance of sharing these emotions which are apparently considered by some 'macho' individuals to be unworthy of them. Christians sometimes seem to be unwilling to accept practical and spiritual ways of being comforted. They are like Rachel in the Old Testament who, having lost her children, refuses to be comforted and prefers to weep alone. It is often necessary to find ways in which one can overcome the obstacles to receiving comfort.

There is an art in expressing sympathy in words which not all of us have, and some find it easier to write a carefully composed letter than to make telephone call or a visit since they feel they may be lost for words. For some friends who want to strengthen and uphold the person they are visiting, there are thoughts that lie too deep for tears, and they can only express their concern in practical ways such as giving their time in preparing food to help the family which may be paralysed by the anxiety and pain of their grief, or finding a dozen small ways in which concern can be expressed. In the parable of the good Samaritan in the Bible, he is not portrayed as saying much, but he is shown as someone who does a great deal and puts himself to some trouble and expense. The good neighbour does the same, and often does so unobtrusively in order to demonstrate the love that is felt.

The root meaning of comfort is to make strong. Many in the initial phases of acute grief are helped through the strains of loss simply by feeling that in their weakness those around them are supplying strength. There is a story about a clergyman's son who was frightened of the coming night and wanted his father to stay with him. His father told him to bear in mind that God was always present and would comfort him. His son replied that at that precise moment he wanted to feel a god with skin on. It was an appeal for his father's love to be demonstrated in a practical way. It is sadly true that Christians may repeat to each other the ancient and comforting words of the Book of Deuteronomy which tell us that 'underneath are the everlasting arms', simply because to say such things is easier than to demonstrate, albeit in a small and human way, our reflection of God's care and comfort for us. Many Christians inevitably feel that they must reach for a suitable card or message to send to friends who are in the pangs of acute grief. It is easy to descend into a rather sickly sentimentality when what is really needed is that the one trying to comfort the sufferer appreciates the sense of desolation which is being felt. It was a wise remark of Aldous Huxley's that we cannot really experience the consolations of religion until we have first experienced some sense of desolation.

*To console*
There are immediate and practical ways in which we seek to comfort those who grieve, but consolation implies that we seek to relieve their mental suffering. While comforting is something that may be needed in the first weeks, consolation seems to me to be something that can make a great deal of difference in the months following a bereavement or loss.

I remember talking to a man whose skill with words and in interviews was well known to anyone who watched television in his native country, and I was surprised to hear him say that when he was a Christian minister he frequently visited the bereaved and felt he had no idea what to say to them. He found this very distressing in spite of his considerable ability and an immense facility in expressing ideas and using words. If such a person can find it hard to offer consolation, what can the rest of us do who frequently find it hard to put difficult thoughts into meaningful words?

I think one answer is that the skill which is needed first and foremost is the skill of listening sympathetically. Those who have lost someone or something desperately need to recount in great detail the circumstances surrounding the loss. It seems to give them great relief, and although listening to them may be in itself a strain, it will lead to relieving the pain of the sufferer.

When a loved one has died, one of their first steps is this detailed recounting of what led up to it. It will frequently be an opportunity to release some of the anger and hostility which has been described earlier in this chapter as a feature of the strain of loss. The careful listener will by implication accept both the reality and the justification for these feelings. This in itself provides relief.

Often one of the next few steps in the consoling process is to review the whole relationship with the person who has now gone. It is a great help if the bereaved person can speak frankly both of the good and bad aspects of the relationship. The intelligent and caring listener is in this process sharing the pain of separation. It is important also to share the bereaved person's frequent sense of guilt that more was not done to help the one who has died. This anger directed towards oneself in the form of guilt, shame and other negative feelings is very like the anger which is felt towards innocent participants, like the ambulance driver who may not have got the patient to hospital in time, or the doctors and nurses who did everything they could and yet are perceived as being partly to blame for the death.

The listening may sound a simple matter, but it is costly

both in terms of time and emotional energy. Yet there is no doubt that it is one aspect of what St Paul describes as bearing one another's burdens and so fulfilling the law of Christ.

Because Christians share the same beliefs, the same faith and the same hope, a truer consolation with greater depth and meaning can be offered. And yet one often feels that sharing the suffering and the desolation simply as human beings is a necessary part of arriving later at the comforts and consolation that the Christian faith imparts.

It is probably the book of Job, out of all the books in the Bible, which describes most clearly the way in which an upright, wealthy and remarkable man was allowed to be subjected to many savage losses. It is from this book that the expression 'Job's comforters' has become part of our language. We can learn from these false comforters that we should not argue with those who are going through a process of loss similar to Job's, and that we should not give such pieces of advice as 'Curse God and die'. There are many pieces of advice which may seem more Christian, but when they are given with a glib self-assurance to the person who has suffered loss, can only be felt as insulting since they are registered as showing how little has been appreciated by those offering such slick words about the depth of distress that is being felt at the time.

It seems to me that we should always feel a sense of our inadequacy to console, since this is at least a recognition of our limitations. Anything that we can do in our contacts with those who grieve which shows how much we feel the mystery of suffering, the inexplicable nature of much of the distress which befalls us, is preferable to offering a formula or panacea which does nothing to soothe or heal. Eventually, one of the main results of true consolation is that we help the bereaved person to accept the reality of the final loss, and help them to give up clinging to the lost relationship and go on to make a new beginning.

*Counselling in grief*

It is the aim of comfort and consolation to help the bereaved person get through the first weeks and months of grief. Counselling becomes important when there is a query about whether the mourning process is going on normally. It is important to try and make it easier for the process of grieving to be completed, but even more important to have some facilities for special help when the bereavement gets into difficult waters. I think this is a matter for skilled professional advice, not necessarily from doctors or psychologists but certainly from those who have had experience of bereavement and some training in offering help for it.

It is worth mentioning some special techniques which explain why counselling can have fruitful results.

Morbid grief and chronic grief present very severe challenges; without proper counselling they can lead the bereaved person to many physical illnesses of a psychosomatic kind, or drive them to drink or other drugs.

I saw one man who told me how his brother had died two years earlier in a fire in a hospital where all the children in that ward had perished, and where the doctor in charge had killed himself as a result of what he felt was his dereliction of duty. The reason the man had been referred to me was because of persistent pain in the face which the dental surgeons were quite sure was not due to any physical disorder. In the course of talking about the history of his pain, he told me how he had been instrumental in persuading his mother to let his younger brother go to this hospital. It was therefore clear to him that he was ultimately to blame for the horrible manner in which his brother had perished in the fire. Suddenly he exclaimed, speaking of his younger brother, 'John is my pain!' It took many years of treatment before a well-entrenched physical disorder which was linked with the grief could be treated and relieved.

A woman was referred to me by a liver specialist because

tests in his unit had shown that she was drinking enough to cause some liver damage. It was clear that her attachment to her husband had been strong and deep, and that the only way she had been able to cope with his sudden death from a heart attack was by drinking herself to sleep every night, and gradually drinking more during the day. By a prolonged period of counselling she was able to understand this and take steps to give up her excessive drinking. At first she expressed a wish to go on causing herself liver disease since in this way she would die sooner and join her husband earlier.

It is a common wish to join the dead person, and some suicides have occurred simply because the wife cannot bear life without her husband. In India, before the British put a stop to the practice, many a young widow was forced to throw herself on her husband's funeral pyre in the practice of 'suttee'.

Another form of suffering which may be prevented by counselling is the experiencing of symptoms such as pain which are exactly the same as those that the bereaved person had suffered. I recall an old lady of seventy who seemed extremely depressed and who had many physical symptoms. I began to understand why she was suffering in that particular way when she asked me if cancer was infectious. She felt she was having exactly the same symptoms as those of her late sister. These were 'identification' symptoms. When she understood this it helped her back to normal health.

The aim of such counselling is to promote better insight and understanding in the mind of the grieving person. The process of treatment is also designed to help the bereaved person to come to terms with the loss. Two methods which have become well known in recent years may appear cruel at first sight.

*Regrief Therapy* is designed to help the patient to re-experience the grief which has gone wrong after the loss. It has two goals: (1) to help the patient to understand why he has been unable to mourn properly, and (2) to help in an intensive way to complete the mourning process.

The patient is seen several times a week for months. Although this may seem too harsh and demanding a programme, anyone who has seen the awful results after many years of a grief reaction that has gone wrong will perhaps accept it as a method of being cruel to be kind.

Another closely related form of regrief treatment is a type of behaviour therapy. This depends on seeing the person who has closed the door on life outside and withdrawn into his grief, as having a kind of phobia. His fear of talking about the lost person leads to avoidances of various kinds. To get over it, the patient is asked to bring photographs and other objects which link him to the lost one. These are talked about in a two-hour interview once a week. If there are tears, and anger and other feelings are released, so much the better. If we return to the picture of the grieving person locking up all their emotional money in the bank of the lost person, then this is a strong-arm method of breaking into that bank and helping the patient to use his feelings more constructively in the future. It is hard for the therapist, and may call for exceptional skill and firmness of purpose.

*Who cares for the carers?*
Much thought should be given to helping the helpers and supporting those who seek to offer counselling to the bereaved. One minister, at the end of a discussion of this subject, told me that he was completely drained if he visited a grieving, bereaved family for a week after the death of one of its members.

The burdens shared are very heavy ones. A therapist of whatever kind should be sure of three kinds of help.

1. The support of colleagues. This is vital, and is one reason why many of us prefer to work in a team. Each problem has many facets, and no one person can see or comprehend them all. It is very helpful to discuss a case with another team member, and

often new light on what should be tackled next may be thrown on the problem in an unexpected way.

2. Supervision of counselling. This is not only good but, in my view, necessary. Older generations of Christians recognised this. Some would arrange for a personal 'spiritual director' to be available to those in training. It is good that groups should recognise those of their number who are gifted in teaching by a process of regular supervision: informal meetings are necessary to share the progress and the problems of each case. The most experienced therapist also knows how good it is to share a problem with another, often younger, colleague who may make useful comments and suggestions.

3. The personal life of those offering this kind of help on a voluntary or professional basis needs affectionate caring and support. Friends and family are vitally important, not only as people to escape with from the hard work, but even more to give the love and understanding the therapist needs. I recall a friend of mine in training, whose wife had flown off to see her sick father, putting it thus: 'I can't care for anybody properly this week, since there is no one to care for me.' The therapist who looks mainly to his clients for supplies of interest and affection which are absent in his personal life is heading for disaster.

We should all learn what are, for us, the limits to the help we can offer others. We need to live and work within those limits and not feel that we can do everything – we are not all-powerful, except in our fantasies. With patience and perseverance we can come to feel that we are adequate helpers for each successive crisis. We can learn to cope with being carers, and thus be models for others to cope.

# 7

## STRESS, SADNESS AND SORROW

Be ye angry, and sin not: let not the sun go down upon
your wrath (Eph. 4:26 AV).

The experience of severe depression as a result of stress is one
of the most disabling things we can suffer. Depression affects
us in so many ways: we feel like giving up; everything seems
hopeless; we feel unable to do anything about it. These feelings
may be overwhelming for a short time only, or they may last for
weeks and months. Sometimes they issue in an experience
which can last for years and be as severe and crippling as any
other illness.

Such depression may start as the simple and obvious reaction
to such stresses as loss, rejection or a blow to our self-esteem.
We must be careful to say, almost in the same breath, that
depression may also follow physical stresses such as a virus or
influenza or an attack of pneumonia. The causes are many, but
the final common path that the experience of depression follows
may well be the same.

Is depression really the 'blue plague', as it has been called?
Certainly it is a modern curse, but it nevertheless resembles
the experiences described in the book of Psalms or in such lives
as those of Elijah the prophet, or Jonah. Modern life, with its

lonely crowds, its lack of proper support from friends and family may make the experience of depression worse. Many have been driven to despair, and this has prompted the Samaritans to provide an open telephone link. Those seeking help find in these voluntary organisations a listening ear and a chance to talk over their problems that may prevent a suicide attempt.

## What does it feel like to be depressed?

That is what a young woman wrote to me recently:

> Last week you asked: 'Do you feel ill?' I do not feel well, therefore I suppose I must be ill. I find that anxiety manifests itself most noticeably in headaches and in my stomach, where I feel a kind of knot which loosens and tightens but never goes away. But because depression is not a tangible thing, I don't think of myself as ill in the same way as if I had the measles. It is, nevertheless, painful beyond belief. At times I wish I had some form of extreme physical pain instead of this depression, because I believe it would be easier to endure and to explain, and therefore to treat and ultimately cure. If I had the courage I would have put an end to it by now, but I don't (I even condemn myself for that fact).
>
> Everything is so much of an effort. I dawdle along now where before I went at things full speed. At times I just cannot be bothered. Pathetic isn't it? I hate this attitude, it's so negative, but it's how I feel. The enthusiasm I had for anything has deserted me, so too my sense of humour and my ability to enjoy and be happy appears to have been impeded for ever.
>
> When I look to the future it appears very bleak. That there is nothing to build on in my present state makes it all the more bleak, and quite hopeless. And that leads me to the awful clichés: 'What's life all about? What's the point of it?'
>
> The answer, of course, eludes me. But it seems to be a fruitless pursuit, and it scares me to think I'll feel this way for ever.

In my view, the young woman who wrote this letter was ill – she had a depressive illness.

In this chapter I want to describe some features of depression which may affect any one of us *without* our being ill. Each of us has a capacity to feel depressed. If we can understand our own bad feelings better, I think it will help us to understand even the most severe depressive illness.

### 'Painful beyond belief'

How is depression painful? Is there such a thing as mental pain? When our feelings are hurt, how do we register that hurt?

To many people, perhaps most of us, pain is a physical thing produced by an injury, a blow or a cut. But we all know how, in a relationship, we may be cut to the quick or our self-esteem may suffer a severe blow. These are not mere metaphors – the suffering is real.

In fact, it is often through physical sensations that we register mental pain. The symptoms of anxiety are nausea, sickness, sweating, a fast pulse, and a giddy or dizzy feeling. These may be how we feel pain which originates in our minds when we are affected by bad feelings of a sorrowful kind. We may not have spots like measles, by which we may recognise that sadness is getting out of hand. But there are recognisable features if we care to note them.

One of the commonest feelings, and perhaps the earliest we experience, is the pain of *separation*.

The person whose letter I have quoted began to feel depressed when her grandmother died. Her links with this mothering, caring figure in her life were powerful. When they were severed at her death she thought of killing herself. There was no fellow-feeling of any kind from her own mother, only envy of the special relationship between the grandmother and the young woman.

Warmth, comfort and companionship had been lost. Her

whole life was dominated by a feeling of being a lost, abandoned child whom no one could ever love again in that way.

The pain of rejection is, perhaps, the hardest of all to bear. In our hospital some five hundred patients a year are brought to our casualty department because they have tried to harm themselves because of a disrupted personal relationship. Studies of these distressed and despairing folk show that they are feeling bitterly resentful because a girlfriend or a boyfriend has rejected them. A wife or husband may feel the same awful sense of not being wanted and loved and therefore rejected. A parent or child may have a similar experience. They may all, at times, feel that ending it all and choosing oblivion is better than continuing to feel rejected and separated and without love.

Closely linked to the sense of being abandoned (either by rejection or separation from those we love) is the *low self-esteem* that many of us suffer. Is it a result of the experience of depression or the cause of it? Why does someone say, ' I am a failure,' when what they might more accurately think of themselves is 'I have failed on this occasion, but I am not a failure'?

A man was sent to me by his heart specialist as someone who, because of the stresses of success in business, was very depressed and thought he was having a heart attack. He described himself (with some truth) as the biggest private investor in his home country. Yet what he told me was that he felt an empty shell, a worthless failure. His self-esteem had reached rock-bottom. It was good to see him recover totally with appropriate help for his depression and anxiety.

### Anger turned inwards

Few people understand the important role anger has in the process of going through deep sorrow and sadness. Nice people feel depressed more often, it seems, because their niceness includes having been taught not to show anger or aggression.

They have learned, unfortunately, to 'bottle it all up'. Sometimes, alas, it is the pent-up anger that not only blows out the cork but breaks the bottle itself.

To have controlled explosions, to blame and hurt other people, is the way many of us avoid getting really sad about anything. The bad feelings are not contained at all, let alone bottled up. Many people get rid of their bad feelings simply by putting them outside themselves, by blaming other people and other things. St Paul puts it very pithily: 'Be ye angry, and sin not' (Eph. 4:26, AV). He was thinking of the fourth Psalm which tells us: 'In your anger do not sin' (Ps. 4:4).

Many who have been well brought up (as the saying is) have been taught that they must never express anger or bad feelings because this is bad form and unacceptable. A child who has been constantly told by a parent: 'How dare you speak to me like that!' may learn never to express angry feelings – even if they are fully justified.

A splendid Christian wife and mother told her husband after two decades of marriage: '*You* are allowed to be angry, but *I* am not.' This is far more common that we might think. It may well be connected with the statistical fact that twice as many women become seriously depressed as men. It is part of many cultural and social settings that the wife should keep silent about her bad feelings. It would be much better to learn to express anger without feeling that in doing so some irreparable harm is being done.

A very difficult situation is when we feel impotent rage, as if we are infants or children who have been 'put in the wrong' by a superior parent, brother or sister. To be unjustly blamed is productive of destructive anger, especially if one cannot answer back.

How often, in the setting of an office with its petty hierarchy of power, a business, a family or a church this anger may be produced and felt as an inward threat of great severity. If the anger has to be contained not once or twice but constantly, it produces suffering and both physical and mental distress.

One of the peculiar distortions of the depressive thinking is to make the sufferer feel that the only person they can be angry with is themselves. This process can contribute to chronic depression. In severe attacks of depressive illness, the process of directing the aggressive feelings inwards becomes quite irrational and self-destructive. Such a person can become his own executioner. Like the Queen in Alice in Wonderland his twisted judgment on himself makes him say, 'Off with his head.' It is vital – literally a matter of life and death for some – to be able to stop being so angry with themselves and to direct the anger more properly elsewhere to the places and people where it rightly belongs. If done in the right spirit, this is not destructive but rather a valid response.

## Mea culpa, mea culpa

It is part of some religious rituals to beat one's breast and loudly proclaim one's guilt in public. Now, I do not deny for a moment the value of being able to confess, in the words of the Book of Common Prayer, that we are miserable sinners. In such a setting it is part of the process of repentance and being reminded of the powerful facts about the divine forgiveness, renewal and reparation that may follow an experience of God's grace.

But there is an experience of guilt and shame which is quite different from the positive religious acts which may lead to new beginnings as a result of wrong things being put right. Some sad people blame themselves for everything that goes wrong in their own lives and in the lives of those with whom they come into contact. They are quite unlike those characters whom we may meet in fiction and in real life who say, 'I shall never forgive myself!' and to whom the proper response is 'Oh yes you will, you always do.' Unlike those who make a show of self-blame, the chronically depressed person never feels wholly free from a sense of guilt in his own mind, a sense of shame in the presence of others, and an all-pervasive feeling of failure. He may hide it, and yet behind what may be a string of successes there is a ghastly sinking feeling that they are never good enough.

This person may be a mother who constantly returns to the theme in her own mind of not having been good enough to care for her children or her husband adequately. She may have the most terrible feelings of inferiority because she thinks she has failed in some aspects of her duties. It takes little for such a person to be pushed over into a frank and frightening attack of depression.

Does religion contribute to such improper guilt or shame? Unfortunately, it has often played a major part in creating unnecessary guilt in the past which many then carry around with them for years.

## Law and grace

I consider that it is not the Christian religion in itself but the use parents, leaders or institutions make of religion that produces so much guilt. Parents may use their faith as a stick to beat their children into subjection and submission.

As I was preparing this chapter I heard the story of a man who, in his profession, was much loved and respected. In his home, however, he behaved with ruthless violence. He would lecture his sons with savage words, often accompanied by verses from the Bible, and sometimes beat them about the head in fury. To do this all in the name of Christian religion is manifestly self-contradictory. Sometimes the pressures are non-violent but equally bad, as described in books such as Edmund Gosse's *Father and Son*.

There is a proper, caring application of the laws of God as we understand them. Even at its most severe, the law is seen in the New Testament as a schoolmaster that leads one to Christ. The image is of a gentle yet efficient teacher taking his pupil by the hand. Religion should educate a growing child's mind to cope properly with guilt and find forgiveness, trust and acceptance. In my view it is a healthy process, dealing as it does with real guilt and creating a sound basis for the growing moral sense of the young person. It is the very opposite of creating bad feelings and wreaking havoc on others by inflicting on them our own poorly understood feelings.

I found it hard to accept an explanation offered to me which stated that much religious depression occurs when we turn to justification by works and not by faith. On reflection, I think there is much truth in it. We all feel a need to make ourselves better and to *deserve* forgiveness. The Christian faith starts at the other extreme, offering us forgiveness and new life in Christ which we can never deserve. When we slip back into non-Christian ways of thinking, we return to trying to establish our own worth instead of seeing ourselves as always 'accepted in the beloved' (Eph. 1:6, AV) as St Paul describes it.

Is this to say that what we need to deal with our bad feelings is more of God's grace? In a sense, yes it is. We are *given* a constant assurance of being loved and accepted. That feeling has to come to us through our friends and fellow Christians. It is made evident in the Sacraments, and constantly made clear and explicit in the Words of Scripture.

## Parasuicide

This is not, as some wit suggested, a new word to describe parachutists who do not pull their rip-cords in time. Parasuicide is the modern term for what used to be called attempted suicide. Many people harm themselves by taking an overdose of drugs or cutting themselves on the wrists, often without any real intention of killing themselves. Theirs is a separate kind of behaviour, alongside the more serious suicide risks – hence the term *para*suicide (para meaning alongside).

At times, such an act is a cry for hope and help, and it is vital to respond to it in an appropriate way. Nearly always it is an angry and aggressive act, directed not only at the person but also at the one most important to him. A minority (a fifth to a third) of those who attempt some self-harm have an illness like depression. Most have a close relationship which has been disrupted or is threatened with being ended. A wife or girlfriend may be very angry with a husband whom she feels may have been betraying her with another woman.

A woman had found a lipstick-stained handkerchief in her husband's pocket. The next evening she took a large overdose of tablets so that her husband would be shocked when he found her, and would behave properly again. The husband was delayed and arrived late, and found her not sleepy but unconscious. The hospital was able to treat her and she recovered without brain damage. She made it clear that dying was not her intention, but that she thought it was the only kind of language her husband would understand. A similar story is told by A. Alvarez in his book *The Savage God*. He describes how the poet, Sylvia Plath, died when her life might have been saved if the daily help had a key, or the nearby telephones had not been vandalised. The delay in getting into the sealed room filled with coal gas was fatal.

The wise counsellor will try to effect a reconciliation in such a case, or at least try to ventilate the bad feelings. If anger can be put into words it may then not need to be expressed in destructive acts.

There are often social, financial, family and religious pressures which add to the difficulty that the person in a state of despair feels. A listening ear, as the Samaritans have shown, may be a crucial step away from self-harm. It may be just as important for a problem-solving approach to follow the listening. Many helpers may be needed to resolve different aspects of the crisis that has led to the parasuicide.

# 8

## PERSONALITY PROBLEMS:
## BUILT-IN STRESSES

Nearly all the wisdom we possess, that is to say, true
and sound wisdom, consists of two parts: the
knowledge of God and of ourselves
> John Calvin, *Institutes of the Christian Religion*

Our temperaments may make a very large contribution to the
stresses that we face. That is why learning to know ourselves
better is so vital if we wish to cope with life more effectively.
But if we get to know ourselves better, can we then change our
personality or our temperament? As far as our basic personality
structure is concerned, I do not think we can change much. We
may, of course, adapt: in the process of growth and development
we may appear to be very different from one year to the next. Yet,
underneath the changes in lifestyle, both real and apparent, I
believe that our temperament remains the same.

Such talk may seem offensive to many. What about the many
statements in the New Testament that say we become new
creatures in Christ? Surely this means that old things pass away
and all things become new when we experience God's grace in
the process of conversion and new birth? I think this is certainly
true, but I do not think that such statements refer to our basic,

God-given personalities, I believe they refer to what *we do* with our personalities. If we speak of character rather than personality, we may see the point. For character does develop and change. Character has been described as personality evaluated: it is a reference again to what *we do* with ourselves in life, the origin of the word being a description of what impression we make, as in written or engraved characters.

## What is personality?

Personality is what makes us tick. When we know someone well we see that he has ways of thinking, feeling and responding to any given situation which are uniquely his own. The better we know him, the more accurate may be our predictions about the way he ticks and how he is likely to behave.

It goes without saying that this use of the word is very different from that reflected in, let us say, the term 'television personality'. The building up of a man's ego by the mass media is another matter altogether, and his real personality may be quite different from the media's representation of him.

How do we get our personalities? When we describe someone we know as very like her father, and quite like her aunt, we are implying that there is a large part of anyone's personality that is inherited. Thomas Hardy put it well:

> I am the family face;
> Flesh perishes, I live on,
> Projecting trait and trace
> Through time to times anon,
> And leaping from place to place
> Over oblivion.

We are all more aware of genetics than we used to be, but we are also more aware of how we learn to be the sort of persons we are. Upbringing and nurture are important, even if they are not quite such key issues as nature and what is laid down in our genes. Those who hope to change people by changing their environment are in a constant battle with those who aim to show how our genes affect the way we live and the way we are. Most people take refuge from this endless fight in the fact that, for everyone, there is an interaction between our natural endowment and the way our families, schools and work experience shape us.

If we are all unique individuals, quite unlike others in every detail, what is the point of talking of *types* of temperament? It is because we all tend to share certain traits of personality. Galen, in the second century, based his four temperaments on the notion of the way humours affect the body (blood, phlegm and bile both yellow and black). Thus he spoke of the sanguine, the phlegmatic, the choleric and the melancholic.

## What personality type are you?

I will confine the question of personality type to an account of how the two words extravert and introvert have become so popular. We will then look at one personality type (called Type A personality) since this has been thought to be closely linked with an increased risk of dying of a heart attack. It will help us to ask how we can change and lessen the risks attached to each one of our personalities to some degree.

The extravert has been well described by C. G. Jung whose book *Psychological Types* first made the word popular. He says:

> The extravert is characterised by interest in the external object … a desire to influence and be influenced by events, a need to join in and get 'with it' … constant attention to the surrounding world, the cultivation of friends and acquaintances, none too carefully selected, and finally by the great importance attached to the figure one cuts, and hence by a strong tendency to make a show of oneself.
>
> His conscience is in large measure dependent on public opinion. Moral misgivings arise mainly when 'other people

know'. His religious convictions are determined, so to speak, by majority vote.

The disinclination to subject his own motives to critical examination is very pronounced. He has no secrets he has not long since shared with others. Should something unmentionable nevertheless befall him, he prefers to forget it.... Whatever he thinks, intends, and does is displayed with conviction and warmth.... He lives in and through others; all self-communings give him the creeps.

I find many people use the word extravert as if it simply meant what a good type the person is, whereas this brief quotation from Jung shows that the extravert has as many bad as good points. Professor H. J. Eysenck has studied the extravert and introvert for many years, and teams of his researchers have produced a body of useful knowledge which reveals that we may predict a person's behaviour from the degree of extraversion he shows. Eysenck's popular books give a good account of all this, and his critics have also written a great deal about extraversion. By contrast, this is what Jung wrote in his original description of the introvert:

The introvert is not forthcoming ... does not join in ... in a large gathering he feels lonely and lost ... he is not in the least 'with it', and he has no love of enthusiastic get-togethers. He is not a good mixer. He is apt to appear awkward, often seeming inhibited ... his better qualities he keeps to himself, and generally does everything he can to dissemble them. He is easily mistrustful, self-willed, often suffers from inferiority feelings and for this reason is also envious.... He is usually very touchy and surrounds himself with a barbed wire entanglement so dense and impenetrable that finally he himself would rather do anything than sit behind it. He confronts the world with an elaborate defensive system compounded of scrupulosity, pedantry, frugality, cautiousness, painful conscientiousness, stiff-lipped rectitude, politeness and open-eyed distrust. His picture of the world lacks rosy lines, and he is over-critical and finds a hair in every soup . . .

For him self-communings are a pleasure. His own world is a safe harbour, a carefully tended and walled-in garden, closed to the public and hidden from prying eyes. His own company is the best.... Crowds, majority views ... never convince him of anything, but merely make him creep still deeper into his shell.

These extracts give only a hint of the rich descriptive and sharply observed views that led Jung to his use of these types. He thought we could all be placed to some extent on a line between the extremes of extraversion and introversion. He described two axes on which the way we function might be shown: either as thinking or feeling types on a rational axis, crossed by an irrational axis consisting of either sensation or intuition. So we might find ourselves classified, for instance, as extravert intuitive or as introvert thinking types. It is, as a reader of the original book will see, a much more delicately balanced matter than a black-and-white division into plain extravert or introvert – these days they seem to be seen as natural goodies and baddies in our estimation. This should not be so.

### Strengths and weaknesses
It is possible to use paper and pencil questionnaires to measure whether we are predominantly extravert or introvert personalities. When we know the answers, what then?

The value of knowing what type of person we are is linked to the different ways these two types react to stress. Introverts, when their brain activity is measured, have a high level of activity, excitation and arousal, so they prefer low levels of outside stimulation. If they are in an atmosphere where the social stimulation is too arousing, their tendency will be to isolate themselves from it. That is why the introvert is happier alone, or in a one-to-one relationship, than in a group.

By contrast, extraverts who *seek* stimulation, and who are

easily bored, will look for activities which increase their level of mental activity and arousal. They enjoy anything that stimulates and interests them, and they feel better for it.

Such facts affect the way we learn (at school and later on), and how we enjoy our work and our lives in general. They are relevant to choice of career and vocation. Extraverts, because of their strengths, usually do well in early training. They are good at working closely with people. Extraverts make good ministers, counsellors and administrators. The introvert may be better at planning deliberately – he is good at the kind of 'inward looking' work that many intellectual tasks require. It is said, therefore, that introverts make good scientists, and that they may excel as architects or engineers. Their consistent and stable pattern of thought and life draws admiration from their colleagues even though, in other ways, introverts may be rather remote as friends.

The weaknesses of both types must also be noted. The extravert's very sociability becomes a problem. He is more vulnerable to social pressures and to being manipulated by a group. His good capacity for taking risks may be a virtue in an entrepreneur, but it may become an impulsive chasing after thrills. A minority of extraverts can become antisocial – they break the rules and slip into criminal ways often concealed by their charm in social relationships. The Christian church has had its share of those who have the capacity to take new initiatives – a fact at first welcomed. Later, such a person may become a law to himself, and break the rules in such a way as to make a shipwreck of his life and cause pain and scandal to others.

The introvert has weaknesses that may make him uncertain and indecisive, and very aware of many bad and negative feelings. He will tend to devalue himself and his carefulness may turn into a slow, obsessional deliberation. He may become rigid and hide-bound. Indeed, his hide may turn into a skeleton like that of a crab – a thick skin to protect himself from the outside world. When he fails to cope, his anxieties rise and depression is never far away with thoughts of failure, destruction and death.

Self-examination has an honourable tradition in the Christian church. The introvert may easily overdo this practice and may then become sad and anxious. A counsellor should therefore be cautious in advising it, and may need to be more supportive to the introvert. By contrast, the extravert may need to be urged to more self-examination and to the kind of counselling which is sometimes sought from a spiritual director.

## Making the sensitive plant hardy

It is a sad fact that many of us are oversensitive and that we may wilt and seem to be threatened by any changed wind of circumstance that may blow on us. Whatever personality type we may be, this risk of an over-sensitivity is there – and it applies to Christians as much as to anyone else. How can we become more sturdy as Christians? The Bible makes much of our needs to build up the inner man, to strengthen our personalities so that, whatever our weaknesses, we may be made more hardy and survive the stresses we meet. Studies of stress have recently looked at this same problem, and it is worth looking at two traits in our personalities that need to be developed.

The first trait has been described as *hardiness*, the second is *coherence*.

The hardy plant, as the good gardener knows, survives changes of weather, moisture or the transplanting from one place to another. Is hardiness in humans something similar to that in plants? Dr Kobasa, a worker in the field of stress research, tried to find out how it is that some people do not fall ill under stress. She concluded that the hardy person had a strong sense of meaningfulness and commitment to self, a vigorous attitude to life, and a feeling that they had, within them, the capacity to control things.

Christians may learn from unbelievers in this matter, for we are too often upset by the least threat of change. The Spartans trained their children to be hardy. In their spirit the famous physician, Sir William Osler, told young doctors in an address called *Aéquanimitas* to 'cultivate a judicious measure of obtuseness', and to grow a slightly thicker skin to protect themselves from the criticisms and pressures they were bound to meet. I believe the very sensitive Apostle Paul exhibits this kind of hardiness in his refusal to be seriously upset by the many detractors that he met.

There is some overlap in the way *coherence* is described: those who have it are said to view the world as comprehensible, manageable and meaningful. The Christian, above all, should be able to show this trait of coherence. When I find, in talking with Christians in emotional distress, that they cannot make sense of their lives, it is often because they are leaving out some important data from their thinking. They are not applying their faith – what they know about God and man and themselves – to their current situation.

By sharing our anxieties with other Christians we may learn something about how, in practice, we come to comprehend God's love for us. We are helped to do this by growing in our understanding of our own personalities and their problems. We are helped to see life steadily and see it whole, and not with the built-in bias which our personality traits may produce without the corrective of a shared faith. I am reminded of the first paragraph of *The Institutes of the Christian Religion* which runs as follows: 'Nearly all the wisdom we possess, that is to say, true and sound wisdom, consists of two parts: the knowledge of God and of ourselves.' After discussing the connection between these two kinds of knowledge, John Calvin ends the paragraph by saying: 'Accordingly, the knowledge of ourselves not only arouses us to seek God, but also, as it were, leads us by the hand to find him.'

Calvin and his followers have often been criticised by those who know little of the strong Christian characters produced by their teaching of the Bible. To know oneself, and to develop a measure of hardiness and coherence, may lead us to know more of the constancy and continuance of our lives in Christ. We may then feel, as Paul puts it in his famous passage in the letter to the Romans (Rom. 8:35-38), that nothing – no stress or strain – can separate us from the love of Christ.

## The Type A personality

It is important to consider in more detail how our Christian faith and understanding may affect the way our personalities function. A modern example is what two cardiologists in 1959 called the Type A personality: a man who was at greater risk of dying in middle age of a heart attack.

Coronary thrombosis has been called a modern epidemic. Millions are afflicted and deaths from such heart diseases account for almost half the deaths in the modern world. Many die younger than they might be expected to die. Many risk factors have been rightly blamed: diet (hence the wish to lower cholesterol levels); cigarette smoking; high blood pressure; and lack of regular physical exercise. But in addition to this is our personality – and the kind that shows Type A behaviour is at greater risk.

The man who shows Type A behaviour is extremely ambitious and has a great sense of time urgency. He is competitive and aggressive, punctual and impatient. He is often rather cynical of those around him and finds it very hard to trust anyone. Is this the profile of a potential killer? Yes – there is much evidence that this person's lifestyle may lead him to an early death unless he modifies it.

People such as this are often high achievers and are much valued by society. Are we to ask them to become the opposite of the very things that have made them so much admired? Of course not. We must continue to prize highly those who show great drive and who meet their deadlines promptly. But need they be deadlines that carry a truly fatal risk because they are almost impossible to achieve?

No cardiologist suggests that we should become dull, boring and listless people who achieve little by their efforts, simply in order to avoid heart attacks. That would be too high a price to pay, even if it did secure us total immunity from such an illness. What may be useful is to study the underlying beliefs that a Type A person holds. This was done by Dr V. A. Price who wrote a book on changing such a life-style, after she had worked with the cardiologists (Rosenman and Friedman) who first launched the research that has gone on in this field for twenty-six years.

## Our beliefs and fears

Three themes were found to occur regularly in the beliefs and fears of those who are at high risk for heart attacks. How do we compare with them in our own beliefs?

1. I must constantly prove myself, or I will be thought to be unsuccessful and I will be disapproved.

2. There is no universal principle in the world to ensure that good will triumph; in fact, good guys finish last.

3. I know that all resources are scarce; it is right to fear that there will be insufficient time, not enough achievement, and not enough recognition of me.

Dr Price, after working as a psychologist with such patients, felt that we could see a close connection between the behaviour of men at risk of heart attacks and these fears and beliefs that lay beneath the surface.

How does a man who believes such things behave? He tries to do more and more in less time, working faster than he should and for longer hours. With less time to relax, he may become more impatient and irritable. Hostility and an unpleasant aggression may dominate his life. He may feel as if his mind is revving rather pointlessly like a car engine which is not linked by its transmission to any purposeful driving. The physical consequences are inevitable: a raised outflow of adrenaline, a higher pulse and blood pressure. Other blood levels also go up: cholesterol, free fatty acids and some steroids. The risks of a coronary thrombosis rise steeply.

Many doctors consider that an important way to lessen the risks of such heart attacks in these vulnerable people is to change their behaviour by re-educating them and changing their core beliefs. This is precisely where a Christian response may fit in. To believe in the just and good purpose of God, that 'in all things God works for the good of those who love him' (Rom. 8:28) as St Paul tells his Roman readers, is a basic Christian tenet. To know and to feel that you are accepted as a person, both by God and by those who love and care for you – this Christian theme gives the lie direct to some of the Type A beliefs. To know that God's grace provides ample resources for all our needs is a final guarantee against the fear that all resources are scarce.

### The case of Dr Barnardo

It is sometimes said that we do not breed heroes nowadays – but perhaps we do not recognise them. It is hard to be frank about those still living, but we may all profit by a fresh look at the life of Dr Thomas J. Barnardo whose name has become a household word because of his pioneer work with destitute children in London's East End.

A recent biography by Gillian Wagner called *Barnardo* shows how he illustrates the strong and weak points of the Type A personality. Lady Wagner, as a chairman of the Barnardo Council, is well placed to write about him, and she brings much new material to bear upon the story of the great man's achievements.

Dr Barnardo suffered his first heart attack two months before his fiftieth birthday. After violent paroxysms of chest pain, he was fully aware of what it meant for him. Ten years later he died, in spite of much treatment and a number of further heart attacks.

A man of exceptional gifts, he started his charitable work while still a medical student at the London Hospital. He was autocratic by nature, and took upon himself the task of creating the organisation that bears his name. He was able to succeed, single handed at many times, in forming the largest voluntary child-care group in Britain.

His faults were evident. He never became a properly qualified doctor, he was careless about his publicity methods, and he took little notice of helpful criticism. As a result there was opposition – some of it justified, but most savage and unmerited – from prominent men in rather similar charitable work who became his sworn enemies.

A three months' trial and court case, looking at the accusation made against Dr Barnardo, is the centre-piece of the book. But Dr Barnardo was his own worst enemy, like so many who show Type A behaviour. He moved on to fresh efforts, and sought to meet new deadlines, before the debts on his last venture had been settled. The fact that he was a dedicated and convinced Christian did not make his lifestyle any less unhappy as an example.

Gillian Wagner's description of how Dr Barnardo felt at fifty, after his first heart attack, may be compared with what he himself said at sixty years of age.

[He] knew that for the sake of his health he should avoid mental and physical strain, that undue exertion and stress could bring on a further attack and that repeated attacks could prove fatal. But it was not in his nature, with his excitable energy, to relax and abandon any project to which he had put his hand. Resting only when he was physically unable to keep going, Barnardo drove himself on, making only minimal alterations in his life-style.[1]

Later, after ten years of illness, Barnardo wrote: 'Although only sixty years of age, we have in the exigencies of our work "burned the candle at both ends" and we are, in consequence, now being forcibly reminded of our limitations.'

The question that arises in reflecting on such achievement as Dr Barnardo's is this: was he saying, like a bishop who lived a hundred years earlier, that 'I would rather wear out than rust out'? Or, like the famous young missionary Henry Martyn, 'Here let me burn out for God'? Compared to such heroic figures, our beliefs can seem half-hearted and our enthusiasm lukewarm. Yet we may rightly feel that there is a balance we need to achieve in order to avoid some of the pitfalls into which our personality traits may lead us. We must not conform to the modern rat race but recognise it as part of the 'strange disease of modern life, with its sick hurry and its divided aims'.

If we accept the insights and criticisms offered by friends, family and professional advisers we will often be able to correct our lifestyle in such a way that we avoid the tendencies which our forefathers might have called our besetting sins. When we do that it makes us more able to run with patience the race that is set before us.

---

1. Gillian Wagner, *Barnardo* (London, Eyre and Spottiswoode, 1980).

# 9

# Counselling and Stress

> We took sweet counsel together, and walked unto
> the house of God in company (Ps. 55:14, AV).

> Everyone should be quick to listen, slow to speak
> and slow to become angry (Jas. 1:19).

If you ask for help with problems in your life which are causing
stress, someone is sure to advise you to seek some counselling.
What is it, and who is competent to counsel? Many varieties
are on offer; how can we tell one counsellor from another?

There has been a mushrooming of movements with
counselling as their aim. Many have led to valuable work being
done. Good people have felt that they should seek training as
counsellors. Yet we meet those who, having been counselled,
may feel worse. They blame themselves even more, and have
had solutions offered to them rather than being helped to solve
their own problems constructively.

## A health warning
First a word about the possible dangers of counselling. It may
damage your health, just as it may help it greatly. For Christians
the warning note is this: a powerful personality may do a power

of good, but he may also cause a lot of harm. I believe we have ample evidence that it is the counsellor himself which is more important than any of the impedimenta that surround the counselling professions.

This was emphasised in the teaching of Dr Michael Balint who did so much to help doctors to be better counsellors and therapists. He put it like this: 'The drug most often used is the doctor himself.' He taught that it was, therefore, important that the doctor or counsellor should know himself in his contacts with those who come for his help. He should also be on the lookout for any side-effects that his counselling might produce. He should observe the first principle of any therapy – do no harm.

It is almost impossible in our fallen world to stick to such a principle since harm, just as much as good, may follow the most well-meaning counselling. The counselling relationship is a very important one in the fight to avoid the bad effects of stress. But counselling is not a panacea, and should not be offered wholesale as a cure-all.

## What is counselling?

If I go to a counsellor we sit down and talk. But what happens at depth? First, we share a good deal of time. Whereas a family doctor (according to studies in Britain) may give me a six-minute appointment, a counsellor will often need an hour or so to hear me out. Thus time is of the essence. I cannot begin to unburden myself if the counsellor cannot listen because of pressures on his time. Too often a patient feels there are others with more important problems than he has, and that he is wasting the counsellor's time.

Counselling is not just 'talking about me'; the listening part is vital. By careful listening the counsellor is responding to the words of James: 'My dear brothers, take note of this: Everyone should be quick to listen, slow to speak and slow to become angry' (Jas. 1:19). So we should all take heed how we hear. Yet I believe that to be a good counsellor you have to listen properly. To give total attention to the person we seek to help is not easy. Is it an inborn skill? Certainly, we can recognise some potential counsellors at school by the way their fellow pupils confide in them. But even if it is a gift, it is one which can be improved with training and experience.

The process of listening involves grasping the facts, feelings and difficulties which make up the problem. In the course of conversation, counsellor and counselled will gradually understand what the stress feels like and what effects it is having on the patient's life. By being allowed to air my problems I may take some steps towards clarifying them. To come to a better understanding of my problems will lead to an opportunity to solve them for myself.

Can any 'one-off' interview be called counselling? I doubt it. Care and commitment to help must be offered, I believe on a continuing basis. This is another way of saying that counselling must give time for a relationship to be formed. This involves trust and understanding. There should be a professional respect for my needs, and there should also be a professional love. My needs should not be exploited, but love, in the sense of a caring, charitable relationship, offered. As has often been said, this love should not be possessive, just as it should not be exploiting.

Counselling is like a deep, professional friendship, in that it involves acceptance and time to listen, and offers help which is more than simply advice. Good counselling, like true friendship, is not easy to find.

### History: battles long ago

To know something of the history of counselling may help us avoid some pitfalls. The historians of counselling are many, and they often contradict each other in their accounts. Each writer tends to be dominated by the point of view he has taken up, or by his training. We may easily, like the early heretics, take up one aspect of truth and try and make it into the whole truth.

Dr Roger Hurding's book *Roots and Shoots* (London, Hodder and Stoughton, 1986) gives a balanced and helpful account of the history of counselling. Dr Hurding describes the 'forest of teaching'. He gives a brief account of each movement in the history of counselling, and also a Christian critique of each. At times I consider that he is too kind – he is like a woodsman who spares some trees that should be severely pruned if not cut down. However, it is a fact that many odd and unusual counsellors have helped many; and that, perhaps, is why Dr Hurding is not as angry as some who have seen the harm done by certain kinds of counselling.

We can look at the field of counselling not only as a place where roots and shoots may be traced and described, but also as a battlefield. For many enemies (and friends) have chosen to fight right here. The fight is about how, precisely, we should seek to help others to sort out the problems which have caused them so much stress and suffering. The protagonists have famous names: Freud, Jung and Adler and their followers; Carl Rogers, Maslow and others in the USA. Christians like Jay Adams have done battle here too. But although these battles were fought long ago, their effects are still with us. Frontiers have been defined in counselling and psychotherapy: you may need a passport or shibboleth to cross a border or gain admittance to a hard-won field of practice. This may be inevitable as in many other kinds of work.

Consider a basic question: should a counsellor advise? Many lawyers, ministers of religion and doctors would say they are paid precisely to do just that. At the end of the day their counselling means offering a client advice. After Freud, it has been widely taught that proper counselling should not offer advice, but be *non-directive*.

The theory behind the new counselling had admirable

features. Above all, the counsellor was to keep himself out of the picture. His aim was to help the client gain insight and understanding of himself. One tool in this process was 'free association', meaning that the client could say anything that came into his mind without being censored at all. The counsellor then analysed and interpreted what was said. Dreams, slips of the tongue, all that is part of the relationship between the counsellor and the client becomes the material to be analysed and discussed.

Those whose stresses arise from deep levels of conflict in the personality have been greatly helped by such a psycho-analytic approach. It is a branch of counselling which has grown into many variants which are available today. Such counselling, based (however loosely) on Freudian and similar training, is expensive, and often difficult to procure. To benefit from it requires a skill with words and ideas which many needy people suffering from stress do not have. It is, thus, of limited value.

*The one thing that psychoanalytic counselling is not, is the non-directive thing it claims to be.* In many subtle ways, and by the very method itself, the person seeking help may be very clearly directed. Long before students and researchers established the fact that to be non-directive was almost impossible, there were wise Christian thinkers who considered Freudian counselling a menace for the reason that, under a cloak of not giving advice, it almost seemed to brainwash some who went through the process, and in so doing seriously affected their Christian faith.

Many therapists now accept that there is a great debt owed to Freud and the other pioneers in counselling. They would also admit, as most of us do, that we should be explicit about how, in counselling, we seek to modify behaviour and help with problem solving. We should, perhaps, be more explicit in discussing openly with the patient or client the choices before him. We should not shelter behind any counselling mystique of any kind.

## A Christian reactionary: Dr Jay Adams

I have already mentioned that many Christians have expressed doubts about Freudian counselling. None has been more violent in his reactions, or more prolific in book and journal production, than Dr Jay Adams. In such books as *Competent to Counsel* (Grand Rapids, MI, Baker, 1970) he gives us, in trenchant style, his views.

For Dr Adams, biblical counselling means to admonish, rebuke, reprove and warn. He calls it *nouthetic* from a Greek word used in that sense in the New Testament. His style is well suited to this view of counselling as rebuking. His American Christian critics ask, rightly, why he missed the relevance of the word *paraclete* to the process of counselling. Is not the counsellor one called alongside to help and to comfort, as well as to warn and reprove?

Dr Adams, as a reactionary, goes further than most Christians in his attacks on psychiatry. He has no time for empathy. He questions whether Christians should grieve, and argues that grief reactions should not be seen as necessary. He goes further, saying that the Bible gives no warrant for psychiatry. He states: 'There are, in the Scriptures, only three specified sources of personal problems in living: demonic activity (principally possession), personal sin, and organic illness. These three are interrelated. All options are covered under these heads, leaving no room for a fourth: non-organic mental illness.' I believe this is a sadly inadequate statement. An enormous amount of distress and illness is seen by psychiatrists and counsellors of other kinds. These illnesses can be helped, but not by ignoring what many professors of psychiatry (who are also believing Christians) would be happy to discuss with Dr Adams.

The hard-won knowledge which is the basis of clinical psychiatry should not be dismissed in this way. All truth is God's truth. I believe, like many Christians, that medicine and psychiatry are part of God's goodness (common grace if you wish) in revealing his truth in general revelation. This need not contradict the special revelation in the Bible. God's common grace has much to do with the common sense that many honest workers in psychiatry and the allied caring professions use to sort out the problems presented to them by their over-stressed patients.

### The counsellor himself

The battles will go on raging between rival schools of counsellors. Those who need help from them will not be impressed by such in-fighting. If they are Christians they will be asking how they can be sure of some help if they do go for some counselling, and what they should be looking for. I have already said that the personal qualities of the counsellor seem to me to matter more than his theories. One of the clearest descriptions of some Christian aspects of this matter was given by Dr Martyn Lloyd-Jones in his book *Healing and Medicine* (Eastbourne, Kingsway, 1987). He describes the ideal character and personality of the counsellor. He needs a mind that is quiet and at rest in itself, and informed by a grasp of how Christian doctrine affects the whole life. He must listen patiently: 'You must be ready to give yourself to listening.'

Sympathy and a real concern for the patient are basic to counselling. But what about advice on the basis of Christian teaching? This is Dr Lloyd-Jones' answer:

> The advisor must not hold to his own rigid position otherwise the patient will simply become a tangent to a closed circle. The adviser may end up feeling that he has taken a 'Christian stand' and said all that was right....
>
> The point is that we must be very careful not to foist our opinions on others. The counsellor is not a dictator, he is simply there to give help. While he may give his views and, with care, put them quite strongly if asked, yet all that is put to the patient must be in a spirit of real sympathy, love and understanding.

As counsellors we must never be in the position of dictating to another person's conscience. We have no right to imagine ourselves as 'the conscience' of another! We are there to share with those who consult us our experience, knowledge, wisdom and suggestions concerning the way of cure. There are, unfortunately, Christians who feel it their duty to impose their own legalistic views on others. Our business, however, is to persuade, never to force. We must always be careful to avoid condemnation – especially in the case of a sick or agitated person. If the plain truth of the situation comes home to the patient that is one thing: but it is not our place to condemn.

How I wish these words might burn themselves into the hearts and minds of all those of us who have to listen and counsel. So often, to the patient, client or friend who has come to be helped, we appear to be in the role of the critic – the one who warns, the superior person who condemns. Most who seek help already have a bruised and accusing conscience – they can do without our anger, disguised as it sometimes is as the wrath of God.

Courage is crucial to fighting and coping successfully with stress. The last thing we need, therefore, is the muscular Christians who have never felt a bruise and who end up discouraging the person whom they should be encouraging. To help to bring comfort and support is an essential preliminary to helping the confused person to sort out his thoughts and feelings, and finally to solve his problems more constructively.

## Practical Points

My colleague, Professor R. H. Cawley, is quoted in *Roots and Shoots* as describing four levels of psychotherapy.

First, what any caring person offers by way of support. Secondly, the deeper level of helping with the person's coping techniques and his emotional defences against stress. Thirdly, dynamic methods, which I have described as Freudian in origin, using the relationship and what is usually called the transference phenomenon. Here, previous relationships may be explored in the light of what is developing between the client and the therapist. Fourthly, the level where re-learning occurs, as in behaviour therapy for phobias and fears, and old habits are dealt with and new patterns of behaviour emerge from the process.

Cawley gives an amusing and provocative picture of the customs and excise officer to illustrate what should be going on at every level of counselling. He says that every helper, counsellor and therapist should be asked to proceed through a customs barrier where he must declare his contraband. By this he implied that there are beliefs and assumptions which are never declared. Yet they, in the end, govern the effect of the counselling. The point is that a Christian believer has a right to know whether part of his counsellor's contraband includes a wish to destroy his faith.

I believe many counsellors are aware that they carry much contraband in their mental luggage. The aim of going through training is to understand what is unhelpful in our mental make-up, and to be, as a result, more useful in our work. The Samaritans show that friends may become good counsellors after limited training, and that those who have been through an experience of despair may better help the despairing. The same is true at every level of counselling.

Perhaps it does not matter so much what system of training a counsellor goes through, as long as he is helped in two ways. First, by a sensible system of psychology which will help him to know his own mind and personality better and therefore avoid mistakes which could be very harmful. Secondly, for a Christian, by understanding the principles mentioned in the quotations from Dr Lloyd-Jones: the counsellor must be sufficiently mature and aware in his own Christian thinking so as to avoid thoughtless condemnation and harsh judgement.

Again, I commend the book *Roots and Shoots* for its mini-encyclopaedic account of this area. Dr Roger Hurding suggests, perhaps rightly, that we can borrow the idea that we, as mini-Christs, have a prophetic, pastoral and priestly function in counselling our fellow believers. Personally, I think this is putting the function on too high a plane. A minister is a servant, and a pastor is (in Amy Carmichael's phrase) an under-shepherd rather than a mini-Christ. Being over-ambitious and highfalutin are the besetting sins of the counsellor. The aim should be a modest one: to bear one another's burdens, so fulfilling the law of Christ. The spirit of humility that informs those therapists who have the greatest knowledge, wisdom and experience always amazes me. That, in my view, is what we need to strive for in counselling those who are distressed. We should, perhaps, be as afraid of apparent success as of failure, since all we are required to be is good stewards of whatever gifts in helping we have been given.

# 10

# THE STRESSES OF GUILT:
# COPING WITH CONSCIENCE

The goal of this command is love, which comes
from a pure heart and a good conscience and a
sincere faith (1 Tim. 1:5).

So conscience doth make cowards of us all
Shakespeare, *Hamlet.*

Ours is not an age of guilt, we are sometimes told. We have
outgrown the need to feel the claims of God's law upon us. Some
say that the shadow of a possible nuclear holocaust leaves them
no time to be concerned with trivial failings. Sin, they say, is a
concept that is out of fashion and redundant.

In contrast, there is great sensitivity of conscience about the
environment. Ecology stresses the need to preserve, and not
violate, our world. Animals are given more care, and the animal
rights movement goes to great lengths to protest about animals
who are being ill-treated. Greenpeace is one of the many
movements which speaks to the consciences of people all over
the world about the greed and folly of such things as killing
seals and whaling indiscriminately.

It is shocking that conscience may seem to sleep. We may
be amazed that some parents can brutally batter or kill their

young children. Every trial and punishment of such an act surely reminds us of the Christian teaching that we all have this potential for sinning. Our consciences do not always deter us effectively.

How guilty should we feel in our modern world? Should we in the West still feel badly about Hiroshima or the bombing of Dresden? Do Germans still feel guilty about the camps in Belsen and Auschwitz, and the holocaust that killed millions of Jews? Do Russians feel guilty about the purges of Stalin's day, and the labour camps in Siberia that destroyed lives galore?

It sometimes seems that the greater the guilt, the less conscience speaks or bites. Did Adolf Eichman, tried at last in Israel for his part in the holocaust, show remorse, guilt or repentance? Those who have supped full of horrors may well have lost the benefits of a well-functioning conscience.

The consulting rooms of doctors and other therapists show that guilt and problems of conscience are very much a part of our lives today. Why should this be? What is conscience, and why is it so important in stress?

Some would describe conscience as an umpire in the mind, telling us whether we are playing the game according to the rules. We may see, if we watch some tennis matches on television, how an umpire may attract both anger and anxiety. Conscience is a focal point, rather like a mirror reflecting the light shining upon it. If we allow it, conscience can reflect on the moral quality of our actions. It may reflect only the light from the rules of the family or group to which we belong. That is, it may show the laws or accepted patterns of our own society. Or it may do much more. For million of people in the world, conscience reflects, in an awesome way, the laws of God.

Conscience may cause much suffering, and we will try and show how it may go wrong. It may be oversensitive, or it may not apparently function at all. But it may, as a 'good conscience', be both sensitive and robust.

## Cases of conscience

There are three main ways in which we can recognise some problem with conscience. One of the commonest is when depression settles like a black cloud and we may feel we will never be happy again. The role of conscience in such a case is to condemn, often quite unjustly. It makes the person who suffers from such a black period think only in black and white: like the Red Queen in *Alice in Wonderland* it shouts, 'Off with her head.' Although some in such a mood know that they can get back to normal, there are a good many who do not. They become their own executioner because their conscience tells them that for them there is no forgiveness.

The opposite problem of conscience is found in the con man who appears to have mislaid his conscience – at any rate, it does not seem to be functioning. He will cheat and deceive without apparently feeling any guilt at all. If he is caught, often not for the first time, he will be referred to as a psychopathic personality disorder. But for every such person who is caught, there are many who continue to cheat and lie, never learning from their mistakes.

There is a third problem of conscience which involves having excessive scruples. The house-proud woman, for example, will never be happy that the house is clean enough. She will dust and polish, plump up the cushions when a guest gets up, and her life will be an incessant round of cleaning and keeping her home tidy. Again, a business man may be so punctual that the office clock can be set by his movements, he may be mean with the firm's money as well as his own, and he may find himself slowing down in middle age because he must do everything meticulously. He not only dots the i's and crosses the t's, but he has to check over and over again that he has done so. And even then, the folly of doubting all the time sends him back to check yet again.

Here then are three clear types. The people who fall into

these categories are not ill, but many who develop such cases of conscience do break down under strain, as further examples will show. When they get better, they will only remain well if their consciences function in a healthier manner. We must therefore look at the way conscience is formed and how it grows.

## What is conscience?

Conscience is often thought of as the moral sense we have within ourselves, telling us how to distinguish right from wrong. How does such a sense, or faculty of the mind as it used to be called, get to be there? I find it helps to remember that the two separate elements that make up the word 'conscience' mean 'to know – with'. In other words, the sort of knowledge that conscience has is *reflected* – it depends, very much like a mirror, on what knowledge is allowed to shine on it.

Whether we are born with a true knowledge of right and wrong built in to our hearts and minds, or whether we are born with a *tabula rasa*, a clean slate on which parents, teachers and friends can write what they will, has been much debated. In practice it seems certain that the growing infant has to learn from his parents and later his society, how to behave according to correct criteria and standards which are acceptable to his group.

How does such learning come about? Does an infant take in morality with his mother's milk? Hardly so early, but the toddler soon learns what is acceptable in his limited world. B. F. Skinner, the noted behavioural psychologist, believes that the history of each of our lives is the story of how we have been rewarded or punished. He calls it the schedules of negative and positive reinforcements. When we think about it, a mother's smile or frown are very strong influences on a young child's behaviour. Later, rewards will take on more definite, and infinitely more subtle forms. But their purpose, as far as moral learning is concerned, is to shape a sense of duty which will govern behaviour.

How much, then, depends on the way parents (and those who function in a similar relationship to the young child) use their power to teach by carrot and stick, rewards and punishments. What kind of light and images from culture and society must they allow to shine onto the mirror of the young conscience? Should they be permissive or rigorous? Should they use a sense of guilt or shame to induce a change of behaviour in the growing child?

Great care must be exercised, since the love which the child looks for is a most powerful force, and to withdraw it in disapproval can feel devastating. The magazine *Punch* had a classic cartoon which exemplifies one attitude to moral training: a mother says to an older child about her little brother, 'Go and find Johnny, see what he is doing and tell him not to.' Such has been the prohibitive and repressive approach of many parents in the past, and in modified ways the belief still continues that it is safer to stop children following their natural inclinations.

It was Freud and his followers who added a great deal to what is meant by children's natural inclinations. They dwelt mainly on the prevalence of aggressive and sexual impulses which were not allowed to be expressed, and which were not acceptable in most societies. Freud considered that within every child is a boiling cauldron of desires which has to be battened down by means of the 'super-ego.' The super-ego, he believed, has the function of repressing these unacceptable impulses, thus we are mostly unaware of how savagely it functions. Whether we find Freud's views on the super-ego useful or not, it seems certain that there is a part in each one of us that can contribute to a very morbid conscience. It needs to be educated, to be modified and softened in its self-punitive effects if we are to feel comfortable with ourselves.

In contrast, there is a part of conscience which Freud called the 'ego-ideal': the model that we build up over the years of what sort of person we would like to be and how we would like to behave. We are more or less fully aware of this. It can be a rational, conscious part of our learning. However, it is important to remember that we may identify with someone (or some pattern of living) without being fully aware of what we are doing or of its power to affect us quite profoundly. It therefore matters greatly what ideals and models there are at critical times in a young person's development for him to identify with and make a part of his own personality.

Another way of putting it is that it is through conscience that we develop a sense of *belonging* which is so important to well-being. If we are in a cohesive group, sharing its values, ideals and hopes then we will be able to bear the strains that come to us much more easily. We all need to feel approved by those we like, admire and love. To feel isolated is a bad feeling, and it is worse when it is accompanied by an accusing conscience.

## Some hazards

Some parents bring up their children with severity and narrow-mindedness. This is not confined to religious folk – I have known liberal, agnostic parents who laid the law down so strictly that the growing child develops a far too over-sensitive conscience. Such a child can grow up anxious, scrupulous and over-controlled, sometimes unable to feel free from the excessive inner constraints which have been imposed by a rigid and unbalanced upbringing. Of course, in families where the sanctions added to the parental ones involve invoking God's punishments, the child may grow up with a conscience weighed down with unfounded feelings of guilt. It is one thing for a mother or father to show disapproval or to withdraw their love as a token of displeasure; it is quite another to say, 'If you do that, God won't love you.'

We have to consider carefully what law we lay down in the home for basic rules of conduct. If the unspoken background rules followed by parents and others reflect a balanced appreciation of right and wrong, the growing child's moral sense will be shaped very much by this awareness. He will recognise the major sanctions, and will realise that there is a good deal of freedom in many areas of life. In a great deal of the Western world the power of the ten commandments in influencing conduct is still very considerable. In many homes it is appreciated that to love is to fulfil the law.

Many hazards of moral training, therefore, are avoided if the parents create and live out a loving atmosphere, and if they spell out clearly the limits on misbehaviour, the sanctions that can be expected, and then stick to them in the same caring and concerned way.

The growing child meets parental figures like teachers and other powerful figures in his life and moral conflicts begin. The home rules may be questioned, rebellion tests out the limits of how far differences in behaviour can go. Such conflicts lead to a refinement of conscience from just being an absolute yes or no to being able to cope with grey areas of life, and to decide what is right in such situations.

## Some examples of malfunctioning conscience

In Walt Disney's film *Pinocchio* the character of Jiminy Cricket represents conscience, and the song about always letting conscience be our guide has impressed many film-goers over the years. But is it true? There are times when we should not let our conscience guide us, because it is not properly informed at the time. It is not reflecting in a true and real way the rules we should be following, rather it is being distorted by our depressed, sad mood – this is a common state of affairs.

In a survey (by kerbside questioning) well over half the people interviewed admitted to having had serious thoughts of suicide. The reasons for killing oneself, or trying to do so, are many. One important type of suicide is that associated with a sense of failure and unworthiness. Often those who seriously entertain such thoughts or plans have an overactive conscience which is accusing them of a capital offence on very trivial grounds.

A lady of impeccable morality was admitted to our hospital following an overdose of tablets in an attempt to end her life. The reason she gave for wanting to die was that she was a wicked person. Her crime was that she had not declared (for tax purposes) the interest she had received on a small amount of money in her bank account. In spite of having coped with the strains of living with an alcoholic husband and a drug-taking son, when she became depressed her conscience functioned in a distorted way and led to a nearly fatal overdose.

We can all feel terribly guilty about small things. It is often said that this problem affects the nice and the good more than many others. This is true, and while depression (as in this lady's case) responded to treatment, it might be prevented by a more balanced and enlightened conscience.

It is strange that many people who believe in forgiveness cannot, when they are suffering from the blue plague of depression, *feel* themselves forgiven. They desperately need, until they recover, the strong and constant reassurance of trusted friends, as well as professional carers, that they are forgiven, and that the damage they feel they have done can be repaired. But the power of the accusing conscience is very difficult for the most skilled carers to counteract. Eventually, when the sadness passes, they see things in a normal light again, and their conscience functions well once more.

### The loss of conscience
Some men develop into psychopaths without any sign of an active conscience. There are many reasons for this. It may be that they have been brought up in a criminal family or a sub-culture where the law they learn is the law of the underworld

of illegal activities. But the most tragic form is where someone, having been well brought up, drifts into a life where conscience is not listened to and its voice becomes silent to all intents and purposes.

A young man had been brought up by his grandmother in poor circumstances. When he got to college his ability and charm led him to be an official of the students' union with control of their funds. One day he went off to Sweden, claiming that the funds he had embezzled were a legacy from his grandmother. He was arrested, and after a brief prison sentence he became an official of a small branch of a political party. He again stole their funds and lost his job. He moved south, enlisted at another college, and again found a position where he could steal funds and take a girlfriend for a luxury holiday.

In a court case such a young man might have reports made by social workers or doctors to explain his behaviour: they might well call him a 'hysterical psychopath'. This is simply a label to describe sociopathic or antisocial conduct where the man seems to get a great deal out of living in a kind of fantasy world.

Another very similar case was brought to my notice. A man aged nearly forty had never stopped getting into trouble – something which had started at school when he was quite unable to keep the rules. The man had been an adopted baby, and the woman who had mothered him with so little reward found herself wondering about theories of 'bad blood'. It does appear from some studies that a tendency to such unrelieved absence of conscience – no remorse, no attempt to learn – may run in families.

When such genetic questions are raised, we need to look at the theory that in such families bad behaviour is learned. This is seen in such extreme examples as the Mafia, where there may be fierce loyalty to the family and its head but no conscience about killing. There will be no compunction about many illegal activities organised by such families in many parts of the world.

This lack of guilt or moral sense is, in connection with the problem of conscience, partly due to the wrong education which has been received in the first place. In the second place, not listening to conscience when a clearer light shines upon it seems to result, in time, in a loss of function, an atrophy and shrinking of conscience, until it is virtually dead.

Few of us will go to court for our actions, and fewer still will have any dealings with families like the Mafia, but in some parts of our lives (by a process of putting our activities in compartments that is described more fully elsewhere) we can find conscience losing its power over us. We are more fully ourselves when it is allowed to wake up again and function – even if conscience then makes us feel uncomfortable.

### Ritual and rigidity: the oversensitive person

There is no aspect of our lives where some degree of ritual does not play its part. The most free and easy society still develops rules, a system and a pattern of living. The routine pattern for preparing and eating food is one example – many feel upset if the time of their regular meals is altered. In schools and education, patterns for learning and living are usually spelt our in a careful and deliberate way. Religious patterns vary greatly, yet the way they are practised becomes a set pattern which those who come to belong to a group quickly learn. It does not matter whether the religious tradition is liturgical as in the Catholic or Orthodox church, or simple as in the Quaker meeting or charismatic house church – all of these have a kind of ritual which may easily become rigid and institutionalised. The same can be seen in sports of many kinds – the games have rules and everything about them can become a ritual of preparing, playing and then analysing what happened.

When the young adult faces life on his own, with all the possibilities for using such routines and rituals, some who have an oversensitive conscience can take one of two paths. They may become well-integrated people who are quite obsessional in their attention to detail. However this *suits them* and they do not feel anxious since there are many external and well-recognised patterns of behaviour they can use to control their anxiety. The second path is a less happy one which leads to an obsessive-compulsive neurosis. Here the young adult fails to adapt to the demands of life and retreats into rituals of washing, checking and other forms of careful control. He breaks down and is unable to function well in many areas.

Well-controlled and well-organised people may be recognised by their ability to get things done efficiently – they are the salt of the earth. In private they may feel at times that they have failed, for their pass mark is 100% and no one can achieve that all the time. They may regret a certain lack of freedom in their lives because their conscience makes them bound to follow a prescribed path. Some people like this go on to be as rigid as a crab, with an outside skeleton of immense insensitivity that protects their inner, very sensitive, selves. But whatever their problems they go on functioning well, even though they are prone to intense sadness and feelings of self-punishment when they do not heed the voice of duty which speaks very clearly in their conscience.

An example of the breakdown of an obsessional was in a simple case of compulsive hand washing habit. She was the wife of an air force officer. Although he loved good order and discipline, he recognised that his wife's repeated washing and rinsing of her hands, and her slow bathroom routines were not normal. Gradually her cleaning extended to the house, and her dusting, tidying and washing of everything in her kitchen would occupy her to the early hours of the morning. Her mind became totally pre-occupied with being free of contamination and dirt.

Only a rigorous course of behaviour therapy was able to help her. This involved being with the patient and helping her to tolerate the feeling of dirt being there without having to clean incessantly. It sounds simple, but it was very time consuming. The skilful nurse therapist who worked with this patient fully deserved the television award as 'Nurse of the Year'.

Fortunately, the principles of behaviour therapy are becoming better known, but their application requires a great deal of time and skill. It can be carried out in schools as well as clinics.

## A good conscience

To live with a good conscience requires two types of help. First, we need to know when our shame or guilt feelings are irrational, by which I mean that they are derived from parental pressures which may be unjustified. We receive this kind of help in the process of growing up, yet our consciences can remain childish in a very unhappy way. To educate them is a long-continuing process.

The second kind of help is that traditionally provided by religion and faith. I am surprised how often patients are really asking their doctors for help in obtaining forgiveness and absolution. Their symptoms have arisen because they do not feel good enough (as mothers, wives, fathers or whatever role they are bothered about), and they want to feel all right about themselves.

Doctors cannot help when the strain of conscience leads to a certain kind of sadness and despair. I find it important that Christians have recognised that the 'awakening' of a conscience leads to another kind of sadness: for them this often leads to faith and forgiveness. It is a welcome development that doctors and ministers of religion are working together more often to help such people, for crises of conscience are often repeated and require the help of a spiritual counsellor as well as a doctor. Some call this a process of healing, and refer to sorting out bad influences on conscience as healing of the memories. I think it is just as well to see it as a process of learning and growth, when our consciences go through a process of development resulting in a greater ability to bear the strains of living with its many moral dilemmas.

## Some Christian examples

In the New Testament conscience is seen as either excusing or accusing us in the light of God's law and judgment.

John Bunyan speaks of the *bruised conscience*. I take this to refer to the paradox that one of the first things that happens when God's word and Spirit affects the human heart is that it awakens a sense of guilt and shame. It has been said that faith enters a man's life at the point of his conscience. This is how he comes to feel any need at all for forgiveness or repentance towards God or reparation towards those whom he has hurt or damaged.

At one point in Christian history, in the eighteenth century, the word 'whole-hearted' acquired a bad meaning. This was because Christians recognised the need to be broken-hearted, as David described it in Psalm 51, not whole-hearted in the sense of being full of yourself.

It is through an experience of a proper sense of guilt that we come to know Christ. We can only know him through his saving benefits, as the famous phrase in the time of the Reformation put it. Martin Luther, perhaps because he was such a sensitive and scrupulous monk in his early years, achieved an unrivalled grasp of the way the gospel of Christ should result in true liberty and freedom of conscience for us as Christians. It is through conscience that we are freed from real guilt, by repentance and faith in Christ. We learn that his death and sacrifice cleanses all guilt in a way that the sacrifices of Old Testament days could not.

## Maintaining a good conscience

It is inevitable that even the best Christian is troubled by his conscience. As his knowledge of God's demands grows, his insight of himself should deepen. So, as Henry Twells correctly observed in his hymn:

> And they who fain would serve Thee best
> Are conscious most of wrong within.

I often find that good people cannot distinguish between real guilt and a sense of guilt which has been induced by a parent's wrong approach. I think the process of education of conscience is a continuing one. The possibility of the corruption and even death of a conscience is real.

Educating our conscience includes knowing that when we are justified by faith and made right with God it is a once-for-all act affecting the length and breadth of our lives. Certainty of this may vary. Our assurance is bound to be affected by many things, and sometimes our conscience speaks loudly about a failure or fault. If justification is a once-for-all act, by the same token confession, repentance, and putting right by repairing the damage we have done are daily acts. It is by the discipline of faithful obedience according to our best light and knowledge that we keep a good conscience.

I wish that some Christian friends, whose consciences lead them to be extremely punctilious about some religious practices, knew more about the freedom of conscience that Christ brings from the demands of petty laws and observances. Some Christians carry Sabbath observances much too far. Other Christians, in matters of dress, make-up, entertainment etc., can be bound by their consciences to what they perceive as a proper 'other worldliness'. One does not need to go to such sects as the Amish in the United States to find a harsh legalism where the consciences of those involved are constantly harassed by punitive guilt. They may be weaker brethren (in the way St Paul describes those who could not eat certain meats which had been offered in pagan temples), but we should surely hope that they will come closer to the ideal that God in Christ wants for us all: to live on his forgiveness and to be both strong and free, with consciences 'void of offence'.

## 11

## Sex and Stress: Love and Law

For this reason a man will leave his father and mother
and be united to his wife, and the two will become
one flesh (Mark 10:7).

He has taken me to the banquet hall, and his banner
over me is love (Song 2:4).

Sex is seen as one of the particular issues of our modern time.
Perhaps the contraceptive pill, pornography and the explosion
of social pressure for more liberation from restraint are a
specially modern mix. The AIDS epidemic, with all its horrors,
has placed modern sexual behaviour under a huge magnifying
glass, compelling millions to examine their permissive
assumptions. In spite of all the unusual features of our day, made
worse by living in a global village where the mass media transmit
values and air travel permits easy movement of both people and
their sexual habits, there are basic aspects of our sexual lives
which have been present from time immemorial.

Are the swinging cities of London and Los Angeles so far
removed from first-century Corinth and Ephesus? I doubt it.
Today, when we may hear far more about incest and other forms
of sexual abuse, it is easy to forget that incest was also present

in the church at Corinth to which the Apostle Paul wrote his first letter (1 Cor. 5:1). Rape is writ large across many pages of the Old Testament.

The Bible is extremely frank about the potential of sex and love both for delight and for distress. It not only sets out the ideals, the rules (God's law), it also describes the problems, and the failures to live up to the ideals set out.

For Christians there is an important connection between sex and love, and love and law. In sexual matters, perhaps more clearly than in most areas of life, it can be said that love is the fulfilment of the law. The rules are not there to cause suppression of what is good and lovely in sexual life. The laws and sanctions – not only in the Bible, but also in other societies untouched by its influence – are meant to be a gossamer-like fabric to preserve what is good. To those who honour the rules, this gossamer serves to preserve them from the destructive potential that seems built into the sexual drives, perhaps more than any other in our lives. But the same rules are very easily broken, and that can lead to great and continuing distress and pain to many.

One of the most moving psalms of David, Psalm 51, was written by a man who had been not only a flagrant adulterer but also a murderer. David's killing of Bathsheba's husband by putting him in the front-line of battle would surely make headlines in a tabloid such as the *News of the World*. Yet King David, after repentance, renewal and the loss of Bathsheba's first child, continued in his place in the history of salvation. David is one of the many examples of sex and violence in the Bible.

We miss the point entirely when we say that we should have a Bible fit for children to read. The Bible is starkly true to life. It portrays vivid pictures of humans failing to live up to the basic rules; human experience is illuminated by God's law and judgments.

In the New Testament the light becomes brighter, and the

ideals are spelt out more explicitly. Thus the Sermon on the Mount stresses thoughts and desires, not simply sexual acts. Does all this mean that stresses due to sex are greater? Have we as Christians any right to speak about what normal Christian life should be?

## Truths and perversions

Recently, Christians have had to fight even more for an acceptance of a normal sexual life with traditional teaching and standards. Attacks have come from vocal groups who blame the ideals of the family, marriage and fidelity for our modern ills.

From homosexual movements, including gay Christian liberation groups, there have been concerted destructive criticisms. They maintain (and want schools to teach this) that homosexuality should be a desirable alternative to heterosexuality and marriage. They go further, and wish it to be a legal offence to discriminate against homosexuals in any way.

Feminists and those who argue for women's liberation have many truths on their side. But it is tragic that some should reject the ideal of marriage because of men's age-long abuse of the marriage tie in many lands.

Pornographers have never had it so good – magazines, videos and books have flooded the market. Vast fortunes have been made form soft and hard pornography. For many, feminists as well as Christians, such pornography debases and devalues sex. Men, women and children are simply turned into things to be enjoyed without love, affection, respect or tenderness. Sex and violence form a sordid chapter in its history – we do not yet know the full extent of pornography in the damaging link it exploits between destructive, aggressive drives and sexual ones.

But, alas, some perversions of the truth about sex and love are present in the church too. The Victorians, and others, seemed to think they could lie about sex. Not only religious books, such as *What a Young Man Ought to Know*, but also leading psychiatrists, like Henry Maudsley, thought masturbation should be treated as a grievous aberration – it was commonly taught that it led to blindness and madness. But the church has also taught – or hinted implicitly, that normal sexual feelings are wrong in themselves. To its credit, the belief that the body and its desires are sinful was labelled heresy, but such beliefs do not die easily. In practice millions of churchgoers have been led to think that a celibate life as a nun or monk, doing without sex altogether, is better than the rough and tumble of marriage. I think we must recover Martin Luther's view that marriage should be a school for character. As Christians we may claim both biological, spiritual and emotional value for marriage.

The most basic affirmation is surely that sex is a matter for full and joyful acceptance. Its ideal fulfilment is in marriage where it should be embedded in a matrix of tenderness, affection and loyalty. The rules and laws which hedge it about are for the protection of this highly prized relationship.

Chastity before marriage and fidelity within it may seem quite impossible to attain, yet millions have attained to just that. However, they do not deny that striving to keep the ideals leads to distress and frustration at times. The positive, enriching and fulfilling potential of sex can lead to solid joys and lasting pleasures.

Of course, guilt and anxiety may result from the struggle, especially when young people are pressurised to conform to alternative lifestyles. With proper, sympathetic understanding and support, the negative side of doing without immediate sexual gratification can be coped with well and lead to relationships which are lasting and enjoyable.

### Stresses in marriage

The Apostle Paul's remark that those who are married will suffer 'troubles in the flesh' is part of Christian teaching. He dwells, too, on the problems of dual allegiance: wanting to give his life and time to God, but having obligations to his wife and children. His fellow apostle, Peter, says that we should not neglect our sexual obligations. This part of married life must not be withheld 'so that nothing will hinder your prayers' (1 Pet. 3:7). Such remarks about the importance of the physical expression of love in marriage are a small part of a wider discussion. But we should not neglect to make proper note of them.

In our day three aspects of marriage have been much studied for their stress potential: the social aspect, the bond of affection, and the bond of pleasure. We will look briefly at each of these aspects.

But first, Christians would say that a marriage contract is a thing God not only blesses but, in a way, makes. We say that 'marriages are made in heaven'. The first and most important fact about marriage is that God, in creation, ordained it.

Sexual harassment at work is no new thing, and it is not only women who are harassed. One story from ancient times is that of Joseph (Gen. 39). The wife of Potiphar, Joseph's master, felt it was part of her fringe benefits to seduce the attractive young Hebrew man in his twenties. It was doubtless normal practice at the time. Joseph's protest to her, and his refusal to make love to his master's wife, ends with the words: 'How then could I do such a wicked thing and sin against God?' (Gen. 39:9). Then Joseph was framed, her allegations were believed, and Joseph went to gaol. He suffered for his allegiance to what he thought was an important part of God's will: correct sexual behaviour.

King David, whom we have already mentioned for his flouting the rules of sexual behaviour, accepted that he had wronged both Bathsheba and her dead husband, Uriah. And yet, after his bitter experience and repentance, what stands out in Psalm 51 is that he mourns the fact that 'against you, you only, have I sinned and done what is evil in your sight' (Ps. 51:4).

Both Joseph and David show how, in the first and final sense, marriage is about fulfilling the will of God. We must now consider how it fulfils his will for us in social, spiritual and biological ways.

## Social stresses

Problems arise in the way marriage functions as a social unit. I will highlight just a few, without trying to be exhaustive.

The husband may take a rigid view about his right to be the head of the wife, in Paul's words. He may quote Milton's famous line: 'He for God only, she for God in him.' Men can abuse biblical truth and use it as an excuse for selfish male aggression. It is easy to be a male chauvinist pig with a surface gloss of religion.

A man caused great concern with his insistence that his wife and children should be in subjection to him. He required extreme deference from all members of his family. His insistence on submission to his every whim led, perhaps inevitably, to some abuses of his powers as a father.

It is a sad scandal when social workers and child guidance workers have to intervene to protect children or wives. Yet many men, claiming the Bible's sanction, neglect their plain duty to love and to cherish their wives and children. In the matter of subjection, the Bible's teaching is clearly linked to the duties of loving, caring and cherishing as well (Eph. 5:28-29).

Many couples happily accept a division of responsibility and power for the family unit to function well. But it is crucial that the integrity and personality of a wife or child should not be steam-rollered in the name of alleged Bible teaching.

One partner may remain excessively dependent on his or her parents. He or she does not leave father and mother and cleave to the other partner. In small, close communities parents may be unwilling to let their son or daughter leave properly. How often the telephone cord is used as an umbilical cord to keep the grown child from proper independence. There must be a healthy separation, both emotional and physical, from the parents if a true marriage is to result.

A young man with a good job, a most helpful wife, and two young children came to hospital with severe anxiety and depression. I could not, at first, see why his marriage was at risk. It became clear that when any problem cropped up he went running back to his parents. When his tensions built up he had, for a time, to sleep at his parents' home.

His illness responded to medication and counselling. Then it became important to help him to separate from his parents and have a life of his own. Maturity is always an ongoing process. I could not decide whether his clinging to his parents, or their unwillingness to let him go, was the most difficult thing to deal with. Attention was paid to both, and his wife patiently waited for his progress. He did recover, and leaving his parents was certainly an important part of the process.

A young Christian minister told me that his answer to men who would not let their wives live an independent life was to direct them to the last chapter of the book of Proverbs. There the wife is seen as an active entrepreneur. There are many strong wives who gladly let their husbands be the titular heads of their families while they are often the real mainstay of their families. Their husbands could not have functioned well without them, and the best husbands readily admit their own dependence on their true helpmeets.

Marriage, like friendship, must be kept in constant repair. Social pressures put marriages under strain. Two bonds which keep the couple together: the bond of affection and of pleasure, merit special attention.

### The bond of affection

How do we choose our marriage partners? Dr Jack Dominian, a Roman Catholic psychiatrist, describes three factors which seem to lead to successful marriage or 'assortative mating'. First, we seem to choose someone who is like us in important respects, and we are both aware of sharing similar characteristics even before we are attracted to each other in a romantic sense. A second reason for choosing a partner is nearness: we live near each other in the same locality, or we have similar social backgrounds. A third reason is that we complement each other's needs as partners.

There has been a huge increase in marital counselling and family therapy. One reason is that each partner brings to the marriage many problems which derive from the family which brought him up. Each partner has, for this reason, personal vulnerabilities of varying degrees. Sharing a life together, having children and bringing them up, all impinge on insecurities which may go a long way back in one's life-history. There are common financial pressures, such as mortgages and job promotions and demotions which are among the top ten stresses in any chart that measures life events and the strains which they produce.

No wonder so many marriages end in failure. Even those who will not accept divorce for religious reasons may suffer such misery and hardship because of the pressures on the bond of affection which could keep the couple together. Christians share with many other people of goodwill the belief that marriage is a total commitment and that lifelong fidelity to one's partner is of the essence of the contract. There are many failures to live up to this in thought, word and deed. Yet the Christian position is that it is better to admit our failures rather than lower the standards. To alter the ideal is to de-value the whole currency of marriage. Easy divorce may do this.

This chapter cannot begin to deal properly with the issues involved in divorce, neither can the problems presented by abortion be considered. Other issues in family life, important though they are, cannot be covered. The comment must be made, however, that Christians who are equally devout and committed to their standards do have different points of view. We cannot treat those who disagree with us as renegades from the truth, but should take a charitable and understanding attitude. Some doctors who have chosen to differ from a party line (on abortion for example) have been treated as if the Holy Inquisition was still in existence. This is a sad and unacceptable state of affairs. Let every man be fully persuaded in his own mind.

### The pleasure bond

Is it possible to domesticate Eros? For some Christians, Eros (physical pleasure) is an alien god – they consider that it has little or no place in marriage. Are we guilty, like some Jewish folk, of trying to exclude the Song of Songs from the canon of Scripture?

The Song celebrates the delights of sexual love: 'He has taken me to the banquet hall, and his banner over me is love' (Song 2:4). I do not deny its allegorical value as a picture of Christ and the church, but its primary meaning should also be accepted. The same song speaks of the girl as 'a garden locked up' (Song 4:12). The walls and locks are there to protect a delicate and erotic relationship from harm and illicit entry.

What, then, are we to make of two modern American gynaecologists, Masters and Johnson, who have done so much to study human sexual responses and their related problems? Is all sex therapy out of court for the Christian? One answer can be found in Tim and Beverly La Haye's book *The Act of Marriage* (London, Marshall Pickering, 1984). They take what is useful in sex therapy and set it in a biblical context, as other writers have also done. There are absurdities in sex therapy at times. However, it is important that we place a proper, though not undue, emphasis on the role of pleasure in marriage. Here, in brief summary, are some points.

A couple must learn to 'give to get.' To know how good it is to hug, touch and cuddle without genital contact is another vital point. Masters and Johnson use a verb 'to pleasure' to describe how each must learn what pleases his or her partner. They have also coined the phrase 'sensate focussing', meaning being able to concentrate on what pleases the other partner in a sexual relationship. Simple advice, and a few interviews with a sympathetic, knowledgeable counsellor, can work wonders. To ease the pain and suffering caused by the absence or inability to achieve a good mutual response is a very praise-worthy task. Silly inhibitions, which have nothing to do with Christian faith, make some couples try and drive with the hand-brake tightly on, so to speak.

It is not hard to find proper warrant for this approach in the New Testament. The Apostle Paul, thought to be no lover of women by the ignorant, puts it clearly in 1 Corinthians 7:4 – 'The wife's body does not belong to her alone but also to her husband. In the same way, the husband's body does not belong to him alone but also to his wife.' He is quite explicit: 'Do not deprive each other except by mutual consent and for a time, so that you may devote yourselves to prayer' (1 Cor. 7:5).

## Sexual development
The issue of 'normal' sexual development is queried by those, particularly of a homosexual persuasion, who believe that anything goes and that we should not rigidly insist that there is a proper course of sexual growth for men and women. Christians who look to the Bible for guidance should not forget the approach implied in Paul's words: 'Does not the very nature of things teach you ... ? (1 Cor. 11:14).

Those who think, with modern popular psychology, that Freud advocated sexual licence, are wide of the mark. Consider the way Dr Balint presents the Freudian view in *Marital Tensions*, a book by H. V. Dicks. He says there that a mature adult sexual relationship means 'genital mutuality in a setting of tenderness and affection' – that is his norm. He describes the so-called stages in development thus: the person (man or woman) simply looking for sexual conquests is still fixated in the phallic stage; he who uses a partner to be dirtied or degraded in sexual activity has not got over the anal stage. And an excessive dependence in a sexual relationship means that the oral stage is still unresolved from early infant development.

Of course, a proper understanding of sexual perversions is much more complex than this simple statement. But using psychoanalytical ideas does not mean sexual chaos. On the contrary, the aim is to understand what went wrong on the road to sexual maturity. We all take with us some unresolved problems met at early stages on that long, and sometimes difficult, road.

There are other models for understanding why some have an easy progress in sexual development and others run into trouble. Critical periods occur throughout childhood where things may go wrong. Proper mothering, and parenting in general, has been much emphasised in recent decades. The importance of good models – in loving parents, in older brothers and sisters, aunts and uncles, friends in the local church and society – is paramount, for all influence how we develop and how we handle sexual stresses.

Perhaps there has been too much emphasis at times on 'bad models'. For example, those who are men among boys and boys among men may hinder some boys from negotiating a normal adolescent phase. Powerful personalities may imprint their own approach to sex on others at periods when they are vulnerable or young. We would do well to protect, as far as we can, those who are still growing sexually from such predatory and potentially destructive influences.

## Homosexuality: a Christian view
For many, the Christian emphasis on love and law is something they cannot accept when it comes to homosexuality.

Traditionally, Christians have said that there is nothing wrong with warm, loving relationships between people of the same sex. But, based on Old and New Testament prohibitions, homosexual acts have been forbidden. The AIDS epidemic, as we shall see, gives a new urgency and incomparably greater, life-threatening stresses, to this problem. How are we to cope with these?

First, let us look at the relationship between David and Jonathan. It clearly shows that love between men can be an important part of life without being sinful. David said: 'I grieve for you, Jonathan my brother; you were very dear to me. Your love for me was wonderful, more wonderful than that of women' (2 Sam. 1:26).

Sir John Wolfenden, whose report some consider as having led to the legalising of homosexual acts between consenting adults in private, said in that report that, whatever the direction and strength of our drives sexually, we are all required to exercise control over their expression.

Secondly, what can we say of the swing in favour of believing that we cannot take the biblical prohibitions seriously? This problem is covered by David Field in his booklet *The Homosexual Way: A Christian Option?* (Nottingham, Grove Books, 1976). I recall Dr Sherwin Bailey's books with their views that Sodom did not actually have anything to do with homosexual acts but simply sins against hospitality. By the same token, St Paul's protests were seen by this school of writers as only being against promiscuous homosexual acts, not a loving relationship.

I believe that we cannot, as so many fifth columnists in the church have done, abandon the traditional prohibitions. It is important, while being charitable to those in the large homosexual minority, to stick to the proper rules. We cannot move the goalposts to help one side win. We cannot change what the Bible describes as God's laws, and what nature itself teaches us is unnatural regarding homosexual practices.

Homosexuality is a substantial problem, as it has been since the explicit depiction of it in the literature and paintings of ancient Greece and Rome. It was an established problem when the early Christians met it head on. It is nothing new. What has been new in recent years is the growth of homosexual Christian movements. They have been extremely vocal.

I consider that we have a clear duty to oppose the ways in which many homosexual groups seek to press-gang others to join them. It is time to cry halt to those who feel they have total licence to proselytise and seduce vulnerable people to join their way of life.

Such words are emotive. I use them because I think there is a place for righteous indignation towards those who have misused positions of trust and freedom to put over a minority view as if it were quite normal and acceptable. Again, I would point out that homosexuals are angry with those doctors and psychologists who show, on the basis of much study, how much homosexuals are outside the line of normal development. They hate words like perversion, and yet much of what they advocate is, precisely, a perversion of normal sexual drives.

## The AIDS factor

The spread of knowledge about AIDS has resembled saturation bombing too much for me to dwell on it. Yet the magnitude of the problem merits comment. In the next few years all of us are going to be affected by the way resources will be diverted to dealing with AIDS victims. Hysteria is not a proper response, but rather careful consideration.

Acquired Immune Deficiency Syndrome started in Africa. It has had three phases. The predominant first phase was its spread among promiscuous homosexuals in the United States of America. These men were the vanguard of the Gay Liberation movement. Many would expect some twenty thousand partners during their active sexual lifetime. Practices like fisting were common, and damaging to the partner. I have heard doctors who were in San Francisco in the 70s saying that even Charles Darwin would have said that a species living in such a way did not deserve to survive.

The second epidemic, a minor one in comparison, is being spread through drug addicts using needles contaminated by an AIDS sufferer. The third, and potentially much more difficult epidemic, is due to the spread of AIDS through heterosexual intercourse. When this fact was first known, it seemed difficult to accept. The common finding that homosexual men may also be bisexual and have women lovers, or be married as well as being promiscuous with men, has led to our present sad state as much as anything. We read daily news items of increasingly alarming import about the numbers infected and the numbers who have died and who may do so in the near future.

Bigotry is back. I think it is sad if we fail to be compassionate to sufferers because we feel a new right to be bigoted about how justified we are in believing homosexual acts are wrong. Such self-righteousness, and a certain satisfaction that they are getting what they deserve, is no proper human response, let alone a Christian one. But we are justified in saying that the present alarming epidemic should make it more easy for people to see the sense in traditional behaviour. Perhaps the behaviour of courtship will return. Surely it is subhuman simply to 'have sex' with someone you do not know?

The fear of AIDS is an added stress for many. We must incorporate new knowledge about AIDS into our repertoire of behaviour, avoiding foolish and unwarranted fears. Society will have to make some major decisions about how to use its resources. Christians should not be afraid to speak out on the basis of their traditional beliefs with renewed force, but with charity and compassion too.

## Pornography

Pornography adds many stresses to sex. Just look at the magazines stacked in most corner shops with other newspapers. Professor John H. Court's book *Pornography: A Christian Critique* is a mine of information on the current position.

It is not just a question of whether we see pornography as merely erotica without style – which is the attitude of many liberal, intelligent people. We need to go further and see how, in many kinds of pornography, any connection between love and sex is ruled out. To 'have sex' is the point – whether with woman, child or beast is just a matter of personal taste. To gratify desires is the thing – love, affection and tenderness are immaterial.

Lord Longford's definition of pornography is 'that which exploits and dehumanises sex, so that human beings are treated as things, and women in particular as sex objects'. In the USA a Presidential Report (1970) spent two million dollars on researching the effects of pornography.

Dr Court gives a critical assessment of all this. His final position is against censorship but in favour of quality control. He describes pornography as being anti-life in the following ways:

> It is against the family and against women in degrading and humiliating women.
>
> It is against children, and in a welcome way it is shown that pressing a glamourised adult sexuality on them barely allows them the pleasures of childhood.
>
> It is anti-human: parts of the body, not the whole person, are focussed upon; people are denied proper emotional potential.
>
> It is anti-sex since it takes away the joy, intimacy and fulfilment that sex may bring in a loving bond.
>
> It is anti-social in its repercussions, whether we accept the links between pornography and violence or not.

It pollutes the environment with posters and unwanted material.

It damages communities by supporting a multi-million dollar industry: this links to police corruption, drug addiction and other evils.

It is against culture because the 'obligatory explicit sexual scenes' displace other considerations from books and films all too often.

Finally, it is against conscience: it leads to a lack of any care about the abuses of sexuality that pornography delights in.[1]

Recent events show how pornographers think nothing of attacking Christ. A Danish film-maker attempted to make a pornographic film about our Lord in England, but this failed, thanks to a concerted action.

It is not enough to say that much of what is on sale in newspaper shops is simply fantasy material for lonely men, or a stimulus for normal sexual activity for others. This is all true. But the way in which pornographers act, becoming more and more daring in the depiction of whatever they think is stimulating sexually, is a reflection of our society as a whole. We as Christians, though in a minority, can unite with many men and women of goodwill to make the sexual stresses due to pornography less and less offensive.

We are called, as our Lord reminded us, to be both salt – to restrain corruption, and as light – to help provide guidance in the growing darkness. Perhaps those of us who have no public role can show 'the most excellent way' that the Apostle Paul describes in his great hymn to love in 1 Corinthians 13. By rooting our sexual behaviour in genuine and selfless love, and showing in our daily lives that such love is the fulfilling of God's law in a joyful way, we may do much to counter the effects of those who devalue and debase the currency of love.

---

1. John Court, *Pornography: A Christian Critique* (Exeter, Paternoster, 1980).

## 1 2

# THE HOARY HEAD:
# COPING WITH OLD AGE

Grow old along with me!
The best is yet to be,
The last of life, for which the first was made:
Our times are in His hand
Who saith 'A whole I planned,
Youth shows but half; trust God: see all, nor be afraid!'
Robert Browning, *Rabbi Ben Ezra*

Today in the West the life expectancy is increasing, producing a larger population of elderly people. In the Western world men may live to sixty-nine, and women to seventy-five. In Great Britain some 12% of the adult population are over sixty-five and a third of these are over seventy-five. Some may suffer loneliness and deprivation. Those of us who have not yet joined them must share the enormous burden of care that they may impose on society, on their own families and also on themselves.

### Who cares?
As we approach sixty-five, we find that we lose more friends, we lose our health, we may lose our jobs, and we may miss our customary roles in society as we become senior citizens. Old

folk lose some of their senses, for they seldom see and hear as well as they would like to do. More often they lose some mobility and it is most irksome for many of them not to be able to get about freely as they used to do.

The Christian inherits the command to honour his father and mother. He is to 'rise up before the hoary head, and honour the face of the old man' (Lev. 19:32 AV). The Christian is also part of a society which should care for the old in a positive way. Old age should be a time when wisdom, experience and sheer staying power are all recognised and honoured.

Yet how difficult this can be! The old can be an enormous burden for the family, for neighbours, and for the caring professions. If we ask anyone who has cared for an ill relative aged over seventy, we will learn a lot. It drains their strength, taxes their patience, and sometimes drives them to sheer despair. The violence of granny-bashing may be just as scandalous as baby-battering, but the pressures that can lead to it are easy to understand. It is easier for those who have been through a period of such caring for an ageing relative to understand how violent the feelings about it all can become.

This is sometimes due to missing the emotional and mental changes that occur in the elderly. It is easier to spot deafness or blindness than depression or dementia.

An old man of seventy was in tears in my clinic: he had struck his wife for the first time in forty-five years together. 'I can't cope with her stupidity,' he said. She could not do the simplest of things asked of her. It was clear from a brief examination that his wife had lost nearly all her memory. She was, in fact, in an advanced stage of senile decay or dementia. No one had noticed this, and the husband had borne the whole strain of trying to cope with her single-handed.

Pressure groups like Help the Aged and Age Concern have made us more aware of such needs. They remind us that although our hospitals have so many old folk unable to care for themselves, there are between five and ten times as many out in the community who are often neglected and survive only with difficulty. Governments may spend more, but to little effect. Old people still think of the institutions to which they are invited to go as the poor houses of the time of Charles Dickens. They are not far wrong. Even new institutions can be overcrowded and rather smelly. Much depends on how good those who look after them are. Diligent and dedicated staff – often largely untrained – may produce a model centre which at its best is like an extended good home. But where the staff lose their morale because of the pressures under which they work, they may become patronising, treating their patients like children and omitting the respect and decent care which is their due.

Scandal and concern has been caused by the exploitation of the care of the old for financial gain. Laws may be tightened and inspections of premises and practices started, but vigilance is required since the corruption of human nature may lead to all kinds of evasions of responsibility. Christians, like all people of goodwill, can do something to safeguard the elderly and improve their lot. In order to do this we need to know something more about their special problems and how to recognise them.

### Growing old gracefully

Most of those over sixty-five are well and healthy much of the time. Faced with the enormous problems of the minority, it is easy to lose sight of this fact. What is it that helps some elderly people to enjoy retirement, to love life even when it has limitations, and to continue to show a joy and peace which has a greater depth and power as they grow older?

'We grow more like ourselves as we get older.' If this saying is true, it is a hard one to accept. It may lead us to think that we should prepare for our later years by seeking to resolve problems as they arise. If we postpone dealing with these problems, they will be there to disturb and depress us in later years.

It always amazes me when I hear two sisters in their eighties quarrelling as if they were eighteen. The childhood jealousies, the envy of sibling rivalries, have been barely recognised or sorted out, resulting in an inharmonious relationship. In the same way a brother and sister may hold bitter enmity and seem to cherish each grudge and every hurt. The quarrels of early life rumble on, like battles long ago, as if forgiveness, reparation and reconciliation were quite impossible for them to achieve or enjoy.

The positive answer to such sad observations is to say that there are many who find it easier to be tolerant and forgiving to each other. Philip Doddridge wrote of how 'my last hours of life confess, His love has animating power'. Older Christians may find new ways of applying love as a positive force in their lives.

Many older folk are happy to reap the benefits of caring for themselves through their long lives. They will have made provision with savings and pensions, which in spite of the inflation that has been going on for generations, still remove some of the fear of poverty that haunts even the affluent elderly. Those who have prepared in other ways to fill their retirement with diverse activities say, in jest, that they cannot see how they ever found time for work since their leisure activities give them so many hours of pleasure.

T. S. Eliot said that old men should be explorers. This advice was taken literally by a vicar who, on his retirement at seventy, fulfilled his ambition of going up the Amazon. He joined, for a time, his two sons who were working in that part of South America. Many have similar dreams which they may have to wait until retirement to fulfil.

Others start a second career when they are well into middle age. It may be in the church or in voluntary work. There is no doubt that ability exercised in one sphere can be later used in another career with much pleasure and satisfaction. Perhaps

Konrad Adenauer ruling West Germany at ninety, or Charles de Gaulle ruling France, are the exceptions to the rule, but they indicate what is possible. The righteous, according to the psalmist, shall 'still bear fruit in old age, they will still stay fresh and green' (Ps. 92:14). The elderly can be fertile in their contributions to local groups, to the churches, and to society. Their accumulated wisdom and experience should be welcome.

## Old men forget

We may try to grow old graciously, but we still face problems. Many of them surround the way we begin to forget things: recent memories which we might prefer to retain, give place to a tendency to dwell on the past. There is a benign forgetting which helps: old folks may not choose to register some memories, and this may be because they no longer want to clutter their minds with useless knowledge. To stick to thinking and retaining interest in what is of vital concern is well and good. The forgetting that causes trouble is caused by the death of our brain cells. Such loss of memory may herald the slow onset of senile decay or dementia. It will then be a progressive and irreversible loss not only of memory but also of all mental powers, leading in a few years to an inability to care for oneself.

Grandmother may be on a visit to a daughter's home, and while out for a walk she may lose her way. The local shops do not have anyone who knows her and policeman may be lucky to find a name and address in her handbag and then lead her to the home where she is staying. She or her family may have noticed these early changes, but have failed to realise their true significance. They may go on denying the facts of evident and slow deterioration for a long time, seeking to keep alive the still-functioning part of the mind and the person whom they loved.

A husband with memory loss may have a wife who is well and acts as a kind of extra memory for him. But if the spouse who is well has to go to hospital suddenly, the true extent of the husband's senile changes is shown, and an emergency develops since he cannot really care for himself at all. It is common to find that many who are in a dementing process can spend three to five years happily at home. But certain cautions must be given about the dangers inherent in such a situation.

The burdens in the home must not be underestimated. One grandmother inadequately cared for at home may ruin a daughter's marriage or cause much harm to the grandchildren. The guilt, anger and anxieties will reverberate around the family that is trying to cope with the heavy stresses of the decay in the health and personality of the grandmother. Other sons and daughters may be made to feel badly about the years of care given by one member of the family. This caring person may, unwittingly, push away offers of help from others in the family or outside it. A cycle of unforgiving recrimination may be set up, and the unhappy results may long outlast the death of the parent.

Such cases, and the facts that they bring to light, have alerted many to the need for such caring families to have intense support, day by day and week in, week out. Such carers do the state some service, and indeed save the welfare state very large amounts of money. They should be relieved by regular holiday admissions to hospital, by nurses, home visitors, day centres and many other agencies.

Early and full assessment by one of the new teams of old age specialists (sometimes called psychogeriatricians, but much better called those involved in the health care of the elderly) is important. The teams that work now from many hospitals have grown rapidly in numbers and expertise. But their resources are woefully limited, and their work must be supplemented by many agencies which provide practical help and moral support. It is a challenge to each local church to take its heavy responsibility in this area, and to care with knowledge and enthusiasm for the old among them and in their community.

## Stiffer, sadder and more suspicious

Many more elderly people suffer from other effects of ageing. Three common ones are: becoming more fixed and rigid in their ways; more sad and depressed after many losses; and more suspicious and paranoid of those about them. Each development is a strain, especially if the Christian's faith is affected. They may lose their assurance of faith and suffer much distress as they come to the end of their lives and face death.

*Stiffness* affects not only the joints – we all become more set in our ways as we get older. There is less emotional and spiritual responsiveness. Many change from being outgoing to being inward-looking and turn, in ever decreasing circles, around their own personal needs. Rigidity may have been a hidden feature of their lives, but it now becomes more evident and explicit. It becomes less easy to bend with the winds of change; a new situation or demand may lead to a breakdown, to a snapping under the strain.

How can it be prevented? Keeping in close touch with others helps, especially if they are younger and have more supple minds. It is important to remain curious and to be willing to explore by reading, radio or watching television. New interests and fresh enthusiasms may prevent retrenchment in old attitudes or retreating behind barricades of our own making. Christians may continue to rejoice in old, traditional beliefs and yet find new meanings and applications of them.

*Sadness* is the inevitable result of so much loss. It may lead to a frank depressive illness which it is easy not to recognise. Such illness may respond well to small amounts of medication with antidepressants. Support for the elderly is more important than anything. Christian comfort and consolation must be shown in practical ways.

One has to spoon-feed them with love as if they were children again – they often express a child-like feeling of being abandoned when dear ones die or leave.

Grief deals cruelly with the old, for they lack the resilience of younger days. Hence the need for those who can be both patient and tender with them. Nothing is easier than to slip into harshness of word or action. Somehow we who are younger forget that the elderly cannot always use a lifetime's experience to help themselves: they need our help.

*Suspicion* may sometimes lead to persecutory anxiety and frank paranoid states of mind. Sometimes it is only a mislaid handbag or wallet that leads to a son or a home-help being accused of having stolen it. Bad feelings are often put into another person by a simple process of projection, and then the other person is felt to be a persecutor. Some, who have always been suspicious, become more obviously so in old age. When, on occasions, there is a systematic development of the beliefs that neighbours, family or friends are involved in the persecution, then a psychotic disorder may be suspected and the right treatment may include medication and often a brief admission to hospital.

The suspiciousness of the elderly, like the sadness, often contains or implies a request for help. The patient is asking to be reassured, held and comforted in different ways. At such times the intensity of suspicion may fade or pass completely, and calm may be restored.

### 'Our people die well'

John Wesley said of the early Methodists that they died well. In a century where, for many poor Christians, life was nasty, brutish and short this was no small triumph. In our century death used to be a taboo subject, like sex, but both have moved from being part of a conspiracy of silence to being freely talked about. Much has been written about facing death. It is easy to think of the stages in facing death, such as a denial of our approaching death, anger over it, bargaining with God about it, and acceptance of it, in too rigid a way. These stages need not follow any special order, but thinking of them may help to clarify our minds.

When we learn that we may die soon, it is good to distinguish between the actual fear of death itself and the fear of the process of dying. Many Christians who have no real fear of death still feel with the writer of the Negro spiritual: 'River, stay away from my door.' Dr Cicely Saunders and other pioneers of the Hospice movement have shown that the pain, indignity and suffering of the physical process of dying may be dealt with successfully. We may be proud and grateful for such a practical application of medical and nursing care with evident Christian motivation. The hospices have resulted in a general improvement in the care of the dying at whatever age. But what of our personal reaction to death?

We may deny the fact of our impending death: we do not wish to know about it – at least, not just yet. *Denial* used to be thought of as a bad thing, but many have come to realise that it has value. For a while we defend ourselves against the overwhelming anxiety that full knowledge of our death may bring. It gives us a short breathing space to marshal our resources, both of body, mind and spirit.

We may be *angry*. Like the poet Dylan Thomas in a moving poem addressed to his dying father, we may 'rage, rage against the dying of the light'. It is not wrong to be angry. It may be a necessary step to acceptance of death. Some react with the semi-stoical acceptance of Tennyson when he wrote of 'sunset and evening star, and one clear call for me.'

We must all aspire to the confident assertion of the Apostle Paul that for him to die was gain, since it was to be with Christ which is far better. Perhaps, before we can face death as St Paul did, we must learn to live more like him and the other Christian exemplars of the faith.

I find the gentle and moving account of John Bunyan a most helpful way of remembering how, in a sense, it is an easy thing to die. In his *Pilgrim's Progress* the image of death is the familiar one of the river Jordan. Bunyan describes how the pilgrims ponder about when they will be called to make the final crossing. He describes their conversation as they stand on the bank of the Jordan:

> 'Then they asked the men if the waters were all of the same depth? They said, No; yet they could not help them in that case; for, said they, you shall find it deeper or shallower, as you believe in the King of that place.'

This is a pictorial way of saying that 'he who dies believing dies safely in His love'.

### Exit or entrance?

The euthanasia movement is always with us. The word 'euthanasia' means an easy death, but what the movement has stood for is the legalising of the process of hastening one's own death or that of another. An organisation called EXIT was formed in London to provide a suicide kit for those who needed it. After a court case in which a person offering such a kit to suicidal persons was prosecuted, the organisation has been disbanded. Yet many believe that the right to aid a person to kill himself persists. The predominant Christian tradition is that life is a sacred trust and that we have no right to kill ourselves or others.

In contrast the Christian view is that death is not only an exit but also an entrance into new life. The Apostle Peter, writing in his second letter, speaks of the 'rich welcome into the eternal kingdom of our Lord and Saviour Jesus Christ' (2 Pet. 1:11). Many elderly Christians approach this entrance with fear. There may be many reasons for a lack of assurance of faith: physical weakness and depressive illness may be just as important as other spiritual factors.

Dr Samuel Johnson, the eighteenth-century writer and critic, is a good example. He had championed the Christian cause in many London coffee houses. Yet as he grew older, Dr Johnson was terrified of death. He sent for a modest Anglican clergyman who was loath to counsel him. He was persuaded to come, and his talks with Dr Johnson led to his assurance of salvation. In the book of prayers that he had always kept and written in, Johnson wrote a new prayer: 'Forgive and accept my late conversion.' He described what was, it seems, an experience of Christian certainty. His somewhat bigoted editor removed the prayer from the published book, though his biographers have restored it, since it is in the original manuscript. Johnson died well, after a lifetime of depression and obsessive indecision.

Another great historical figure who was something of an expert on death was John Donne who became Dean of St Paul's Cathedral in London. One of his books *Biothanatos* examines the differing view of famous writers in the Christian tradition on the matter of suicide. Donne feared greatly as he contemplated his own death, in spite of his many sermons on the subject, and such famous sonnets as that which ends with the words: 'Death thou must die.' His last poem is a remarkable prayer which, in moments of weakness and lack of faith, anyone may adopt as his own:

> I have a sin of fear, that when I have spun
> My last thread, I shall perish on the shore;
> But swear by thyself, that at my death Thy son
> Shall shine as He shines now, and heretofore;
> And, having done that, thou hast done,
> I fear no more.

# PART THREE

## PATTERNS OF
## BREAKDOWN

# 13

## STRESS AND SEVERE DEPRESSION

Where is the blessedness I knew
When first I saw the Lord?
Where is the soul-refreshing view
Of Jesus and his word?

William Cowper, *Olney Hymns*

I was a stricken deer, that left the herd
Long since....
There I was found by One who had himself
Been hurt by the archers....
He drew them forth, and heal'd, and bade me live.

William Cowper *The Task*, Book 3, 11, 108-117

I remember being surprised, thirty-eight years ago, when a colleague told me he could never sing the hymn at the head of this chapter. It is the first of the Olney Hymns, and begins: 'O for a closer walk with God.' His reason for not singing it was that Cowper, he believed, wrote it when he was depressed. I think my friend missed an important point, but our conversation led to my reading more of Cowper and about his life.

Cowper is a remarkable example of a man who suffered at least six bouts of severe depression. His first was before he became a Christian, when he tried to kill himself. He saw himself as a stricken deer. Yet, as David Cecil shows in his life of Cowper entitled *The Stricken Deer*, he never blamed the herd. Cowper became a best-selling poet of his time, rather like John Betjeman in our day. The fact of his depression played an important part in his way of life, his style of thinking, and his long association with John Newton who helped to look after him.

We all know someone like Cowper, who may suddenly be plunged into deep black depression. Urgent treatment may be needed. There may have been a crisis at work because he has been agitated, or slowed up, and is unable to cope. His family life may have been disrupted by his extreme irritability. He may have been finding fault constantly, or lashing out with cruel words or even physical aggression.

If we do not know these details, we may find news of the illness unexpected and puzzling. We may simply know that a friend is out of circulation for some months. If we visit him, the ward will seem very different from what we expected. The nurses wear no uniform, and the pattern of care may seem very different from that of the ordinary hospital. When this happens again and again, with a return of the symptoms of depression, it becomes harder to understand. Just as my doctor friend felt Cowper's illness made him alien and strange, so we may feel it is hard to approach someone who is depressed.

The chronically depressed person who has not responded to any attempt to care for him is one of a small minority. Most cases of depression get better quickly with proper care. But there are, in Christian circles, those who seem hopeless cases, because the most enlightened approach has done very little to help them. Some, alas, commit suicide, for part of their depression (like William Cowper's at times) involves losing the assurance of faith. They believe themselves lost or wicked, and lose the very faith that has sustained them. This should be seen as part of the illness, and it will be a great help to the depressed person if we provide support for him till his normal feelings, and his usual faith, return.

Why does severe depression come?

## Melancholia: some explanations

Popular theories to explain depression come thick and fast. They are often wide of the mark. To say it runs in the family, and to blame blue genes, is only part of the story. Some are happy simply to say that there is a depressive constitution: the kind of person, like Puddleglum in C. S. Lewis' Narnia stories, who always expects the worst and looks on the gloomy side all the time.

Because so much has been written about the importance of social factors like unemployment, it is easy to get even that aspect out of proportion. Although depression and suicide figure more largely in the area of unemployment than many others, to blame crises like job loss or retirement, bereavement or the departure of a wife or husband does not wholly explain a catastrophic illness of depression. When some social disgrace leads to suicide (more common in certain countries than others, and dependent on many cultural attitudes like those of Japan), we must look deeper than the surface incident.

It is sad when some Christians think of depression as a punishment for some secret sin.

Perhaps we should avoid the questions which were put to Jesus: 'Who sinned, this man or his parents, that he was born blind?' When similar questions occur about depression, we should remember the answer that Jesus gave: 'Neither this man nor his parents sinned, but this happened so that the work of God might be displayed in his life' (John 9:2-3).

We know a good deal about the physical and biological aspects of depression. The old theory, which gave rise to the word *melancholia* (meaning black bile), was that there are fluids in the body which affect our state of mind. Modern research has shown that there are such substances: they are called 'amines' (rather like adrenaline, which is involved in so many feelings, particular anger and anxiety). These amines are vital because they form the neurotransmitters in the brain and nervous system. They enable the brain's myriad computers to work properly. In depression, their levels become low and need to be restored to normal with the use of antidepressants.

This was discovered when patients with high blood pressure were treated with the extract from a root from India which had long been used as a sedative (rauwolfia – producing reserpine). A minority (some 15%) became severely ill with depression. Further research showed this was due to the way reserpine lowered the brain amines. It was an important step in building up the amine theory of depression.

Those who find it hard to think that substances which they know nothing about (like noradrenaline, dopamine and serotonin) can lead to a belief that they have committed some unpardonable sin, may be helped by thinking of a physical disease like Parkinson's. Here the patient becomes stiffened, trembles a lot, and his gait and his mood are affected. Yet, giving the Parkinsonian patient l-dopa tablets, so that the dopamine level in his brain rises to normal, leads to amazing improvement in cases where it works. This process was described by Dr Oliver Sachs in his book *Awakenings* (London, Penguin, 1976). An extra bonus for many of these patients was getting rid of their depression. This striking picture may help to illustrate the changes which occur more slowly, but no less dramatically, when antidepressants work in severe depression.

### Blue genes
Depression often runs in families. Some kinds of illness, like true manic depression or bipolar disorders, does so more than others. Does that mean it is inherited, pure and simple? Do we learn to be depressed by modelling ourselves on parents or

grandparents that we grow up with and inevitably imitate?

A colleague of mine has written: 'The evidence for a genetic contribution to typical manic depressive illness is consistent and compelling.' The key word is contribution. What we inherit is a tendency, a predisposition. What we make of it is entirely up to us. We must not hide behind our chromosomes.

In my first five minutes with him a thirty-year-old man said to me, 'I've been depressed for nine years. Doctors in France, New York and Los Angeles have treated me. No one can help me because it's genetic. My mother and my uncle both committed suicide. Besides, my brother is a psychiatrist and even he gets depressed.'

In spite of protesting so much and saying he could not be helped, a change of approach and medication led to a vast improvement in his health.

A well-documented example from the famous Huxley family is described in Dr Julian Huxley's memoirs. His father had no illness, but his grandfather (T. H. Huxley, friend and expositor of Charles Darwin) suffered from depression. While describing his own illness and that of his brother, Francis (who killed himself), he also makes it quite clear that the advent of such physical treatments as ECT and antidepressants helped enormously to cut short his depression.

Christians may find such facts about the inherited part of depression disturbing. This may be because they make the prior mistake of confusing illness with sin and punishment. It is surely mistaken to think of the words amplifying one of the Ten Commandments as if they applied to depressive illness: 'For I, the Lord your God, am a jealous God, punishing the children for the sin of the fathers to the third and fourth generation of those who hate me' (Exod. 20:5). It is equally misleading to point to the proverb quoted by Ezekiel: 'The fathers eat sour grapes, and the children's teeth are set on edge' (Ezek. 18:2).

Depression is *not* punishment. I was appalled when one Strict and Particular Baptist minister told a patient that her depression was God's judgment on her for moving away from his church. Those of us who are well may laugh off such incredibly insensitive and unchristian remarks, but when we feel low and anxious, we may not. Caring and compassion are called for, not judgment and condemnation. James Denney, that splendid Christian thinker writing in the hey-day of views derived from Ibsen and Darwin, said:

> The inherited bias may be strong, but it is not everything in man's nature.... What we inherit, strictly speaking, may be said to fix our trial, but not our fate. His natural ancestry determines the mode of it.... But it does not depend on them what the issue of this trial is to be.

If we know of a person's 'bad' family history, it should alert us to his need. It should not make us, or him, sit down and wait for his fate and his inevitable illness. To guard against stresses in his case, particularly those to do with loss, is vital. He will need more support for longer periods than most people, but he can learn to fight the tendency to depression and accept all kinds of help to do so. Not only medication wisely used, but the social support of friends and fellowship may help him to cope better and not fall into unconstructive habits of thought and behaviour.

## Recognising severe depression

A glance may reveal more than a long gaze. Many of us are adept at hiding sadness. We look animated, smile and talk of other things, but in repose the depressive sadness may show. The old saying to help medical students was: 'If he looks depressed, says he is depressed, and makes you feel sad then he probably *is* depressed.' This is true as far as it goes, but it implies a certain skill in tuning into and appreciating the feelings of another, and not all of us have such empathy. It is often difficult to read the mind's construction in the face or in the tone of voice. To be a little more sure we need to look for depressive patterns in the life of the person we try to help.

Dr John Pollitt put it well when he described the *shift* we can recognise in serious depression. It is a biological shift in our lives. We may list some changes that occur: Appetite for food is less: weight may be lost. The sleep pattern is changed: often the person goes to sleep quickly, only to wake frequently in the night and in the early morning – usually feeling dreadful. Concentration and memory become less efficient: a man may fear that his brain is deteriorating into decay. Sexual interest is less, and the usual capacity to perform sexually may be lost temporarily. Grooming behaviour is affected: a man or woman will become careless of the appearance they show to others.

Such features may be recognised if we bear the pattern in mind and perhaps ask a few questions. The patient may burst into tears when any of the above features are mentioned, and more facts may then be forthcoming. He may say how he cannot see the bright side of anything any more, and how his sense of humour has been lost or become cynical. His irritability and anger, particularly towards those he loves, and the unhappy results of this with family and friends, may be the thing which bothers him most.

Our self-image is important to us all, and a little sadness may affect it badly. Serious depression, however, makes the person feel a total failure. For religious folk this includes the feeling that their faith and profession is not genuine and never has been. It is amazing how such strong feelings lead to fixed depressive beliefs or delusions. They may also affect the sense of taste and smell.

A lady who was impressively and impeccably turned out asked me in the hospital consulting room if I noticed the awful smell of bad drains. I could not, and she said that her husband could not smell anything strange either. It was in fact a hallucination of smell quite often found in severe, prolonged depression. Another man said he could taste the decay inside himself. This was no mere figure of speech, for our mood, when disordered, affects our very senses. It is not only that things look different to us when we are cheerful or unhappy, all the other senses may be affected as well.

Should we seek to persuade or argue such a person out of his state of mind? It is unwise to attempt this, and usually fails, except on a very temporary basis, to change the firmly held views which are determined by the fixed depressive mood. With Christians it is so tempting simply to reassure them, but it does not work.

The man sitting with me told me he was worse than a criminal. All he had done in his richly useful Christian life was 'for show'. He said, 'I would kill myself but for my fear of facing God in judgment.' He believed his whole body was affected by his terrible moral state, and his inability to eat proper food.

Eighteen years earlier, he had been successfully treated for a similar illness. His wife confirmed what his church minister had written of his excellent qualities such as a faithful church member, but discussion alone did not help. Physical treatment with medication gradually enabled us to talk more sensibly about the illness, which had wide-ranging effects on the man's life and that of his family. He became more normal once again, after some months of out-patient care.

Such thoughts of guilt, self-blame and spiritual despair are often difficult to learn about: the person keeps them tightly to himself. Slight hints may be given, but only with patience and time can we establish sufficient trust for some patients to talk about the blackness within. Once recognised, such severe depression – where thoughts may lie too deep for tears – *must* be taken seriously and expert help obtained. For the outlook with treatment is good, but without it such patients may progress to further depths of illness such as we find in depressive stupor (where the patient refuses to talk or eat) and death may result.

### Helping the severely depressed

Much serious depression (about ninety per cent) is treated by family doctors without recourse to any psychiatric specialist. Results may be very good. It seems true that, the more serious the depressive symptoms, the more likely they are to get better with physical treatment. It is evident that the family doctor may be the key member (the captain, often) of a small team that can help the seriously depressed person.

There is now a wide range of medication available for depression. The wise doctor will choose what he thinks is most likely to help the patient. For some, where anxiety is very high, help will be given in that direction, often by totally non-psychiatric drugs like beta-blockers which reduce symptoms of anxiety very well in the short-term. Many patients feel they have already enough problems without adding tablets and their side-effects to them. To explain that a dry mouth and constipation or slight drowsiness may be a problem to bear with for two or three weeks may make it easier for the patient to comply and take the medication without expecting a magical change the next day. Only a few antidepressants require any dietary precaution like avoiding cheese and red wine. Today the degree of risk with most carefully prescribed medication is only small. The risks and the misery of depressive illness are far worse, and may be cut short with treatment.

Medication is only the first step: counselling and support must follow. Many doctors are happy that their practices or hospital departments have a wide range of workers to help. A nurse may often be trained in community psychiatry. A psychologist may provide expert advice and therapy in depression, helping the patient to see and to change patterns of thinking and behaving which have contributed to his illness.

Other helpers and counsellors are available too: not simply professional social workers, but others who may help in the patient's home in many practical ways. When such extra help is not available it puts an extra burden on neighbours, church friends and officers to provide crucial supportive care. The last thing that should happen is that the depressed patient should be treated like a leper, for he already feels alienated by his illness.

All these measures simply help; it is the patient himself who recovers. Where the customary recovery does not take place, then in-patient care and admission to a special unit in hospital or day hospital is advisable. There, more expertise and more time may ensure recovery. Other physical treatment may be considered necessary.

ECT (electroconvulsive therapy) is sometimes used, and can be life-saving. It has had a bad reputation. Some dread the 'shock treatment' while others, knowing how quickly it helped them before, ask for it to be given without delay. It was misused in the 40s and 50s but nowadays it can be highly effective without upsetting the patient. A light, brief anaesthetic is given, followed by a muscle relaxant and a small, brief electrical current is passed through the brain. A twitching of the fingers or lips is often the only evidence of a 'convulsion', and ancient films of ECT do not properly illustrate the present method. It appears that its effectiveness is due to a direct action on brain amines. Whereas tablets have to be swallowed, absorbed, got through the liver to bloodstream and thence to the brain, the application of ECT may be much more direct and certain.

Many other measures contribute to recovery, each of them therapeutic. At first, support – being *held* safely by the care and love of others – is essential. Later, the kind of counselling that looks at painful areas of the patient's life becomes necessary. Continued care from staff who know and understand the patient may be immensely helpful.

## Preventing depression

Much study has been undertaken on the identification of vulnerable groups. It is helpful to look, for instance, at the work of Professor George Brown and his colleagues in London and to apply some of their findings.

Women are more liable to depression than men in our society. Those who have lost a mother before they reached the age of eleven are more at risk than others. It seems obvious, then, to stress the need for mothering in order to prevent depression. Others, such as an aunt, grandmother, father or friends, may have provided a group from which the child who is bereaved expected mothering. But having missed out a true mother, it follows that care may be needed later in life to provide the sort of love they have lost. It is hard work, and the carers (doctor, professional, or friend) will be challenged to the limit.

The role of a confiding, intimate friend is also important in protecting against depression. This may be someone whom the person sees daily, or can phone if she cannot see. Obviously a husband, boyfriend or special woman friend may fill this role. Regrettably, this intimacy may be absent from many relationships. A special sort of befriending is needed – it is expensive in terms of time and effort, but rewarding in the personal growth it may promote in someone who is depressed.

Work may sound an unexpected antidepressant, yet Brown found that part-time or full-time work was a great help. The clue is in what it does for our self-esteem. It is not simply that we are paid for what we do and are appreciated, it is that there is a change of scene from the demands of home. It leads to new horizons and opens up new friendships. In a time of unemployment, the vital role of work cannot be overemphasised.

It may sound obvious to say that if there are three children at home under fourteen years of age, the risk of depression goes up. Any man who has tried to look after one or two young children for a day may admit how little he understood of the many stresses involved. An inexhaustible supply of skills and energy is called for.

To some extent the provisions of help in the form of crèche, day nursery or child-minders is based on recognition that a mother needs to be helped and enabled to work if she wishes. But much more could be done to lessen the stresses of looking after children. Voluntary workers and churches have been inventive in finding ways, and they may help greatly in cutting down the risks of depression.

# 14

## IS STRESS PSYCHOSOMATIC?
## SOME PHYSICAL EFFECTS OF STRESS

The mysterious leap from mind to body.
                                        Sigmund Freud

Leave comfort root room.
                                        Gerard Manley Hopkins

It is a curious fact that some words are used like swear words –
to express bad feelings. Sometimes telling someone that his
problem is psychosomatic is taken to mean that his pain or
distress is not genuine, but in a way faked. It is like saying to a
person, 'Let's face it, you're being rather neurotic' – again a
pejorative use of the word 'neurotic'. I believe that suffering
psychosomatic distress is one of the most unpleasant things in
life. Much of our distress, whether due to a spiritual crisis or a
problem with another person in our lives, is felt physically. How
does this come about with such frequency?

   Freud's description of the problem has been translated as
'the mysterious leap from mind to body'. To me it seems an
awesome as well as an awful thing to find physical symptoms
so disabling when the cause is in the realm of mind and spirit.
In medicine, two kinds of people have been traditionally
recognised as needing help in a special way: the hysteric and

the hypochondriac. However, under stress we may all behave in ways which make others think we are nothing but histrionic (or worse, making it all up and malingering), or so totally preoccupied with our bodies that we are in danger of imagining all sorts of disorders which are not there. We may bore our friends with talk of symptoms, tests, X-rays and operations. It may even become a way of life. (Later in this chapter we'll be looking at the psychosomatic pilgrim's progress.) We should try to understand people, not mock or call them names.

## An extreme example

A doctor or surgeon may face a severe and urgent problem which calls for action. At the back of his mind will be a series of questions. First, is there something physically wrong, an organic problem? Should he operate or treat for that? Then comes the next urgent question: if all tests are normal, is it safe to think that there is no organic problem, but rather a functional one (meaning simply that something is not working properly, yet usually taken to mean it's not important because it isn't obviously physical)? Then the doctor must ask: is the patient hysterical, or malingering, or is it a case of *le malade imaginaire*?

I was asked to see such a case:

A surgeon asked me to see a young man who had been sent to hospital in the hope that he might have his kidney removed. For six years he had suffered pain in his lower abdomen. The first operation was to remove his appendix; the second and the third were to deal with adhesions around the area. The fourth operation was to remove part of the kidney – to no avail. For in spite of it all, the pain persisted.

Family doctors despaired of the frequent calls for visits, requiring injections to relieve the pain. He was told to change doctors several times. He was dependent on pain-relieving drugs. His wife felt very angry and helpless. The future seemed very bleak.

Should the kidney be removed: Clearly, it should not be operated on again. What the surgeon did not know was the long history of the patient. The stresses started when, just prior to the onset of the pain six years earlier, his twin had died in a swimming accident. He heard the news of the twin's tragic death, and it had led to many problems with which the pain had become inextricably connected.

The patient and I were fortunate that a team of doctors and nurses were able to sort out this particular pilgrim's progress. He had fallen into a slough of despond, as so often happens, by not fully disclosing the story behind the pain. By looking to drugs to relieve pain, or to a surgeon to perform miracles in the operating theatre, he had simply got worse and worse.

We will return to a fuller consideration of this case later on in this chapter. First, we must consider the meaning of the word 'psychosomatic' itself.

## The history of a word

A brief look back in anger at how a word has been used is justified. I am angry that those who diligently pursued the road of psychosomatic research found themselves in a blind alley. Much study and research led to hopes which have been dashed. Yet the new meaning of the word 'psychosomatic' is to the effect that all conditions due to stress have a component which is psychosomatic.

The doctor who first used the word in 1818 did so as a reaction to the materialism of the time. He was saying, quite rightly, that man is more than just body: he has a mind, a spirit and a soul (or psyche). The term 'psychosomatic' was first applied to the result of the influence of the spiritual and emotional world on the body. It described the influence of mind over matter as it affected illness. Thus, when the prophet Jeremiah cried out, 'My bowels, my bowels! I am pained at my very heart; my heart maketh a noise in me; I cannot hold my peace' (Jer. 4:19, AV), he was describing psychosomatic pain long before the word was invented. Many other references of a similar kind might, of course, be cited.

The influence of Freud was important, although he never seems to have used the word 'psychosomatic.' His followers, especially in Chicago and the USA generally, used the idea of psychosomatic illness to treat a number of diseases. These came to be called the sacred seven: asthma, peptic ulcer, high blood pressure, colitis, rheumatoid arthritis, thyroid problems and neurodermatitis. Their mistake, looking back on their years of work and writing, seems to have been to fix their eyes mainly on the internal world of the patient. Conflicts, such as how to handle anger, were used to explain symptoms and diseases.

Inevitably, newer discoveries have led to this limited view of psychosomatic disease being abandoned. The work on the immune system of the body has brought the nature of the sacred seven diseases into a clearer light. Everyone now knows more about the immune system since the advent of the AIDS epidemic where the immune system breaks down. Diseases such as asthma are now viewed in a different light. Yet it is easy, even today, to succumb to the simple explanation.

A woman of fifty heard on the telephone that the husband from whom she had been separated for many years had died. She immediately had her first attack of severe bronchial asthma. She still suffers, years later, from crippling asthma. Was it just the pent-up anger she had felt over many years towards her husband which caused her to have asthma? It is tempting to think so, but we must consider other factors too.

Nowadays, when a mother takes her child who is wheezing more than usual to see a doctor, he is bound to consider other, non-emotional factors too. Did the asthma follow a cold: should any infection be treated with an antibiotic? Is there an allergic factor which might call for tests leading to the use of a special inhaler? Is it brought on by exertion and cold air? If so, a different treatment might be needed. Many factors may make a child wheeze. Asthma kills 6,000 people in Britain each year, and clinics are trying harder to treat each factor where there is reason to do so. Of course, it is still sometimes necessary to remove a child from his home or mother to clarify the picture. The history of asthma may thus show what has happened to the history of the word 'psychosomatic'. It is no longer wise to use a theory about dynamic unconscious conflicts to say that anger or guilt invariably produces one kind of symptom picture.

Hysteria is not a fashionable term at the present time. One reason for this is that there are patients who exaggerate and dramatise their symptoms – perhaps they should be called histrionic rather than hysterical. Some of these patients, after being told they are hysterical, go on to show evidence of serious organic disease like brain tumours, or multiple sclerosis which were not diagnosable when the first investigations were made. That is why many doctors are nowadays very unwilling to make a diagnosis of hysteria. They may use the adjective hysterical, but they do not want to miss a possible physical condition that is also present – and the drama surrounding the presentation might lead to a failure to diagnose and treat it.

Hysteria may be a learned disorder. The following is a good example of this aspect of the problem:

A boy of sixteen was admitted to our psychiatric ward with a paralysis of his right hand, which he used for writing. Six months earlier he had actually broken his wrist and had six weeks' treatment in a plaster of paris splint.

During the period of treatment the time for his 'mock' examinations had come up, but due to his wrist fracture he was excused from writing the papers.

Now with the real examinations upon him, he realised he was almost certain to fail. As a result, he developed an 'hysterical' paralysis of his wrist. His parents believed, wrongly, that he had a great deal of academic ability. He knew he was unlikely to succeed in passing his examinations or getting into college. He had found that the 'sick role' was useful in his mock examination period, so he had now developed a similar 'hysterical' paralysis of his writing hand. In hospital, the treatment programme was directed at getting him to 'save face' and helping his parents to come to terms with his limited abilities. His arm then recovered without any special treatment directed at that symptom.

Many of us learn in childhood that sickness brings us attention and affection. In later life, when the going gets difficult, we may develop symptoms which enable us to recover the love which being ill in some way brought us when we were younger.

## The hypochondriac
Most of us have been, or will be, hypochondriacs of some kind. Anyone who reads a book about illness – perhaps this one – begins to be preoccupied with the question: have I got that problem? When the *Reader's Digest* started publishing articles of a medical kind, perhaps the seeds of this problem were being sown. Radio and television has broadcast many programmes describing illnesses, and the mystique of medical secrets seems lost for ever. I welcome more knowledge, but it is not always easy to handle it.

A preoccupation with health is one form of hypochondria. Every deviation, however slight, is noted and causes some anxiety.

A hospital colleague asked me to se a young friend who had this problem. The patient played several sports to a high standard. When he noticed a fast pulse he went to three heart specialists in turn. He became more fearful and saddened about what he thought was a dreadful cardiac problem they were concealing from him. He began to believe he was incurable.

Slowly, with help, he came to see that it was his morbid preoccupation with either real or imagined symptoms. People usually become more concerned about dreaded diseases like cancer than health, and very often these symptoms are due to depression (as we have said in other chapters). But it is one thing to recognise that a patient is seriously depressed, and quite another thing to be faced with someone who is totally convinced of the reality of their physical symptoms – such as the belief that they have a brain tumour, or that their bowels are blocked, or that they have incurable syphilis. When all the tests are returned as negative and normal, only then does some wise person ask: could this be part of a depressive disorder? If that is treated, the other symptoms disappear. To reassure the depressed person is never enough: the underlying condition must be effectively cured for reassurance to work at all.

## A psychosomatic pilgrim's progress
I shall try and chart the progress of the man described at the start of this chapter. There may be six stages.

1. The stage when symptoms are felt: in this case, pain in the lower part of the abdomen. This has been called the unformed stage of the illness: there is generalised distress, but no pattern may be discerned. Later we found that the death of the man's twin brother was the immediate precursor of the pain. If the two senior people at his work argued in his hearing, the pain came on. We learned that his adoptive parents had argued a lot, but he could not share his distress with anyone.

2. The stage of seeking help. No one listened to his story, no one wanted to know. Perhaps he did not realise the links between his distress and the death of his twin. So operations on normal organs resulted, but the pain was not relieved.

3. How medical contacts are handled makes a great difference

to the outcome. Doctors often differ, and their attitudes can in turn produce more anxieties in the patient. On the other hand, a patient may go from one doctor to another, trusting the full story to none of them. He manipulates the doctors to do what he wants. One view of the hysteric is of someone who had a good number of unnecessary operations and investigations before the age of thirty. Someone, at this stage, needs to stand back from the drama going on and consider the whole patient and what may be happening. This is a time-consuming and often thankless task.

4. The illness process may often give rise to crises which distract attention from what is really going on. The patient may misuse medication or take an overdose as in the case quoted where the family doctor refused to go on treating him. The hospital and other doctors may be at cross-purposes. The relatives and neighbours feel that 'something must be done'. If these crises are simply treated in turn, the illness goes on. If a team of therapists look at the social set-up and the psychological problems involved, then a clear picture will emerge and appropriate care may be started. Without adequate time for assessment, reflection and getting to know the patient, it is unlikely that a psychosomatic problem will be cured.

5. Convalescence and rehabilitation have to be carefully arranged if relapse is not to follow and the previous good work lost. There will need to be adjustments at home and work, in marriage or sexual life, and money problems may need sorting out. If no proper help is given with rehabilitation, what then? A more chronic disability may result. To cope with such disabilities may prove vastly expensive to family, friends and the caring profession.

6. Failure of proper care may occur in any of the five stages already described. Such failure may lead to severe and chronic illness.

A nurse had developed symptoms affecting both legs which she claimed she could not use. This was diagnosed as a hysterical condition. As the years went by she continued to refuse to use her legs. This led to atrophy from disuse, and the normal muscle capacity was lost. The contractures in both her legs meant that they became fixed in the contracted position and she became bed-ridden. Such may be the long-term result of an imaginary malady.

A note of caution must be sounded. Zeal without sufficient knowledge of the stages of illness may lead to more trouble. The wise attendant (medical, nursing, clerical or just a friend who wants to help) will register the fact that for a time this patient has found his illness to be a valuable thing in itself, therefore it must not be taken away by too sudden a cure.

A keen young family doctor was new to the practice. He found that the middle-aged mother who had a chronic ulcer due to varicose veins called upon all his capacity for intense treatment. The ulcer had been present for ten years, and he succeeded in helping it heal in ten months – but with unhappy results. For ten years the life of the whole extended family had quietly revolved around mother's indolent and fairly harmless ulcer. The physical symptoms of the ulcer on the leg, though unpleasant, had yielded great gains to the patient. A wiser doctor might have anticipated what changes the recovery to normal health and mobility might bring about. The ground would then have been prepared for the ulcer's healing, and proper and necessary adjustments to the family's way of life would have been made in good time.

The person with a psychosomatic illness requires, above all, a contract for continuing care. Without it, sad and tragic results may follow further stress. Such a contract may well be best made with the good family doctor and his practice team. But, alas, such a patient is sure to find fault with the best care and will tend to turn away from it. Friends and neighbours may have to fill the gaps left by such a refusal to accept professional care. The local church and the groups in it that may know such vulnerable patients have a special opportunity to support their weaker brother or sister. The task of sharing one another's burdens in this respect is a hard one, lacking all glamour.

'I was sick and you looked after me,' said our Lord in the parable of the sheep and the goats (Matt. 25:31-46). 'Whatever you did for one for the least of these brothers of mine, you did for me.' Such words are easy to apply to attractive situations, but not to the difficult and unresponsive patients which we have been thinking about in this chapter. Yet it is in bearing one another's burdens in this way, the Apostle Paul tells us, that we fulfil the law of Christ.

The offer of help, on a continuing basis, is vital. But it is not only the illness that makes this so far from easy. The difficulties are often in the prickly personality of the patient who has the illness. All that is part of the challenge: for to help in coping with the stresses of this particular sort of person is help indeed.

# 15

# COPING WITH STRESS IN PSYCHOSIS

> To define true madness
> What is't but to be nothing else but mad?
> William Shakespeare, *Hamlet* 2:2

Can stress drive me crazy? This is the fear that many people keep hidden when their anxieties become severe. They are terrified of losing control and going mad. We must say at once that the vast majority of people who do experience high anxiety do not, ever, become psychotic. They do not lose touch with reality, they do not have any strange experience of hearing voices or believing unusual things, or having severe disorders of thinking. These are some of the hallmarks of psychosis.

One in a hundred of us has a lifetime expectancy of developing schizophrenia. The acute form may be a dreadful crisis for the patient and his family, and yet respond to treatment well. The chronic sufferer is an enormous burden to society – an estimated 17 million in the world suffer from schizophrenia.

## Types and stereotypes
In this chapter we will start with physical states which mimic psychosis, and then describe how to recognise and treat psychotic disorders. We will try to distinguish eccentricity from

illness – for the eccentric may appear mad but not be ill. He is simply different from the rest of us and relatively happy and harmless. Even a little hard data may help us to understand and accept psychosis. It may be cared for and sometimes cured, but often requires support for both the sufferer and his friends and family.

Every church or religious group is likely to have a handful of patients with some degree of psychotic disorder. They may be greatly helped if we know how important it is to subject them to as little criticism, hostility or enthusiasm of an emotional kind as we possibly can. They have rightly looked to Christians for help, and chronic sufferers from schizophrenia are best helped by consistent, quiet and non-threatening care and support.

Our stereotypes and caricatures of those who fall mentally ill under stress are derived from such films as *The Snake Pit* and *One Flew over the Cuckoo's Nest*. As children many of us form views which are based on the fears our parents had of asylums and psychiatric institutions. Phrases like 'being put away' or 'being committed' still occur when thinking of psychotic illness. Let us try and get beyond the jumble of fears and taboos to describe, briefly, what madness is.

We may feel, as Polonius says in *Hamlet*, that 'to define true madness what is't but to be nothing else but mad?' Another way of saying the same thing is to suggest (as many doctors do) that to work in mental health care you must be a little crazy. Of course, there are always some colleagues who love to play out the saga of the mad psychiatrist, but this is generally yet another caricature of a doctor who has simply acquired extra skills. The same suspicions of madness lead many to say that we are all, at times, briefly psychotic. To illustrate this let us look at such ordinary, everyday things as delirium, drug side-effects and sensory deprivation (the experience of being alone, without hearing or seeing other human beings).

## Delirium

A child develops a high fever when he is toxic with an infection. At night he starts seeing things, his mind is disturbed, and his talk rambles all over the place. The wise parent does not send for a psychiatrist but tries to reduce the fever by sponging the child with lukewarm water. A doctor may prescribe for the infection. When the temperature becomes normal, so does the mental state.

With elderly folk the same process causes a more complicated and alarming picture to emerge. Think of a man who suddenly has an emergency operation. It is life-saving and is decided upon in spite of a weak heart and poor lungs. But the anaesthetic and the pain-relieving drugs cause the man to become confused. The brain, with less oxygen than it needs to function properly, plays tricks and the patient seems mad and behaves crazily.

A woman who had always had an expansive, warm and enterprising personality was recovering from a planned operation. Suddenly the next day she began to write letters to the Queen and the Prime Minister. She planned a new business and asked for her cheque book to write large advances of cash which she could not afford to pay. She had a mild but definite manic episode. Her friends felt that her characteristics, normally under some control, had escaped from her grasp and that she was temporarily out of control. Treatment with medication quickly restored her to her normal effervescent (but sane ) self.

The previous life-history and personality traits of a person do seem to determine the pattern of delirium.

A man with life-long traits of being suspicious and solitary developed a serious chest infection. In hospital he started throwing things at the nurses and accused the doctors of poisoning him. Visitors were surprised that he believed they were trying to steal his money and were acting in a grand plot to make him a pauper. He had a paranoid state. But it was only a matter of weeks before he fully recovered (when his physical state was back to normal).

## Drug-induced psychosis

A common problem today is the person who has become psychotic as a result of either taking prescribed medicines which have side-effects or illicitly taking drugs such as amphetamine, LSD or cannabis. At times all the drugs have done is precipitate an illness to which the patient might have been subject anyway. At other occasions the drugs were taken purely to produce an altered state of awareness and to distort perception. The tragedies of young people who, after LSD, think they can fly and kill themselves are well known. But others may hardly be suspected.

After World War II many cheerful and rather overweight women were put on Dexedrine or a similar amphetamine. Most coped with the lift of mood and then the let-down after its appetite-suppressing effect wore off, and they were pleased to lose weight.

A few began to complain that the police were watching and following them, and that their families were persecuting them. After many years it was shown that this amphetamine psychosis was a special kind of paranoid psychosis. The main treatment was simply to stop taking speed (the street-name for amphetamine). The women recovered, and another drug-induced mental state was added to the long list.

Many fairly innocent drugs may cause dramatic illnesses. Those readers who wish to read an excellent account may do so in a book by Evelyn Waugh called *The Ordeal of Gilbert Pinfold.* Waugh, in this autobiographical account, tells of how he took a slow boat from London to the Far East. Two drugs, Carbrital for sleep and a pain reliever for arthritis, combined with his alcohol intake, were to produce a dramatic mental illness. In his cabin he thought he could hear a Salvation Army band playing on deck. He told the captain of the ship that he was tired of hearing a group talking about their sexual guilts. As he ran out of medication at the end of the journey, his state of mind returned to normal.

Most drug-induced states, from the alcoholic's *delirium tremens* to the millions abusing cocaine, heroin, crac and many others now flooding the streets, are a sad and tragic fact of modern life. We know that the poppy has been used in opium dens for centuries and that alcohol abuse is at least as old as Noah and Lot (see Gen. 9:21). But the raging drug abuse epidemic of the late twentieth century threatens to make psychotic states due to drugs a commonplace experience.

### The small black room

In many universities where research on psychological problems is done, there is a comfortable, unlit, sound-proofed room. Here the students and others who go in for a few days (and are well paid for it) see, hear and feel nothing from outside stimulation. Food and drink is provided and toilet facilities are there – nothing more. These sensory deprivation experiments have taught us that many find the experience so stressful that they are forced to press the panic button after two or three days. They have heard voices and started having all sorts of unusual beliefs. Most people recover quickly with a return to normal life.

Many regimes have used such knowledge to torture political prisoners, adding sleep deprivation to the mix and sometimes using special sounds and noise (as in Len Deighton's book and film *The Ipcress File*).

Certain religious communities encourage silence and limit human contact. However, this can be taken too far. Some of the Desert Fathers and other ascetics wrote of their wish to fast and deny themselves social and sexual contact, but instead of inner peace and clarity they found themselves having rich feasts of fantasy and of the very things from which they had fled. The fastness of their solitude was no solution and no protection. The deprivation may, as in the small black room experiments, have made the visions and the voices worse.

A young man, after his university course and training, offered himself to a society which wanted missionaries to teach in an African school. Part of the final preparation was an intensive retreat with talks and study, but also much solitary prayer and meditation. This vulnerable candidate found the strain of being deprived of warm human contact the last straw. Already anxious about the planned new life, the retreat led to his feeling mentally confused and emotionally troubled. So peculiar did he seem that a diagnosis of schizophrenia was considered, but rejected after medical examination. The stresses of early adult life together with the problems of going abroad proved too much when sensory deprivation was added. He recovered but did not pursue his missionary career.

## Recognising the psychotic patient

It is very easy to miss the person who is beginning to have a schizophrenic illness. At school or work, home or church their odd behaviour may be put down to eccentricity, laziness or moral inadequacy. Early treatment, counselling and rehabilitation may thus be denied to the needy young sufferer.

Susan came from a fine family with two working parents who were keen Christians. Her brother and sister had done well at school and made a splendid start in life. Susan had also done well at a good school with excellent examination results at sixteen. Prizes had been won and her musical talent had been nurtured. Everything seemed set for a good college career. Then, after the first year of working for college entrance, her work began to be unsatisfactory. She spent time alone in the laboratory, giggling sometimes or smiling at things with a secret smile.

The headmistress advised specialist help. But the tutor – who was a committed Christian – put it all down to Susan's laziness and lack of discipline. The examination results next time were bad. Yet when her parents sought counselling from a well-organised church they were led to believe that Susan's condition was their fault.

Increasing violence and aggression led to her admission to hospital. It was discovered that, like many schizophrenics, she had private experiences of a hallucinatory kind. She had long conversations with a friend miles away. With appropriate diagnosis and medication, all the abnormal thoughts and experiences disappeared and within some months she started work and has been relatively well for some years.

Susan's case illustrates many of the stresses that have been found to be involved in schizophrenia. She may have been predisposed to schizophrenia since her grandparent had a similar illness – there may have been a genetic factor. But frequently there is nothing to suggest an inherited tendency. As a teenager Susan was pressured by demands to conform to the sexual behaviour of others at school: her excellent Christian parents were aware of the clash between their own high standards and the permissive atmosphere of school. Again, the depressive illness of one of her parents in the period preceding her own breakdown had played its small part in producing her illness.

The lessons are clear: do not blame illness on moral failings, as her tutor wrongly did. Do not blame parents for producing schizophrenia: Susan's parents were not to blame. Start proper medication as soon as a diagnosis is made, and then make plans to get the patient back into the main stream of life as far as he can go.

In many other cases the young psychotic patient shows many more sad effects: the personality may seem to disintegrate and social living becomes almost impossible. Intelligent young men may be left lacking in motivation; they cannot 'get up and go' –

whether to study, train as apprentices, or just work well within their previous capacity. To occupy their day becomes, for such chronic schizophrenics, a major problem. In many parts of the world they drift into a life of boring incapacity to enjoy things as they once did. Recovery may only be partial, and living in a suitable hostel or group home may protect them from being exploited financially or sexually. They may settle down to a pattern of living (as thousands did in the best 'asylums') with work to fit their needs and a lot of custodial care from family, friends and professionals.

We have to sketch such a gloomy picture for it is still a common one. A chronically ill schizophrenic may be institutionalised at home as easily as in a bad psychiatric hospital. The mainstays of care are proper medication and provision of daily activity with well-modulated stimulation (not too little or too much).

The discovery of antipsychotic drugs in the 1950s led to a great improvement in curing psychotic symptoms like hallucinations, delusions and the severely disturbed behaviour that goes with such disturbances of thinking. When drugs could be given by injection, their effects lasting for two to four weeks, another advance was possible, and treatment outside hospital and in the community became more usual and more practicable. But medication alone was soon found to be inadequate.

Care for the psychotic patient is extremely hard for those who find that such mental illness repels them: they cannot begin to understand it or see how to offer sympathetic support. Professional care by nurses, doctors, psychologists and social workers may help a lot. But it is only increased tolerance from all of us and a willingness to learn how to cope with those impaired by chronic illness and disability that will make a lasting contribution to care. Dozens of people in every community need such care – day centres and hospitals cannot begin to provide it all.

## What can we do to help?

Many churches have, in recent years, begun to make great practical improvements in helping to look after psychotic patients who have partially recovered. Such British organisations as *Mind* and the *National Schizophrenic Fellowship* have guided those who want reliable information and guidance in what to do. Much more could be done, and the stigma attached to labels like schizophrenia or manic-depressive might be lessened a great deal if Christians joined with other people of good will in ventures to improve care. Not all can undertake the intensely difficult work with individuals and groups, but we can all do something to lessen prejudice and fear by combating ignorance with accurate data about the needs of these sick folk and the inadequate provision made for them by society.

Protection from excessive stress is important in preventing a recurrence of acute disorders like schizophrenia. Two sorts of information may help. First, a major life event frequently happens in the six weeks before a further relapse or nervous breakdown. We cannot prevent major happenings, but to know that they increase the sufferer's vulnerability may enable us to be more careful with both medication and in supporting him emotionally.

The second kind of discovery is more surprising. It was found that high emotional expression in the family of the schizophrenic patient makes a further breakdown more likely. This means, oddly enough, either too much warmth and over-protection on the one hand, or the expression of hostility and criticism on the other. How hard it is to get parents and others in a family to change their habitual method of talking to the patient! But something must be done. A hostel may be the answer, providing a non-possessive, non-critical home for the patient to try and establish some independence.

In informing ourselves of how to help sufferers from

schizophrenia, it is important not to take heed of those who say that it is simply the result of pressures in the family. Dr R. D. Laing, a psychiatrist who has written many brilliant books, seduced a generation into thinking it was romantic to be schizophrenic. Many years later he speaks favourably of the use of medication, but his views in his early books still influence many who do not know his present beliefs.

To say that the family first identifies the teenager as bad and then makes him mad is simply not true. Many who go through the turmoil of an adolescent crisis of identity and its accompanying confusion and depression are *not* schizophrenic. Fortunately, the so-called Laingian view of the illness has been frequently rebutted by expert evidence.

It is equally false to speak, as some do, of the myth of mental illness. The 17 million schizophrenics in the world are a sad, persistent reminder of the damaging effects of the illness. We know a good deal more about the biochemistry and genetics of the illness than we did fifty years ago. But we have no cure, only much that can be done to alleviate symptoms and help in getting the patient back to normal life. Some patients do get very much better, and some only have an acute episode of psychosis that leaves little in its wake by way of damage to the personality.

We have reason to be wary of attempts to close most hospitals to such patients. In countries like Italy where this has happened, the community cannot cope. Those not cared for drift homelessly and live rough like the vagrants in our inner cities: they are the sad *abandonatti*. It seems that many chronic patients are ending up in prison, a worse kind of asylum.

Community care is going to be a great challenge. The pendulum may well swing back to providing havens for those who cannot cope in hostels, group homes or other places in the district where the new caring system is set up.

## The eccentric
Those who have read this chapter so far may well find it rather

frightening and upsetting. The facts are bound to be sad reading. But it is vital to say that eccentricity is not psychosis and not necessarily any kind of illness. Let us consider one explanation of eccentricity: the over valued idea. This term is used to describe a common experience where someone gets a bee in his bonnet. It may be a highly plausible and indeed quite proper set of beliefs in a Christian or other context. What makes it an over-valued idea is that it dominates the person's life and affects their thinking. It becomes a concern about which he feels with passionate strength. It lead to eccentricity by making him lose any balance in his life: the centre of gravity moves, as it were, to render him constantly 'off centre' and with a bias in favour of his pet views.

However eccentric a person, he seldom loses touch with normal life and reality, he simply becomes taken up with his chosen bit of reality. He is usually able to cope with life as long as he can devote all his spare time to his special interest. He has no true psychotic symptoms at all.

It may be possible to understand the eccentric as one who has allowed a few traits to dominate his personality. His character becomes odd as a result: it may be an exaggerated suspiciousness, a tendency to dramatise everything, or an enthusiasm which is not only infectious but damagingly so. They lead to some eccentrics being seen as suffering from religious mania.

Usually such a condition owes nothing to religion except that, in developing the eccentricity (or illness at times), the flavour, colour and appearance have been influenced by religion. The real cause lies either in a curious personality development or in the kind of biochemical disturbance that can lead to a manic depressive disorder with many other kinds of features involved. Religion gets blamed when it is only the top dressing.

Alexander Cruden, the Scot from Aberdeen whose great work was *Cruden's Concordance*, was probably more eccentric than ill. He was forced to go into asylums on some five occasions. It all started when he left his native city as a young man. The girl he was hoping to marry came to tell him she was pregnant through an incestuous relationship with her brother. He was extremely upset by this, and whenever the possibility of marriage came to him he was ill again.

His eccentricity led him to believe that he was Alexander the Corrector with a mission to reform British morals by stressing the need at every chance that came to him, to keep the Sabbath strictly. But his sad life left a lasting monument. Perhaps his obsession with the words of Scripture was necessary to produce a work which many would consider required a large team.

Eccentrics may often have much to offer those of us who are seen as more normal. We need to tolerate them, offering love and understanding. It may be vital to guard against their excessive influence, especially with the young. Safeguards sometimes need to be offered to the eccentric to prevent damage being caused by them and to set limits which may help them to feel safer and more accepted. Our aim is to preserve balance and prevent excess.

# PART FOUR

# CONTROVERSIAL ISSUES

# 16

## POSSESSION, ILLNESS AND THE DEVIL

> In order that Satan might not outwit us. For we are
> not unaware of his schemes (2 Cor. 2:11).

> There are two equal and opposite errors into which
> our race can fall about devils. One is to disbelieve in
> their existence. The other is to believe, and to feel an
> excessive and unhealthy interest in them.
> > C. S. Lewis. *The Screwtape Letters*

A doctor may be confronted with a patient who believes that
he is possessed by a demon, or by a good spirit. What is the
doctor to do? If he is a Christian physician, believing that the
Bible's account of the powers of Satan is both true and relevant
today, his position is a difficult one. He wants to use his medical knowledge in an honest way. He may recognise a pattern in
the patient's behaviour which his experience has taught him is
typical of certain forms of hysterical illness, or of psychoses like
schizophrenia or severe depression.

On the other hand, his Christian teaching leads him to think
that behind the symptoms there may be a deeper problem. There
may be, in the view of many who meet such cases, some form of
demonic activity either causing possession, or what some call
oppression and obsession.

While I was revising this chapter at a weekend, I received a long and urgent call from a Christian minister. A vicar was troubled about a man who was asking for prayer and exorcism. The case was proving very difficult. As he talked, the minister told me that he had worked as a psychiatric nurse and that he agreed with the diagnosis of schizophrenia. I urged him to use both his ministerial skills and prayer for the patient, but not to neglect his skills in persuading the patient to accept the medication that had proved so useful in helping the patient over previous episodes of illness. There need be no contradiction between his *spiritual and Christian* understanding on the one hand, and his proper and valuable clinical experience on the other.

First, let us look at the medical approach to cases where states of possession are found. These are quite common, and are seen in countries and cultures where there is no Christian faith, as much as they are in Christian circles.

Secondly, let us consider some of the Bible's teaching. In particular, we will note the unbalanced way in which this is often presented. Case studies will help us to examine the problem.

Thirdly, we will suggest ways in which we may try to do justice to both the medical and the spiritual aspects of a case of possession.

## Possession as a medical problem

In a nearby psychiatric centre in London, the professor and his colleagues have a very helpful working arrangement where any case where demon possession is alleged or suspected is also seen by a Christian minister working in a church centre. He is skilled and experienced in using prayer and exorcism where this is needed. Yet he finds that over ninety per cent of the cases he is asked to see suffer from a purely medical condition and do not need spiritual healing or exorcism.

A few weeks ago a general practitioner in London asked me

to come with him to see a young student from Africa who was staying with his sister. His brother-in-law was supporting him in his studies, and he had progressed well. Suddenly, after some months of feeling confused and unable to cope, he felt he was taken over by a spirit which told him to climb a nearby tree, take off his clothes, and wait for the Queen of England to pass by. On a cold December afternoon, this is what he did. His sister became frightened when he threw her two-year-old daughter down the stairs. He also threatened her with a knife after the violent incident to her daughter.

Both of us as doctors, and the social worker who came to see him at the same time, agreed that this was a psychotic illness. His schizophrenia responded to medication, and admission to hospital was needed to protect both the patient and the family.

There was no background, in the African district he came from, of any such experience of spirit possession. Yet it seemed likely that this was an example of the patient *attributing* an illness to a spirit which had taken control of his mind.

For many doctors, such a case would raise the question of the patient's cultural background and his attitude to the world of spirits. They would say that because of his African background, and in spite of his Western education, he would revert to primitive forms of thought. In addition, any severe illness would make him regress and go back to child-like, magical forms of thinking.

Most of those who deal with such cases would agree with much that is said about the importance of a man's beliefs and what he may, in a sense, be programmed to use as an explanation when he falls ill.

The next two cases raise this problem in a Christian setting. Both men were believers who had been well educated and held responsible professional posts. Both had solid spiritual support from local churches and were well known for their Christian commitment.

One of my first experiences was with a middle-aged man whose zeal and knowledge had been a by-word among his friends. But then his enthusiasm began to wane, and after a time he began to doubt if he was even a believer. I happened to meet him while he was in this state and urged him to seek medical help at once. He agreed to see a Christian doctor he knew.

To my surprise, when I returned to the wards of the psychiatric hospital where I worked, I found him there. He accosted me in the corridor and told me, with anguished concern, that the devil had taken possession of his soul. My assurances to the contrary did not help him at all.

I told him he would recover quickly with appropriate physical treatment for his undoubted depressive illness. And such was the happy result. Within a few weeks he had lost his false belief that he was possessed. His former good mood and high spirits had returned. He was again himself and in his right mind. His depressive delusions had disappeared.

This middle-aged man is a fairly typical example of a severe depressive disorder responding quickly to being given hospital care and, in particular, physical treatment that restored his nervous system to normal.

The next case study is of another Christian, working as an executive and belonging to two church fellowships, who believed he was possessed but was treated successfully for a schizophrenic disorder.

His family called me, and I agreed to visit the young man in his flat, where I found him chatting with his girlfriend. As we talked, I discovered that he believed there were demons on the roof which he feared had influenced him and might have taken possession of his soul. I also learned that the girlfriend had heard a well-known Christian doctor speaking of demon possession. I suspected that it was her concern that had triggered off this line of thought.

He came into hospital and we found that he had a psychotic

illness, the symptoms of which included false beliefs that he was influenced by some power. He certainly had strange ideas about the devil. His treatment included tablets which were antipsychotic and he had a good deal of counselling and psychotherapy. His minister (the curate of the church he attended) came in regularly and would speak and pray with him, helping him to understand his illness.

### Exorcism: successes and failures

In many Christian churches there has been an increase in the use of exorcism. I am anxious simply to warn against excesses and problems which arise, and do not want to give the impression that doctors are against exorcism. It has, after all, been used for many centuries in both Christian and non-Christian settings. The fact that psychiatrists have patients sent to them who have failed to benefit from exorcism means only that a wrong assessment may have been made in the first place.

Here is an example of where a non-Christian colleague decided to advise that his patient should seek the help of an exorcist. The woman patient told him that a male demon joined her and her husband in bed at night and did unspeakable and very frightening things. My colleague, after a number of interviews, diagnosed a hysterical state and thought he had little to offer her. When he found she had great trust in a local church staffed by Anglican friars, he approached them. After explaining the woman's problem, the friars kindly arranged a full service of exorcism with bell, book and candle. The psychiatrist attended the service, and was pleased when he learned afterwards that the lady had recovered.

The question remained in his mind: had his patient recovered because a hysterical condition often responds to ritual and to suggestion made in a powerfully impressive setting? Or was it a case of true possession?

Another case illustrates the importance of clergy and ministers being free to work closely with doctors and psychologists. The man concerned was sent to me by his vicar. The patient had first been sent by the same vicar to a free-church minister who was well known for his ministry of exorcism and deliverance from demon possession.

The man was a science graduate who had become depressed after failing to complete a project for a higher degree. The failure in the research study had also been made worse by other personal problems. When I saw him, he was convinced that there was a serpent inside his head which needed to be removed. He was extremely depressed and had been plagued by suicidal thoughts for many months. With appropriate anti-depressant medication and regular help in counselling he improved greatly, although there were relapses from time to time. It seemed evident that the diagnosis of a serious depressive illness with delusions had been missed and that exorcism had not been the best approach to helping him.

Doctors have noted that suggestible patients tend to come to their clinics, showing symptoms of possession, not long after such films as *The Exorcist* have been shown in their area. As well as films and books sensationalising demon possession, there is a good deal of teaching about it in charismatic churches. Many leaders in these churches see exorcism, as well as divine healing, as part of their ministry and calling.

Inevitably there have been excesses which have led to scandal and concern. Many were distressed at the much-publicised case of a man in Yorkshire who, after a long service of exorcism, murdered his wife. Another sad example that I learned of in a seminar on the subject occurred when two quite untrained men decided to exorcise a woman they thought was possessed by a demon. The rough and ready service which they arranged ended tragically. They laid hands on the woman, she struggled physically, and in the struggle which ensued the two men were so rough with her that she died of a ruptured liver.

The men were, quite properly, arrested and made the subject of judicial proceedings and of medical and social reports upon their own mental condition.

Such cases come from the wilder shores of religious life, and one cannot judge the careful use of exorcism from them. Such happenings led a number of churches to set up study groups on the subject of exorcism and to publish guidelines for its use which might – it was hoped – help to prevent such excesses in the future.

## Understanding the Bible's teaching on possession

There are many who dismiss out of hand the teaching of the New Testament about the devil. But I believe the account of the Christian life cannot be understood without accepting fully the teaching given in the Bible about the devil. If we leave out the teaching about Satan's activity we lose a whole dimension about the mission of Christ. We are taught quite explicitly that 'the Son of God appeared for the very purpose of undoing the devil's work' (1 John 3:8, NEB).

The words of C. S. Lewis are worth pondering: 'There are two equal and opposite errors into which our race can fall about the devils. One is to disbelieve in their existence. The other is to believe and then feel an excessive and unhealthy interest in them.'

In a recent book called *Demon Possession* there is much of value. A group of experts write as those who believe the Bible's teaching and have had much experience in dealing with possession. One of these experts writes in strong language of his belief:

> The modern cult of deliverance is gaining ground in many quarters. Generally it flourishes where much is made of demonism, where demons are identified in terms of sickness, the abnormal or the unusual. Fortunes are made – and lives destroyed – by this approach.[1]

1. John Montgomery, *Demon Possession* (Minneapolis, MN, Bethany, 1976), p. 306.

Another expert contributor to the book is Dr John White, writing as both a psychiatrist and a minister. He writes of his concern about what seems an overzealous use of techniques of 'deliverance'. He says: 'I wonder whether some of the advocates of spiritual warfare do more harm than good. I also wonder whether their effectiveness may sometimes be explained in psychological terms alone.' Such a book, with many different viewpoints on demon possession, shows how believers differ, even when their basic acceptance of the Bible is the same. How can we achieve a balance, in our views and in our practice, about whether to attribute some stresses in the Christian life to demon possession?

I would simply like to underline a few facts about the Bible's teaching. I will start with the letters written to the young churches by the Apostles.

I consider that the striking thing about the discussion of possession in the New Testament epistles is their silence about it, and about exorcism generally. Here are letters which, by common consent, reflect the life and practice of the early church. Written before the gospels, we should expect them to give detailed advice if exorcism was the common practice.

The argument from silence is a dangerous one, but let us place it in its context – for much is taught about the devil, often in passing, as it were. In Ephesians we are exhorted to arm ourselves against the wiles of the devil. But even here there is a striking absence of any instruction about healing by exorcism. In fact, the last chapter of Ephesians is a classic example of the balanced view needed in our response, as believers, to satanic activity.

Consider one of the best known books on this passage of Scripture: William Gurnall's classic work *The Christian in Complete Armour*. It is the fruit of rich Puritan teaching. Gurnall was writing over three hundred years ago at a time when witches were still being hunted and burned. In a racy and readable way, the author deals with the practicalities of living the Christian life. The book owes nothing to popular superstition about magic and witches. On the contrary, it sticks closely to how we have to fight the battles of our faith against the devices and deceits which are the result of satanic attack.

The epistles and the great hymns, the creeds and the statement of faith give a very healthy emphasis in describing the works of the devil. By dwelling on the positive aspects of our faith and trust in God and his great salvation, they put all the problems of the devil's work in a proper, subordinate place to that.

Many of our generation have fallen into the trap of a morbid, unhealthy interest in demons which titillates a general interest in the occult. We should seek to return to an older, wiser balance in our understanding of the New Testament.

## Arguments from the gospels

Anyone who has opened one of the many books on the deliverance ministry, exorcism or possession will know that a major appeal is made to our Lord's casting out of demons and his orders to his disciples to do so. This powerful theme cannot be avoided.

I would simply point out that the days of Jesus' ministry as recorded in the gospels were a unique and special period. The incarnate Son of God had to be attested with signs and wonders. It as also a special epoch when there was a great confrontation between our Lord and all forms of satanic activity. In later history there have been periods with a similar but less spectacular confrontation between God and evil. Again, special signs and wonders have appeared.

It is believers, not those who reject the supernatural, who have pointed out in studying the New Testament that there are distinct differences between the special (unique and not to be repeated) ministry in the gospels, and the less spectacular but no less genuine life described in the epistles.

Many questions are raised by the gospel ministry. An epileptic has a demon, for instance. Does this mean that we should regard all epilepsies as of demonic origin? Of course not. Did not our Lord select many everyday illnesses to show how, ultimately, sin and Satan were the great first causes of all disease? There are also secondary causes of illness which we, like Luke the beloved physician, may be expected to treat while still knowing that sometimes divine power can be exercised against the effects of the great primary causes that led to sickness ever being a factor in our fallen world.

We can never prove a point by trading proof texts as if they were party shibboleths. But it is helpful to look at examples in Scripture, such as the case in Mark 2:5 where Jesus is presented with a paralytic man and demonstrates his authority on earth. The paralytic is told by Jesus: 'Son, your sins are forgiven.' The teachers around him object, thinking his words are blasphemous. But the point of the passage is to show the authority with which Jesus Christ, the Son of man, works. By the same token, when he commands evil spirits to come out of those possessed, it is to demonstrate his own special authority over all satanic forces.

In the Old Testament, we are told that Job was plagued with boils. It is made clear in the account that Satan has been permitted by God to afflict Job in this way. No one would argue from this that boils are always of satanic origin. Nor should we argue (in my view) that we should give up the customary treatment of boils in favour of prayer directed against satanic activity.

The case which shows most clearly that prayer for deliverance is sometimes answered in the negative is that of the Apostle Paul. In 2 Corinthians 12:7 we are told that he was given a thorn in the flesh, a messenger of Satan, to torment him. We are not told precisely what the thorn in the flesh was, and it is well that we do not know. The important thing was that, having prayed to be delivered from the suffering three times, he was told: 'My grace is sufficient for you, for my power is made perfect in weakness' (2 Cor. 12:9).

This last case of St Paul's own suffering is, to me, an unfailing antidote to the triumphalistic belief that we are to have all our sufferings, and perhaps all our stresses, removed as if by divine magic. That cannot be, has never been, and never will be the case. Let us return to a more balanced, biblical view and not foster the belief that instant deliverance is always available.

## Can we bring medical and spiritual care together?

I trust that the burden of my brief argument will now be clear. I believe many people may attribute their symptoms to demonic possession when in fact they are suffering from an illness that may be diagnosed and treated in an ordinary way without any recourse to the supernatural. At times, the failure of healing or exorcism confirm this. In that case, it is sad if the failure is put down to lack of faith on the part of the sufferer. I have known this to happen, and the last state of such a badly treated believer is worse than the first.

I believe it might help us to avoid mistakes if those who feel called to exercise a deliverance ministry were to learn more about the physical and psychological stresses which may appear to be spiritual conditions. I could not help noticing that the later books of Trevor Dearing, well known for his exorcism ministry, show this use of modern knowledge to help explain some of what we see in cases coming for help by healing.

Should we not, as Christians, ask for prayer whatever our condition – even when we are seeking treatment by purely medical means? It was a normal part of classical Christian thinking about sickness, not only to see it as part of God's providential permission, but also as something which prayer and proper treatment could help to ease or cure. To call something a natural recovery, in this way of thinking, did not mean one did not thank God for the recovery itself.

Increasingly, prayer is being used as a normal part of the work of the church that is trying to help its sick members. There should be no contradiction between looking for God's blessing on means of treatment which are medical and human, and also praying for a divine and supernatural work to proceed in the same case.

Great spiritual discernment is often needed to decide whether demonic possession is present or not. I consider that this judgement may have to be left to those specially gifted and experienced in that field.

Many doctors, even those with a firm Christian faith, may confess to a sanctified scepticism. Disagreement between doctor and minister is inevitable. But the wise exorcist will take pains to avoid any sensationalism. He will rely heavily on a careful, prayerful faith and a simple service. He will avoid the kind of prolonged pressures – spiritual and physical alike – to which many have been tempted. Such pressures, with long or all-night prayer, have led to tragic and fatal results, some of which we have mentioned in this chapter.

This may seem to be an attempt to have our cake and eat it. To write about any of the topics of this chapter is to confront strong prejudices and beliefs. Why do it at all? Simply because those of us who are Christian doctors should lay special emphasis on the fact that there are many facets to every illness. There are physical and emotional aspects, as well as social and spiritual ones. Those who are Christians should always have a special concern for the spiritual side of illness. This leads, naturally, to prayer and intercession.

Sometimes – rarely, I believe – it is proper to call for a special prayer of faith about possible demonic forces which may be present and active. Such a decision cannot be hasty, and should never be automatic. Even when a special attempt to seek healing is made, it should never exclude seeking help of a social, emotional or physical kind. These areas may call urgently for careful assessment and treatment, just as much as any spiritual problem.

# 17

## THE BORN-AGAIN CHRISTIAN: CONVERSION OR BRAINWASHING?

You should not be surprised at my saying, 'You must be born again' (John 3:7).

Use no constraint in matters of religion. Even those who are farthest out of the way never compel to come in by any other means than reason, truth and love.

John Wesley

If we begin at the beginning, many of the stresses which the Christian is specially liable to suffer have to do with conversion. There may be a majority of Christians who have never known any dramatic change: like Timothy they have grown up with the faith and in due course it has become their own. They may see in their own lives evidence of new, divine life – 'the life of God in the soul of man' (Henry Scougal) – and are content that this should be there without any great crisis preceding it. But whenever a new evangelist appears on the scene, such Christians may be led to doubt if they are anything but nominal believers. They may seek some new form of sudden, striking conversion and repudiate their previous faith.

When presidents in the United States and other prominent figures claim to be born again, the phrase is devalued of some of the original meaning it had when Jesus told the Jewish leader Nicodemus that he must be born again. This change in the use of the phrase has led to an emphasis on the outward nature and evidence of conversion, whereas the inward changes of a new birth are less easy to see. There are many questions which need to be raised about how a person becomes converted or born again. Can we ever be sure it is genuine?

### Evangelistic techniques

It is not always superstar evangelists working within the churches' framework that may provoke a questioning by believers; many other sects and leaders have done so. The early Frank Buchman laid great stress on being changed in a special way. There are countless maverick evangelists in Europe and North America who appear like comets on the Christian scene, leaving a trail of disaster. A leading American evangelist is reputed to have said that he expects nine out of ten of his converts to fall away. This fact of the lapse rate after apparent conversion is evidence of endless psychological problems. It is not those who have been involved in crusades who witness the casualties, but those of us to whom they are later sent.

A new phenomenon is also troubling many: those organisations, calling themselves Christian, who engage in a kind of brainwashing. Working on young people they entice them away from their families and persuade them to make over all their money to the new sect and to belong henceforth only to the new family which expects from them a total allegiance. Great distress has been caused to many when such sects have suddenly invaded their family circle with devastating results.

For all these reasons it is vital to ask what, from a psychiatrist's point of view, is conversion? Is there a normal Christian conversion? Is there a physiology of faith as well as pathology?

To answer any question about conversion we must take some note of the massive figure of Dr William Sargant, a London psychiatrist who wrote a book called *Battle for the Mind* in 1957 and has subsequently been regarded as something of an authority on the subject. His publishers describe the book as a classic authoritative examination of the techniques of religious conversion. Dr Sargant has been an inspiring teacher and has headed a department of psychological medicine in a London teaching hospital. But though many patients and doctors owe him a great deal, he would be the last to expect us not to look critically at his ideas on conversion.

## Battle for the mind

During World War II Dr Sargant was engaged in treating psychiatric casualties, and in 1944 he began to apply some of Pavlov's finding with dogs to his work. He found that 'the brain's slate could be wiped clean'. By this he meant that if drugs were used to heighten excitement while talking to the patient about his experience (say of shell-shock), then the patient would suddenly come to the point of collapse and later recovery. Dr Sargant was thus converted to Dr Ivan Pavlov's views. During a subsequent illness he began to read extensively, and in his father's study found John Wesley's journal, for his father, unlike Sargant, was a devout Methodist. Dr Sargant writes: 'The fear of burning in Hell that he [Wesley] implanted in his congregation corresponded well enough to the suggestions we made to soldiers under abreaction, such as the one about being trapped in a burning tank and having to find a way out.' Later Sargant widened his reading of the literature of sudden conversion to support his belief in this new explanation. Not surprisingly, he found it everywhere.

But were Wesley's converts like Pavlov's dogs? First, it is worth saying that a student of Wesley found only one sermon by him on hell, and that in a register of 7,000 sermons preached between

1747 and 1761 there was no mention of one on hell. But it is estimated that he preached 40,000 times during his lifetime on his favourite theme – the love of God freely offered to all mankind.

Secondly, were the converts then brainwashed in class meetings, as the prisoners of the Chinese communists reportedly were? A quotation from John Wesley is one good answer:

> Beware that you are not a fiery persecuting enthusiast. Do not imagine that God has called you (just contrary to the spirit of Him you style your master) to destroy lives and not to save them. Never dream of forcing men into the ways of God. Think yourself, and let think. Use no constraint in matters of religion. Even those who are farthest out of the way never compel to come in by any other means than reason, truth and love.[1]

Dr Sargant seems to be unaware of how concerned Christian leaders have been about true conversion as opposed to false ones. The outstanding example of a great thinker who was also an evangelist, observed the revivals in North America where he worked, was Jonathan Edwards. Like Wesley he deplored the histrionic outbursts which were sometimes a feature of revival services. In his book *The Religious Affections*, Edwards seems to meet the criticisms of Dr Sargant and his predecessors half-way by describing a revival of religion as a mixed work. The mixture of grace and nature, flesh and spirit, human and divine influences is characteristic of all Christian work, not only at special times of revival. Dr Sargant might be surprised to learn how suspicious Edwards was of much in Christian experience which could well be irrelevant or just dross. But in disposing of the dross, he also describes the gold: the genuine, gracious experiences that are always the result of an encounter with God, his truth and his Spirit. No mere psychological pressures, Pavlovian or otherwise, can produce a true conversion.

---

1. J. Wesley, *Forty Four Sermons*. From *The Nature of Enthusiasm*, p. 427.

## Change as growth

Dr Sargant wrote an early paper entitled: '*The Psychology of Faith*' which I think describes rather the *pathology* of faith, the abnormal and diseased forms and not the healthy, normative Christian experience. In opposing Dr Sargant's over-simplified view, one need only look at the wealth of writing about the life of God in the soul of man. This life is properly called regeneration, and its outward evidence is conversion – a changed life and different behaviour. Like any form of life it is a complex and delicate matter, not a simple process of excitement, fear, collapse and indoctrination. Faith may be described as the truth to be believed, leading to the truth as it is in Jesus. Another aspect of the faith is the assent of the mind, leading to a trust of the heart. Spurgeon said: 'Faith is the hand that lays hold of God's promises.' The faith that leads to a new birth, a new life, may appear unexciting to the outsider who may only see the person professing it as dull and prosaic.

The images of the Bible are those of growth and development: 'First the blade, then the ear, then the full corn in the ear.' These are not spectacular and dramatic, but if we have any sense of awe at creation then surely we will wonder at the new creation. There is a marked element of learning in normal faith: 'Ye have not so learned Christ' (Eph. 4: 20, AV). This is a marked contrast to the glib saying that religion is caught not taught. We are to be imitators or followers of God, as dear children. Training up a child in the way he should go is said to lead not to sudden conversion but to his not departing from it.

There are rarely earthquakes leading to dramatic conversions, as in the prison in Philippi. Saul, on the road to Damascus, is the exception not the rule. The Apostle's later converts are said to have obeyed from the heart the form of teaching given to them. They experienced the common and more usual means of conversion. Had Dr Sargant included them in his research and writings, he might have given an equally graphic but much more balanced account. Instead, Dr Sargant writes: 'I might have to end these long years of research with the conclusion that there are no gods, but only impressions of gods created in man's mind.' It seems to me that Dr Sargant started with this conclusion, for it is not difficult to show how much he neglects evidence which does not suit his purpose.

Dr Sargant seems to be a man of one idea: treat the brain and get results. In his zeal for physical treatments (a zeal his five preaching uncles would have envied), he neglects behavioural approaches, social work and psychotherapy. One might have hoped that someone whose new work in 1944 started with Pavlov might have become interested in the large growth industry of behaviour therapy, but he has not declared any interest in this. He pokes fun at the psychiatric social worker, yet there is a solid body of knowledge about the social causes and correlates of illness. And one often cannot understand how such things as conversions happen without a knowledge of the social network involved. But Sargant's arch-enemy is what he calls psychotherapy, although anyone who has had the benefit of Dr Sargant as their doctor knows how well he practices psychotherapy of one kind. However, there are many ways of developing understanding and insight and of using relationships. Anyone who reads his three books, therefore, must bear in mind that Dr Sargant stands at one end of the psychiatric spectrum, perhaps even, like Athanasius, against the rest of the psychiatric world.

But Dr Sargant's first book would not have sold 200,000 copies in the first ten years (to say nothing of starting a new sect in the Solomon Islands) if there was not something more than one man's hobby-horse being ridden in it. I accept those criticisms which Dr Sargant makes of certain evangelistic techniques. I abhor the audience manipulation practiced by many evangelists, and all ways of bringing psychological pressures to get results and conversions. We should be sceptical of the results of some kinds of evangelising, for they do not rely on the truth and response created to it by God, but on excitement and fear worked up by human means. Christian work should be with the spirit, but with the understanding also. We must hold the balance between word and Spirit. And we must persuade, as Wesley advised, only by reason, truth and love.

### Analysing conversion

To make a riposte to Dr Sargant's attacks on conversion is not too difficult. But there have been many others who have mounted criticism of conversion who show a lack of understanding of the proper teaching on the matter. In the Christian tradition conversion has involved changes in three areas: the mind, the heart and the life.

It is possible to have a change of mind which is purely philosophical – the furniture of ideas being changed. Such an intellectual change is not enough to be termed a Christian conversion. Sometimes a change of heart may be simply a 'peak experience' with oceanic feelings of being at one with the world, or some such genuine and important crisis of emotional life. But unless the feelings are related to Christ in a specific way – unless there is a 'felt Christ' as some of the Fathers put it – it is not Christian. Likewise to those for whom religion is morality tinged with emotion, there may be a change of life that is dramatic and permanent: yet outside any context of belief in or love for Christ.

The only conversion which is Christian, then, is not merely a matter of being changed. It means change of belief, affection, feelings and behaviour, and change within a specific context.

How much belief is essential? It seems to me that the basic commitment is small, while working out the consequences of it has taxed the minds of giants like St Augustine and Pascal. To say, for instance, that 'Jesus is Lord' was something very specific for the early Christians. To say with the Apostle Paul that Christ 'loved me and gave himself for me' (Gal. 2:20) is a huge statement.

The crucial thing is what happened to the perception of the Christian: his eyes have been opened so that he not only sees but also perceives. There has been a process of enlightenment: he understands the basic things about himself in relation to God, and sees Christ in a way that many who actually saw him on earth were unable to see him – as someone who calls for faith and trust. Such a beginning in learning about the faith which must be believed in, and such a first step as using the faith which believes, depend ( in the Christian view) on the action of God. In Pascal's fine statement which he attributes to God: 'Thou wouldst not be seeking Me unless I had already found thee: thy conversion? 'Tis My concern.'

## Taught not caught

Such a high view of the first cause of conversion does not mean (after understanding, enlightenment and perception) that instruction can be left out. If there were a choice between saying whether religion is taught or caught, I would say it is taught. Of course, in true teaching something is also caught.

The early Christians sometimes called converts at this stage in their progress by the name 'catechumen'. Far from the kind of brainwashing which Dr Sargant reports from the practice of certain evangelists, this kind of learning (or catechism) implies settling down to apply the mind to the truth of God's revelation of himself.

Much is rightly made of the open secret through which God's hidden wisdom is made available to any one through God's own revelation of it. But as St Paul frequently points out the natural man regards it all as foolishness without prior perception being granted him. He cannot know the things of God, for they are spiritually discerned. And one of St Paul's great arguments is what happened to our Lord: none of the princes of this world knew Him, for had they known, they would not have crucified the Lord of glory.

There is often a close link between the learning and believing process and what happens to the convert's feelings. Very unpleasant feelings often, if not usually, accompany the process of finding out about yourself in relation to God. Many feel some degree of guilt and shame, anxiety or misery, and some despair of themselves. Later, when there are good feelings such as joy and peace, the earlier gloom is seen differently. Thus Francis Thompson, in a memorable passage in his poem 'The Hound of Heaven' recalls his darkness:

> Halts by me that footfall:
> Is my gloom, after all,
> Shade of his hand, outstretched caressingly?

Thompson, a medical student who had become addicted to morphine, was reduced to sleeping rough on the Thames Embankment (as many still do near Charing Cross). Another version of the same experience may be found in his well-known lines:

> But (when so sad thou canst not sadder)
> Cry; – and upon thy so sore loss
> Shall shine the traffic of Jacob's ladder
> Pitched betwixt Heaven and Charing Cross.

Thompson is far from the tradition of John Bunyan and its many other representatives. But wherever one looks, the true Christian convert describes the mixed feelings which are inextricably linked to the discovery of their need of forgiveness. Perhaps Bunyan (and many like him) suffered more intense feelings because they had an innate capacity for it: the person who is obsessional and depressive may in fact feel a true guilt for sin more deeply. Or is it that the genius of Bunyan enables him to express the burden of guilt and its relief in a way that is universal and applicable to all (though not to the same degree)? This is how he describes Christian in *Pilgrim's Progress*:

> He ran thus ... just as Christian came up with the Cross, his burden loosed from off his back, and began to tumble ... and I saw it no more. Then was Christian glad and lightsome, and said, He hath given me rest by His sorrow, and life by his Death...

> Then Christian gave three leaps for joy, and went on singing ...

> 'Must here be the beginning of my bliss?
> Must here the burden fall from off my back?
> Must here the strings that bound it to me crack?
> Blest Cross! Blest Sepulchre! Blest, rather, be
> The Man that there was put to shame for me!'

I doubt that one can be 'glad and lightsome' when the burden of guilt falls away without first having felt the effects of the burden in our hearts. This is why some teachers used to speak of the work of the law in the human heart as ploughing up man's self-complacency and preparing him for the seed of the gospel. Luther used to refer to God's 'strange work' by which he prepared men for belief and faith in Christ. *'Working by contraries'* was another way in which an earlier generation put it.

### The proper tests

Jonathan Edwards' classic work on the feelings associated with conversion has already been mentioned. He devotes a whole book to an exposition of one passage where St Peter describes the early Christians in their relation to Christ: 'Though you have not seen him, you love him; and even though you do not see him now you believe in him and are filled with an inexpressible and glorious joy' (1 Pet. 1:8). As one might expect from so acute an observer as the first president of Princeton University, Edwards dwells at length on feelings that are 'no sign' of true grace. He then moves on to describe what he calls gracious affections: feelings which, as he puts it, show that your experience will 'beget and promote the temper of Jesus'.

But how is such a temper to be recognised? Generations of Christians have been condemned for being introspective to the point of morbidity. They are seen as taking their spiritual temperature or feeling their psychological pulse to decide if the crisis is past and they have come through. Few of the critics put it as elegantly as Gibbon's sneer: 'I will not, like the fanatics of the last age, attempt to define the moment of grace.' It is not the moment of grace which is the vital thing, but its effects and consequences in the life of the person who experiences it. Notions in the head and feelings in the heart count for nothing unless they issue in a change of life.

Doctors who treat patients with psychological problems now attempt a behavioural analysis. This is a fashionable thing to do today, but it has always been an important part of any decent diagnosis. What does a behavioural analysis of conversion show? In the book of Acts we read that Christians were known as those who 'belong to the way'. 'The way' was a matter of obedience to God's law and following Christ. This always involved radical life changes, whether for the dissolute Corinthian or the devout Pharisee. Ever since then, Christians have been persecuted for being different in their behaviour: sometimes they have been killed for it, but often simply ridiculed or cut dead by their friends or relatives.

Arguments always rage as to how different Christians have to be. For the Quakers and Puritans details of dress were vital – and their point of view has a certain logic, still followed by those like the Hutterites or the Amish in America who dress in black. Liberty of conscience has been more important at some times than others, but there is astonishing agreement about the need for behaviour to reflect the new life, its new allegiances and goals.

William James defined conversion as 'the process, gradual or sudden, by which a self hitherto divided and consciously wrong, inferior and unhappy becomes unified and consciously right, superior and happy in consequence of its firmer hold upon religious reality.'

As a general description of conversion this may be true. But it is too general and too sweeping to be applied to Christian conversion. 'The scandal of the particular' applies to the Christian in his belief in a crucified and risen Christ. The feelings which surround this belief are also more special than James allows in his definition. And the experience of being consciously right, superior and happy does not adequately describe a believer who will rejoice with trembling and in whom a certain fear and awe will coexist with feelings of tenderness, dependence and love.

Some people find it hard to draw a distinction between certain sects, like the 'Moonies', and Christians in their insistence on changes in their converts' lives. After all, did not Christ promise to bring not peace but a sword? And did he not say that a man's foes were to be those of his own household? And yet the clear changes that occur in the lives of those who become Christians happen without the coercion practiced by sects who grab their converts' wealth or property. 'Make them come in,' said Jesus in his parable of the great banquet (Luke 14:23). And reflecting on John the Baptist, he said, 'The Kingdom of heaven has been forcefully advancing, and forceful men lay hold of it' (Matt. 11:12). But the compulsion and the force is a spiritual matter, related to the truth as it is in Jesus; and to the love and obedience which he evokes and demands.

Christians must be extremely careful to avoid the psychological pressures to which the sects (and some unwise evangelists) have sought to subject their converts. We must trust the truth to do its work and leave it to faith working through love to achieve true and lasting spiritual conversion.

Those who are like Timothy who had 'from infancy ... known the holy Scriptures' (2 Tim. 3:15), may wish nostalgically for a dramatic conversion experience. Whatever we have said to try and describe some of the beginnings of the Christian life in faith, feelings and behaviour, we must bear in mind that conversion is only relevant as a door to a much more important home. In that home, the important thing is to share its life, to love its Lord, and to live worthily of it. In other words the new life or regeneration is the God-given process of which conversion in its various forms is the outward and visible manifestation.

# 18

## Healing: a Time to Rethink?

For I am the Lord who heals you (Exod. 15:26).

Do all have gifts of healing? (1 Cor. 12:30).

I dressed the wound, and God healed him.

Ambroise Paré

A doctor is often asked: 'What do you think of faith healing?' I find the real question is about many different kinds of healing. It is important, first of all, to think of the different ways that the word 'healing' is used today.

'Miraculous' is a word used too easily: I may use it about a simple electronic gadget or a computer which is child's play to my son. If the modern healing ministry always dealt with miracles, then we could compare them more easily with those of our Lord in the New Testament. The healings of Jesus were usually immediate, complete and lasting, and often without external means or helps of any kind. Judged thus, only a very small proportion of modern healings could properly lay claim to being miraculous.

I am not thinking of the antics of some television evangelists, whose exposure brings ridiculous scandal and concern. I am thinking rather of genuinely serious attempts to assess healings.

At Lourdes for decades, eminent Roman Catholics have used their medical skill in assessing the healings that take place there. Only a very small percentage are thought to be true miracles of healing. However amazing it seems at first sight, when the full facts are known, such cases lend themselves to natural explanations. Recently the Archbishop of Westminster, speaking at Lourdes, said the place was not about healing but rather about strengthening the faith of those who came there, whether healed or not.

Other terms are used: spiritual healing, divine healing, healing through faith in Christ, or simply faith healing. It can all be very confusing. I would like to clarify some of the underlying problems by thinking about the healer, those who seek healing, and the healing process itself.

Divine healing might be easy to deal with by saying that all healing is ultimately divine (though some immediately think of lying wonders that can be attributed to evil forces). I simply mean that Christians have always believed that God is Creator, Sustainer and, in the ancient words of Moses at the head of this chapter, the Lord who heals. Whatever means are used (medicine and surgery being indirect means), the Christian sees God's goodness behind them, just as much as in any healing by direct means. And he sees the laws of hygiene and healing as God's laws, discovered by men who, like the founders of the Royal Society, believe that in such discoveries they are 'thinking God's thoughts after him'.

When great and astounding claims for healing are made, we are at liberty to doubt the claims without doubting God and his ability to heal anywhere and any time he chooses. Faith in God is very different from credulity. From the earliest days of the church, erroneous, apocryphal and extravagant claims have been made in the name of Christ. Today, as in those days, we are commanded to 'test the spirits' (1 John 4:1), our concern and interest being that nothing should discredit the name of Christ and his gospel. When a doctor or scientist knows that there is a natural explanation to a story of healing, it is hard to see how it can be regarded as a testimony which is likely to glorify God. Even when the situation demands a supernatural explanation, we must not at once say that it is therefore of divine origin. The New Testament speaks of 'lying wonders' (2 Thess. 2:9), and our Lord spoke of prophets who by their wonders would deceive, if it were possible, the elect (Matt. 24:24). Each experience of this kind that we meet must be judged carefully in the light of both natural or scientific knowledge and the Bible and Christian experience.

What are we to say to the question: has faith a place in the hands of the healer today? My answer is an unequivocal, positive yes. The faith of the patient or client is vital, but the faith of the healer in what he is doing is just as important. I completely disagree with Dr Alex Forbes, the chairman of the Healing Research Trust, who states that faith is not necessary and prefers the term 'natural' healing. In a recent interview Forbes stated that his slogan is: 'Natural healing can refresh the parts of man that other therapies cannot reach' – a witty adaptation of an advertising slogan which does less than justice to a complex problem.

## The healer: some modern types

I wish to focus attention first on the healer and the role of faith in his training and approach. Then I will discuss the person who seeks healing, laying particular emphasis on the difference between ignorance and credulity on the one hand, and faith and trust on the other. The healing process has been the subject of much study and we will look at this as well, together with the setting in which the healing takes place. Since the subject of healing has assumed very large proportions in many church circles, the discussion will end with a personal assessment of how the current emphasis on healing compares with a more traditional Christian view of healing.

Is there a type or an archetype of healer? By a healer do we mean the therapeutic personality who, over a cup of coffee, can make us feel better by some mysterious alchemy? Forbes states that 'everyone can heal or be taught to heal and indeed many people are unconscious healers'. Most of us think of the rather exceptional type of person who sets himself up as specially gifted to heal. A list of them would have to include some of the following: Harry Edwards the spiritualist; such Americans as Aimee Semple Macpherson and Kathryn Kuhlman; Christian Scientists like Mary Baker Eddy; parish priests and others following Archbishop William Temple's lead and that of the Churches' Council of Healing; Christians of many denominations who (under the influence of the charismatic movement) believe that the gifts of healing which were found in the early church are available and should be in active use today. This long list might easily be multiplied. To it should be added the large number of native healers, traditional healers, and the 20,000 natural healers whom Dr Alex Forbes estimates are actively or occasionally practising.

The longer the list becomes, the more disparate the figures which appear in it. Should one include, for instance, President Jimmy Carter's sister, Ruth Carter Stapleton, whose books are so popular and describe the 'healing of memories'? Do we include the similar approach of the scientologists? And how many Christians (who should shudder at being in a list that frequently includes colourful and maverick characters) would still quietly regard healing as part of their religion? They might say with the famous French Huguenot surgeon, Ambroise Paré: 'I dressed the wound and God healed him.'

I consider that there is such a thing as the typical healer. One way of delineating him is to consult such an anthropologist as I. M. Lewis who has studied and described the native healer or 'shaman' as he appears in different cultures. Lewis shows how a shaman often has to undergo critical illness and be healed before he then becomes a healer. It is the theme of T. C. Eliot in the *Four Quartets:*

> The wounded surgeon plies the steel
> That questions the distempered part;
> Beneath the bleeding hands we feel
> The sharp compassion of the healer's art
> Resolving the enigma of the fever chart.

Helen Gardner is doubtless correct in seeing the wounded surgeon as a type of Christ, but I also think Lewis is right in seeing others as, in some sense, an imitation of the same process. In fact during a television debate on the subject, Lewis went as far as to say that the psychoanalyst undergoing his training analysis was a modern version of the shaman.

I was offering a contemporary example of the making of one modern healer when a patient gave me an American paperback called *England's Exorcist Tells about Supernatural Superpowers.* This unlikely title is that of a biography of an Anglican priest, Trevor Dearing. He graphically tells how he was 'a mental and physical wreck as a youngster', and how his psychiatrist diagnosed 'intense hysteria, anxiety neurosis, chronic depression, suicidal tendencies and symptoms of paranoia'. Dearing writes: 'medical men had written me off as a hopeless case.' He then describes how at nineteen he became a Christian and was then told by his psychiatrist that he did not need to see him again. Later he is advised to become a preacher; later still to take up a healing ministry; and again, after a while, to become a well-known exorcist. The hopeless case became England's exorcist and healer.

Such a dramatic story might be repeated in more muted tones by many healers who have undergone a 'creative illness' which has changed their lives. It may be but a heightening and an accentuating of the experience of many doctors, nurses and others who have chosen their calling after early illnesses which gave them an insight into the caring professions and a wish to join one of them in later life. It can be argued that what marks out the doctor or therapist of any kind who has special success as a healer is his total faith in himself and the system within which he operates. Inside his own system of belief and work, the healer has a superb capacity for rationalizing any difficulty and for dismissing any failure.

I do not believe any shaman is a total sham; the more honest and open the character, the less will he succumb to the pressures of publicity, flattery and adulation. But within every doctor there is a charlatan struggling to get out. If he succumbs to the temptation to ease up on his professional standards, he may well be taking the first step in the change from medicine-man to mountebank.

## Who seeks healing?

Across the spectrum of all professional and other workers who are engaged in any kind of healing, I find that the most successful have a commitment and a belief in their own calling which may be correctly called faith. It is often a faith which as been arrived at after personal suffering and affliction. What of the person seeking healing? First, they are often, if not anti-doctor, disillusioned by their unrewarding contact with the medical profession. They cannot be expected to honour a physician with the honour due to him since they are like the woman in the gospels who had had a flow of blood for twelve years. As Mark's account puts it, she 'had suffered a great deal under the care of many doctors and had spent all she had, yet instead of getting better she grew worse' (Mark 5:26).

No one can deny the importance of any help that faith can bring to the embittered and frustrated patient. But surely faith, in any true sense, must be distinguished from both ignorance and credulity?

Ignorance of the need for something in addition to faith may be fatal. I recall an early experience with a devout lady who became hoarse: it was evident that she had a carcinoma of the larynx. In spite of her intelligence she was unwilling to be persuaded that surgery or radiotherapy might help her. Either God must heal her or nothing would be done. Her decline and death was a very painful process to observe. It may be that ignorance is only invincible when any new knowledge which contradicts the believer's prejudice is excluded. Certainly it can lead to fear of the 'surgeon's knife', avoidance of curative medication, and thus result in unnecessary suffering.

Credulity – belief founded on weak or insufficient evidence – is endemic in the world of faith healing, even among trained professionals. To be sceptical is to blaspheme sacred tenets. I find that credulity leads to being gullible. In minor matters this may be of little importance, but in life-threatening illness it is a cruel and wanton disregard of basic human rights to tolerate a credulous acceptance of trickery.

I believe that the faith of the patient is something to be greatly valued, and thus it should be distinguished from ignorance and credulity. Faith in this sense may be analysed: it is partly a matter of what makes up the assumptive world of the patient, to use Jerome Frank's phrase. The patient's expectations of the healer and the healing process are vital: if these are built up the results from any healing will be better. His trust may be partly in the healer as a person who deserves and attracts a feeling that he can be depended upon, or it may be built upon his fame, or the fact that he is seen as the agent or channel of a higher power. The permutations and possibilities of faith are endless. No wise surgeon would neglect the importance of his patient's faith in his skill and in the healing possibilities of modern surgery. And the prescription which the patient is given will be greatly helped in its efficacy if the patient believes totally in its value.

What of the diagnosis in the patient's case, and its bearing on faith healing? Frequently healers show a cavalier disregard of diagnosis, since faith is the thing to stress across the board and irrespective of diagnosis. If the prognosis is grave, some healers only accept this as a challenge to the patient's faith. There seems little doubt that in very many cases that have been documented, the diagnosis shows the patient to be suffering from functional rather than organic disorders. There is often a prevalence of hysterical and psychosomatic disorders. Even in frankly organic diseases the emotional component is the one which the healer aims to relieve most often.

## Can we explain healing?

Suggestibility is a personality trait which psychologists can measure. It seems to me one of the most important aspects of whether a patient is going to benefit from healing or not: the more suggestible the client, the more certain the cure is of working. The process and hypotheses that purport to explain healing have been much studied. Three aspects of its study call for comment: the physical basis for healing, the psychological aspects (as in studies of the placebo effect), and psychoanalytical formulations of healing.

Many spiritual healers believe they merely facilitate the natural process of recovery. Thus Dr Christopher Woodward writes: 'To me the most important thing with any kind of disease is to keep your spirit up, and if you can keep above it, you stand a much better chance of neutralising its effect or even reversing the process of the disease.' This line of argument has been used in terms of possible connections between the laying on of hands and the stimulus this produces to release the adreno-corticotrophic hormone, which in turn releases cortisone-type hormones. Thus, in this view, the cripples who throw away their crutches at emotionally-laden healing meetings are merely producing their own internal medication.

The discovery of endorphins has led to speculation of how pain may be relieved by a placebo injection or tablet which contains no active ingredient. It remains to be seen if there are internal mechanisms similar to this process. It is likely that the more we understand the biochemical mechanisms of the body, the less mysterious will be the physical results of faith healing. Sceptical scientists may then feel happy, while believers of various kinds may simply feel that there is 'yet more light to break forth' on how nature, and the God of nature, operates in what used to be called the *vis medicatrix naturae* (the healing power of nature).

Studies of the placebo effect are a good example of how the faith of both patient and doctor are important in achieving results. Thus inert pills may produce not simply good effects but allegedly harmful side-effects, suggesting that it is all in the mind. Red tablets or capsules have been shown to enhance the good effects of such apparently innocuous and ineffective pills. As a result of placebo studies we have scientific evidence for such comments that sage physicians have often made in the past: 'Use a new drug while it works,' and 'It matters less what you prescribe than who prescribes it.' For these reasons any trial of a new treatment has to be doubly blind: both the patient and the doctor should be ignorant of which preparation contains the active ingredient and which is the inert placebo. Clearly such accepted observations as these have great relevance for measuring whether or not the hands of the healer matter and whether faith in them matters. Yet, like adequate trials of psychotherapy, there is a strange resistance to mounting such experiments as might shed light on faith healing.

A mother, when her child is hurt physically, will kiss it better. Is this also a magical touch of faith? I think it is a vivid and early illustration of what many people in later life find out:

that the interest and attention and the genuinely professional affection of the caring professions is what makes them effective. Paul Halmos, a professor of sociology who wrote *The Faith of the Counsellors*, deals with the importance of love in such caring relationships as social workers seek to build up in their work.

In my view it is not simply love (as Halmos describes it) that matters in a caring relationship, but rather what we might call, with apologies to St Paul, faith working through love. This has, within their discipline, been shown amply by psychoanalytical writers. I am not, of course, saying that the psychotherapist is kissing it better and healing the hurt in that way. Indeed, the first thing laid down is that there shall be no physical contact between therapist and client – no healing touch – and certainly no kiss, maternal or otherwise. But the vast literature on what psychoanalysts after Freud have called *the transference* deals with how the client in his sessions develops and feels a close relationship with his analyst. In one view the client is bound to relive, and in some sense to recapitulate, his earlier feelings for his mother or others. Whatever view we take of this, we cannot doubt the affectional bond between the healed and the healer illuminated by psychoanalytical work. It is helpful to remember the possibility of a sexually eroticised transference relationship. And healers of all kinds might be less naïve if they remembered that their feelings for their clients, described as counter-transference, may also become eroticised.

## Some dangers to be avoided

Physical and psychological explanations, then, may help to shed some light on how the hands of the healer may work. There is wide interest (often of an odd kind) in spiritual aspects of this process. It sometimes looks as if we are seeing a recrudescence of medieval and later preoccupations with the demonic and magical aspects of healing. As a soundly based faith has retreated in the West, so magic and superstition seem to threaten to take over. I think of the earlier example of a woman who died after two men tried to exorcise her. Such horrifying results are unusual, but they show the dangers of a faith which is uninformed and has led, as in earlier practices like those of the Inquisition, to hateful violence.

Healing is always a social process to some extent, therefore the social and cultural background of traditional healers is increasingly being studied. I have written from the stand-point of a doctor working in Great Britain who has noted striking changes in expectations about healing in the last twenty-five years. Pressures of time and space limit my final comments to my own culture.

Healing has become an overvalued idea and an overworked word. In a recent review *Healing: Biblical, Medical and Pastoral* (London, Christian Medical Fellowship Publications, 1979), C. G. Scorer refers to the breathtaking comprehensiveness of the word 'healing' as used in the church: 'The Churches are being called to mediate this kind of spiritual influence that will lead to healing of every sort, healing of individuals and communities, healing of society and nations.' The word 'healing' becomes so wide in its application that its true meaning becomes diluted and superficial, and ultimately is lost.

In the process of rediscovering healing, many healers carefully avoid the issue of whether their work involves miraculous or divine healing, yet that is certainly what many who seek healing expect. Earlier generation of Christians were supported by a belief in divine providence and a doctrine of suffering which helped them to bear life's afflictions nobly. There was often a supportive community which shared their beliefs and demonstrated a firm faith working through practical love in action. Faith healing can intrude on such a scene and the healer can appear like a comet leaving a trail of esoteric interest.

## A time to rethink

When the hands of the healer fail to heal, what then? The most cruel assertion is that failure is due to lack of faith in the patient or client. In my experience this can lead to disastrous depression and distress for the individual and his family. I consider that a reappraisal of the headlong rush into healing is long overdue in those churches which have made it a focus of energy which might better be expended elsewhere.

Faith can be tested, and the results can be looked at carefully. Edmunds and Scorer in a valuable recent review, *Some Thoughts on Faith Healing* (London, Christian Medical Fellowship Publications, 1979) show how such studies are readily available. Louis Rose analysed ninety-six cases of purported faith cures and failed to be convinced of the efficacy of faith healing. A surgeon in America worked with Miss Kathryn Kuhlman in her great healing services and wrote that whatever good she was doing was far outweighed by the pain and bitter disappointments she was causing.

There are classic examples of healers who fail to be healed themselves. St Paul the Apostle, who had used the gift of healing, described how his thorn in the flesh was not removed in spite of prayer. It should also be remembered that St Paul sometimes had to leave a sick colleague without being cured. Luke, the beloved physician, was often with St Paul and one cannot but assume that his ministrations were welcome.

Those Christians who are happy to follow in the tradition which St Paul described so well have had, I think, a clearer attitude to faith healing. They have believed that all healing comes from God. And that they may use medical and other means to treat their sicknesses as well as relying on prayer and the ministry of the church. They have not, usually, believed that faith healing is some magic and automatic process: their faith in God (using the word 'faith' in its special Christian sense at this point) leads them to look to him sometimes for miraculous healing if he so wills it.

This is a hard saying for the modern follower of faith healers. I agree with a former Bishop of Durham, H. Hensley Henson, whose words are quoted by Edmunds and Scorer:

> Suffering saddens and perplexes, but it does not alienate us, for under the bitter covenant of pain we all must live and He suffers with us; but the partiality of favouritism, which grants exemptions from the general curse, not on any intelligible principle or in the service of any adequate case, but by mere caprice at this shrine, or at that man's hands, alarms and revolts us. Not the credit of churches, but the character of God is the issue at stake in this controversy. 'Shall not the Judge of all the earth do right?'

Such trenchant words remind us that the hands of the healer beckon us to consider deeper, wider and larger issues. It requires a consideration not only of the nature of faith, but of what we believe about the nature of man and his relationship to God.

### The need for a balanced view

No attempt is made here to belittle those who stress that healing is part of 'the fullness of the blessing of the gospel of Christ'. This conviction, whether seen in the godly lives of simple folk or in the teaching of eminent Christian leaders, has been honoured by God. One of the many reliable books on this subject is *Miraculous Healing* (London, Marshall, Morgan and Scott, 1951) by H. W. Frost. The striking conclusion that Frost's balanced treatment gives is that special healing (when all other means have failed or are not available) has not always been granted to men – even to such men as Hudson Taylor of China and others – although fervent and believing prayer has been offered. A sane, balanced approach must take note of this and realise that the overriding consideration must always be that God's will should be done.

How strange that a blind eye should be turned to the long and noble story of those who have borne pain and suffering! Those who in Scripture and Christian history have found a gracious purpose in sickness that is accepted and borne gladly, would find it hard to believe the modern tale that total health is God's will for every believer now, and that their sin alone prevents them from enjoying perfect health which is their birthright. Some justify this modern oversimplification by referring to Christ as having 'borne our sicknesses', concluding from this that 'by his stripes we are healed' in a physical sense. We have already mentioned the Apostle Paul, who of all men was privileged with an unrivalled insight into the merits of our Redeemer's death. He prayed to the Lord three times for his thorn to be removed but was told rather to glory in his infirmity. This is always the authentic Christian testimony. It recognises that whatever illness or other suffering God may permit, together with all things in our lives it works together for our ultimate good in his hands.

Miraculous healing by faith in Christ has a secure place in the work and ministry of the church. But to concentrate too much on healing is, most certainly, to put second and third things first. Healing should never be the primary concern of the church. Today, when the church is bearing so little fruit, it is important not to spend our energies on one small branch to the detriment of the tree and its roots. Should we not rather hope that the tree will be enabled to bear fruit again? When this happens many, who are not content with much less, will find true healing and rest for their souls. It may well be that once again we shall see 'signs and wonders' accompanying the authoritative ministry of the word. It has often happened in times of advance, even in modern times, as may be seen in the accounts of certain missionaries such as Pastor Hsi in China over a hundred years ago. At these times of revival it is more necessary than ever that we should have a spirit of discernment in order to judge rightly between the true and the false. We should, in my view, seek to be like those who 'by constant use have trained themselves to distinguish good from evil' (Heb. 5:14).

# 19

## How Medication Can Help

> Stop drinking only water, and use a little wine
> because of your stomach and your frequent illnesses
> (1 Tim. 5:23).

> Their fruit will serve for food and their leaves for
> healing (Ezek. 47:12) .

'Why don't you take some Valium like any other normal person?'
This splendid remark comes from the sound-track of a film
released in 1985 which has made millions at the box office. It is
typical of one approach: there is a pill for every problem, so just
take it.

We know this is not the case. It may be best to start with
asking why it is that so many sensible people today do not want
to take any medication for strain and stress. I am frequently
surprised when a patient tells me very firmly that he (or more
often she) has agreed to *talk* to me about the way symptoms of
strain such as anxiety, depression or being unable to sleep are
upsetting the whole of his life. He then adds, 'I don't want to
take any drugs.'

### Over-reaction to misuse

'Why won't you take any medication?' is a question answered
in many ways, and the explicit answers are often as important as

the implicit objections to being 'fobbed off with a prescription'.

A fear of addiction or dependence is frequently mentioned. This is a wholly sensible concern to have. Valium (Diazepam) is a most valuable compound for the relief of anxiety. It has been prescribed to more people than any other drug. It has a small but definite risk of creating a dependence problem. This has been exaggerated, but none the less even a small risk must be considered and weighed carefully against the benefits from taking it for a short period. If a person can trust the doctor to use it discreetly as part of a wider programme of help in solving the problem, then this may overcome a proper reluctance to embark on medication. For the vast majority of properly prescribed drugs there is no problem in finishing with a course of treatment.

A fear of side-effects is another valid worry. Since Noah first drank wine and suffered from its ill effects, the fact that substances which exist in nature and are used to relieve symptoms *also* have side-effects has always been with us. The most ardent herbalist knows this as much as the pharmacist who handles so many compounds that are discovered and synthesized in the laboratory. Aspirin, which can make the agony of arthritis bearable and relieve many physical pains, can also cause massive bleeding from the stomach. Aspirin can kill in an overdose, but it may cause much upset short of that disaster. Yet properly used it is a valuable aid, as are so many other drugs.

Modern medicine relies heavily on the discovery of antibiotics, antihistamines and antidepressants. To be able to kill so many potentially fatal infections with the 'magic bullet' of new drugs has been an enormous blessing. But *all* the drugs that have been discovered have had a potential for misuse. As this fact has become part of public knowledge, it has made many people reluctant to accept orthodox medical methods of treatment.

## The case of Thalidomide

There are some disasters which signal the end of an epoch. The tragic teratogenic effects of Thalidomide may have been one such experience. Babies were born without proper arms and with other deformities because the mother had been given Thalidomide during the first three months of pregnancy. The drug crossed the placenta into the baby's foetal circulation and, at the vital time when organs were being formed, caused the cruel, handicapping result.

It was a sad saga which had enormous impact: never again would it be possible to trust the drug makers to market a new substance without changing the laws and making more stringent tests imperative. The fight for adequate compensation for the children and their families involved a lot of washing of dirty linen in public. It was greatly to the credit of some agencies that Thalidomide had never been freely prescribed until further tested, as in the USA.

I remember the change that Thalidomide produced in the expectations of young mothers-to-be. It had often been difficult to help some symptoms of early pregnancy such as sickness and vomiting. After the news of the potential side-effects became generally knows, it was no longer easy to prescribe *anything* successfully for a pregnant woman. This was, of course, a good thing but sometimes it meant that essential drugs for severe anaemia of pregnancy might be refused by the patient.

The wider effects of the Thalidomide scandal are still with us. A lack of trust in the way drug firms operate and publicise their new discoveries is an obvious result. It has also affected the trust of many patients in their doctor's judgments: after all, it was qualified medical men who gave Thalidomide to patients. Should they not have known better?

Other drug-firm scandals have contributed to distrust in the system. When large Swiss firms are shown not only to make huge profits but also to victimise some employees who draw public attention to what is wrong, there is a knock-on effect that reaches to the pharmacist in the local chemist's shop. Whenever a drug is withdrawn by a committee of safety, there are many people who shake their heads and say, 'I told you so.'

We know that reputable drug firms spend millions of their profits on research, and co-operate fully in safety regulations. And yet the doubts persist. The consumer rightly thinks more than once about whether he wishes to consume this or that particular drug.

Since many effects of stress and strain are minor and self-limiting, the reluctance to take medication can be a healthy and beneficial response. But some who are seriously in need of help, suffer needlessly for a long time. I am amazed to find, at least once in every working week, a patient with a crippling condition like chronic depression who may have endured a year's misery (and a suicide attempt) – things which might have been prevented by proper treatment.

### 'I want to do it on my own'

I cannot help admiring the wish of many good and well-balanced people to get over their problems *without* the help of medication. I find that Christians often seem to be specially keen on avoiding medication for any stress-induced symptoms of a nervous kind. They feel that they are 'letting the side down' by even coming to a doctor for help. They feel their faith and the spiritual resources of grace in the forms of prayer, Bible reading and other things that come from Christian fellowship in the church should be ample support for them in crisis. In addition, they feel insulted that it is considered that an intensely personal problem can be helped by medication. How can tablets be trusted to help to remove feelings of despair and the tortures of anxiety?

I recall a young lawyer who was succeeding well in his career. Two brothers had died from a rare hereditary illness affecting the nervous system. He knew that the second of the brothers (who had lived longer than the first) would die, but when it came to the final separation his grief had surprised him. Now, a year later, the anxiety was affecting his ability to work; he was not sleeping and he was losing his appetite and getting thinner.

After an hour of listening and sorting out why he had become depressed, I felt it right to suggest a mild antidepressant in effective dose at night. He was appalled at the suggestion that a pill should help to restore his peace of mind when it was so clearly related to the loss of the much-loved brothers.

Eventually he came to accept that if his depression were to respond to physical medication he might then sort out his feelings more easily. He did take medication, and he recovered.

Many feel that they are not depressed but simply unhappy. One famous teacher of psychiatry used to say that if a person was unhappy and if he was ill with his unhappiness then he was depressed. That may beg the question of what being ill, in such a case, means.

I mean that the unhappiness which makes you ill gives a recognisable pattern – sleep is disturbed by waking in the night or early morning, for instance. If the person is slowed up mentally and physically, there may be a marked loss of concentration and forgetfulness. Weight is lost because of loss of interest in food. The person's normal sexual interest and performance may also be lost. Frequently there are other physical symptoms in depressive illness.

When such a pattern emerges I think it is correct to tell the patient that a course of antidepressants will very probably help him. The side-effects will be few, and in a month or so he may begin to feel better. He may need medication for six to nine months, but he will not be dependent on it. Once he begins to feel better, the problems that may have led to his depression can be sorted out.

In my view, there is no more personal disgrace in having the help of antidepressants than there would be in having appropriate antibiotics for severe tuberculosis. It is important to treat personal and social aspects of tuberculosis too, but before streptomycin and the other anti-tuberculous drugs, tragic deaths occurred from the disease. Since 1955 antidepressants have helped shorten the period of illness for many, and deaths from both suicide and the effects of depressive illness as such have been reduced in number.

## Crisis and capsules

When Librium was introduced it became common to give these black-and-green capsules to many people who went to the family doctor in crisis. Librium is a most effective drug, very like Valium, and many patients owe a great deal to its makers for the relief from anxiety it has brought.

But if one goes to a doctor in crisis, a capsule three times a day is surely not what is needed most. To listen, to assess the problem, takes time. Many doctors in primary care, working as general practitioners or family doctors, have very little time to spare. Nowadays a happy solution in many group practice centres is the provision of nurses, social workers and psychologists who work as a team and help to sort out the problem. It is ultimately the patient who decides how he will solve the problem, but the skilled counselling of the team members may make a great deal of difference.

Where anxiety is high, all the patient's efforts to help himself may be of no avail until the level of anxiety is reduced. So we come back to the problem of medication. The short-term, carefully adjusted prescription to lower severe anxiety to more normal levels may be an essential part of the plan to provide real help.

This is especially important in crisis care. The wise counselor or helper will, at times, sense that the client's response to a crisis is leading to a nervous breakdown. That is, the client is becoming a patient who will soon be unable to function as a person because of his anxieties. Intervention with adequate medication, or even admission to hospital for a brief period, prevents the crisis from becoming a collapse. As soon as the symptoms are relieved the work of problem-solving can begin again.

For many patients a sedative or mild tranquilliser will help to control the state of anxiety. The amount of sedation they produce varies greatly from patient to patient; the correct dose is the one which relieves the symptoms without producing too many side-effects.

### Controlling anxiety

In recent years it has been possible to control much anxiety – especially its physical symptoms – with a new group of drugs called Beta Blockers. Some experts believe that they should be the first choice since they do not act on the brain but on the peripheral nervous system.

Many who suffer from disabling anxiety do not complain of their worry or tension, but what they feel. It may be nausea or sickness, a fast thumping of the heart, tension headaches, trembling of the hands, or abdominal symptoms such as pain, indigestion or general over-activity of the bowel.

The discovery of receptors in the tissues of the body which respond to adrenaline was followed by the finding of such drugs as Propranolol (Inderal). These drugs, used in much smaller doses than those needed for blood pressure and similar problems, may reduce or abolish anxiety symptoms.

A man who had lost a wife to whom he had been devoted was still suffering with depression two years after her death. He was preoccupied with killing himself in order to join his wife. But what he complained of most was a constant feeling of sickness. For many reasons, including the fact that he believed in homeopathic medicine in preference to anything orthodox medicine could offer, the choice of medication was difficult. Propranolol, in very small doses, abolished his symptoms, and he was then prone to treat his consultant as a witch doctor with magical powers. But abolishing his disabling symptoms was only a preliminary to a long and hard attempt to relieve him of the underlying burden of grief.

A combination of medication, for a short time, may be needed – both Propranolol and sometimes something like Diazepam (Valium). By this means a quicker control of the physical aspects of anxiety is achieved.

I cannot emphasise too strongly that medication is a preliminary to learning new skills to deal with anxiety. Often a psychologist will be able to teach some of the techniques of relaxation, assertion or other social skills. A social worker may perform invaluable case-work involving counselling and other forms of help. In all these therapeutic relationships the aim is to give more understanding and insight so that the patient may make the necessary changes to solve his problems.

The comparison is sometimes made between medication for stress and the early treatment of a broken bone. It is usually essential to immobilise a limb with a splint of plaster of paris. Later it is equally necessary to do other things to achieve full recovery: physiotherapy, exercise and even advice on preventing a recurrence of some fractures and dislocations. The use of medication may be compared to the immobilisation of part of an arm or leg till healing has occurred.

## Drugs and psychosis

Since the early 1950s it has been possible to treat symptoms of psychosis, such as delusions and hallucinations, and to cut short many episodes when the person affected has been quite mad and out of touch with reality. Regrettably, the problems of stigma prevent many from receiving prompt and early help when they become psychotic.

There is still a fear of going to those who work with psychiatric patients, and good will towards the patient may be mixed with a lack of knowledge. In many Christian churches gallant attempts have been made to give support and counselling. In spite of this, old-fashioned madness, with all its well-known psychotic manifestations, may go unrecognised and untreated.

A mother phoned me about the violent behaviour at home of her eighteen-year-old daughter. After a falling off in her high standard of work at school, there had been a relative failure in the examinations necessary for her to follow her quite normal brother and sister in their university careers. This was followed by bizarre changes in behaviour at home and at school, including withdrawal from friends, silly giggling and inappropriate laughter, and odd remarks which led her intelligent parents to fear that she was concealing other symptoms (as indeed she was). She had irrational beliefs (delusions), and was hearing voices (auditory hallucinations).

Counsellors who were doctors and clergymen all said it was some sort of identity crisis and blamed the home and the parents. Thus for many months the proper diagnosis was missed, partly because the patient cleverly concealed her symptoms.

When it became more evident that we were dealing with a schizophrenic illness, it was possible to treat it with drugs such as Largactil (Chlorpromazine) and Depixol injections. The patient recovered substantially and began to work and make progress, needing an injection only every three weeks.

It would not have been possible to improve the lot of many who have psychotic disorders, like schizophrenia and manic depressive illness, without the discovery of Largactil and other similar drugs.

When research was being done in Paris on antihistamines, it was an accident, or a piece of serendipity, which led to Largactil being discovered. In those days there were no strict ethical committees governing research, and the drug (properly called Chlorpromazine) was given to very disturbed manic or schizophrenic patients. For the first time ever these patients lost many of their symptoms and as a result behaved more normally, without showing the sedation other drugs produced.

The rest is history. By being able to control the symptoms, admission to hospital was often avoided and the time in hospital briefer. Later on, being able to give medication by long-acting injection was a further great step forward in community care. Such things as Modecate (fluphenazine) and Depixol (fluphenthixol) have made the acceptance of medication easier and made it more certain that a patient who does not wish to comply and remember his tablets can be treated effectively.

Christians have an honourable record of seeking humane treatment for those who are mentally ill.

How many of those who pass the statue of Eros in London's Piccadilly know of the work of the seventh Earl of Shaftesbury whom the monument commemorates? Some know of his work for children and for reforms in factories. Only recently did I learn of his great work for the mentally ill.

His work with the Lunacy Commissioners included being chairman for forty years. His first Act of Parliament in 1828 was to help the mentally ill, and in the year of his death in 1885 he spoke with authority about another act to improve their lot. His long-sustained efforts did much to improve the lot of psychotic patients in the nineteenth century in England. Florence Nightingale, not a stranger to psychiatric disorders herself, said: 'Had he not devoted himself to reforming asylums, he would have been in one himself.' Such snide remarks are still directed towards those who feel they must work with the mentally ill. But we need more men and women like Shaftesbury today in mental health work.

## The churches' response
Concerned helpers in this difficult field object to medication for psychotic illness: they say it is using a 'drug strait-jacket' instead of the coarse linen jackets used to restrain violent lunatics a few

decades ago. I think the objection is misconceived. Anyone who has seen a newly admitted patient hitting the ward like a tornado and smashing a TV and the furniture, or attacking staff and patients alike, will be glad that such drugs as we now have for psychosis are available and effective.

To me it seems clear that we should use drugs to control psychotic symptoms and behaviour. Then we can start the real work of helping the patient back to his normal life, and supporting his family in this rehabilitation. That work is costly in time, staff and money. Community care is much spoken of, but the absence of proper resources for such care is a cause for scandal and concern. Relapse is common in most of the serious psychiatric disorders and can be prevented only with much careful supervision and support.

Churches have always had a substantial minority of psychotic patients. They are not suffering from 'religious mania', as is often said, but usually have recognized illnesses such as psychotic depression or schizophrenia, with religion simply giving some colour and form to the illness. To regard such illnesses as demonic or the result of major sin is a tragic error in most instances. Ninety-nine per cent require medical care, including drug treatment.

No one denies the value of prayer and the part that faith may play in healing and recovery, but it has always been the Christian's belief that when drugs or surgery are discovered they should be used wisely and well. It is the patient that recovers, and medication only plays its small but important part. In this sense psychiatrists share the approach to treatment that is typified by the remark made by the French surgeon Ambroise Paré. In the wars of his day, Paré used techniques for cleaning and sterilizing wounds which were far in advance of his time – and with excellent results. Asked to explain his success, Paré said: 'I dressed the wound and God healed him.'

It is a great pleasure to see the recovery of people whose minds have been deranged and whose behaviour has been irrational and dangerously insane. Part of the improvement must be credited to the medication which can restore the brain function to normal and give the mind and personality a chance to return to health. The fact that happy accidents have led to new discoveries of such drugs must surely be regarded by believers as providential blessings.

Their side-effects are, of course, a great problem. Weighed against the hazards of psychotic illness, the risk of having side-effects must be taken, for the sake of the patient, his family and others who might be harmed by his psychotic behaviour. Even such writers as R. D. Laing, whose early work was thought of as 'anti-psychiatry', have long since returned to accept the value of medication, as well as seeking to understand the meaning of madness for the psychotic and the society of which he is a member.

# 20

# How Does Alternative Therapy Help?

Test everything. Hold on to the good (1 Thess. 5:21)

Honour the physician with the honour due him,
according to your need of him, for the Lord created
him (Ecclesiasticus 38:1 The Common Bible, RSV).

Many who feel that doctors and hospitals have failed to help
them cope with stress are turning to alternative medicine. This
is not a new thing – many of the alternative therapies have a
long history, like acupuncture in China. Homeopathy has an
honourable tradition and many practitioners have been
attracted by it. In Britain it has had much support from the
Royal Family. However, some alternative therapies are new and
suspect. What can we make of them? Are they all good, or a
mixed bag, or (as some think) dangerous and to be avoided?

## The choice available
It is not one alternative but a whole wide range of therapies
that is now available. Prince Charles, in his address given to
the British Medical Association, said doctors should take

account of 'those sometimes long neglected *complementary* methods of medicine.' A Council for Complementary and Alternative Medicine has been set up by a group of practitioners, who work in this field. They want to set their house in order, and consider training, standards, qualifications and discipline for the public's protection. It is a far cry from the time when doctors might be struck off the list of the General Medical Council for associating with an unqualified practitioner. The 'quacks', as they used to be called somewhat disparagingly, have come in from the cold.

In a recent survey by *The Times* (March 1985), over 100 doctors were asked what alternative therapies they were aware of and what they recommended. The top six in the list were acupuncture, homeopathy, osteopathy, hypnotherapy, medication and medical herbalism. The first four were recommended by a third to a half of the doctors. Others, in decreasing order of importance to the doctor, were chiropractic healing, nutritional medicine, naturopathy, acupressure/shiatsu, gestalt/humanistic psychology, aromatherapy, reflexology, medical radiesthesia, Alexander technique, and clinical ecology.

Before giving a brief account of the main therapies, we must ask *why* there should be a flight to such alternatives from doctors.

## The failures of orthodox medicine

After all the triumphs of modern medicine, it is a fact that many doctors are disillusioned by its failures. The great advances represented by the discoveries of the last fifty years have resulted in simple and effective medical care for previously fatal conditions. The technology has advanced to the edge of the miraculous. Yet some of our best medical students decide not to stay in technologically-based medicine but to become family doctors in the belief that they can do better work there.

Patients, too, come to dislike hospitals for their impersonal approach. They hear of infections, such as Legionnaire's Disease, that may be picked up in the most modern hospitals, and they only stay if hospital care is a matter of life and death. In some countries it is not the danger to health but the financial hazards that keep many away. Without full cover from insurance, an operation may break the family financially. The large cost of 'high-tech' hospitals and doctors' fees has done nothing to endear them as caring for the patient. The consumer response has been to sue the surgeon if the slightest thing goes wrong. Trust between doctor and patient can reach new lows in such a setting, and doctors' insurance against expensive claims increases to astronomical heights.

Doctors in orthodox medicine have failed their patients on a number of grounds, in my view, and have therefore contributed to making many look for alternative help elsewhere.

First, there is hardly ever enough *time*. In Britain, the average time for consultation with the family doctor is six minutes for each patient. Much may be done in that time, but it is not enough. The patient wants to be recognised as a person, listened to, examined and have the treatment explained to him. This does not often happen. A doctor may wait with pen poised to prescribe for the next patient, or to give him his certificate. We know that doctors may give all the time needed for a sick patient, and a home visit may take longer since a doctor is usually called out for more serious conditions.

Secondly, the patient is seen in an almost automatic and perfunctory way, with a tablet dished out for every symptom rather than time given to discover the real problem. With simple, self-limiting things this may be all that is needed. But the universal reaction against the indiscriminate use of tranquillisers is due to their excessive use by doctors, and serves as one example of how their status has changed.

Doctors should not go to the other extreme and feel that every patient requires psychotherapy. One patient with a high fever and sore throat had her tonsillitis properly diagnosed and prescribed for. Then the young doctor leaned forwards and asked, 'Now tell me what is *really* bothering you?' All the patient wanted was to get home to bed and let the antibiotic do its work.

Doctors have often failed to provide *continuity of care*. A group practice of five or seven may be a fine thing, but not if it means that you meet a strange doctor on your next four visits. It seems vital to many patients (and doctors too) that a *relationship* should develop where the doctor knows the patient and his background and the patient can trust his doctor. This is a minimum basis for a treatment contract. In many practices it is difficult to get an appointment with the doctor you know or wish to see. The receptionist and secretary may be like 'dragons at the gate' and seem to be there to protect the doctor rather than help the patient.

## Honour the physician?

It seems evident to most of us who have observed the work of the orthodox doctor since the end of World War II that there have been many decades of decline in his status. The old-style family doctor had an authority that was based on his knowledge and experience and his wisdom and tact in relating to his patients – gifts which made him, to some, a charismatic figure. The doctor of fifty years ago could do so little compared to his counterpart today, but he had a figure of incomparably greater power in the eyes of many of his patients.

Many who have studied the problem would say that fifty years ago the doctor was forced to understand his *personal* role as a physician. He was more of a psychologist and philosopher, a guide and friend. Above all, he was more of a healer: he understood about helping people to recover from their ills.

Many factors are thus involved in explaining why many patients seek help from those who are not doctors. The orthodox doctor, with a previously unheard of therapeutic potential, seems reduced to impotence in the face of many patients' demands. He may be glad to see them seek help elsewhere.

The patient, as the client/customer, still wishes to find a good doctor. Their experience of modern-day practice makes many patients feel that they cannot obey the injunction of the Apocrypha to 'honour the physician with the honour due to him.' They feel let down by their experience so often that they turn elsewhere for help. Anyone who has lived in London for the past twenty years may often have been referred, in the evening or weekend, to an agency which will send a radio-car with a doctor to him. The emergency doctor is of course ignorant of the patient, has no clinical notes and thus no notion of his medical history, and will, at best, be forced to do an inadequate job as a locum covering for the patient's proper doctor. In the next few weeks it will be surprising if the patient does not read of doctors wanting an increase in salary to keep up with comparable professions. The patient may reflect that the vocation which he thought doctors had to follow seems to have changed in character.

Another factor that makes patients look elsewhere is the vast increase in popular knowledge of medical matters as put out by the media. Both television and radio have broadcast excellent material related to health and disease. No longer, then, is orthodox medicine full of secrets dispensed by doctor, nurse and pharmacist. All, or nearly all, is told over and over again, and the secrets are shouted from the roof-tops. I believe it is good that everyone knows about the facts of science, health and disease.

But the mystique, part of every healer's stock-in-trade, is lost for ever when such public knowledge abounds. The holders of the secrets of healing are sought elsewhere and the boom in alternative therapies begins.

### Danger: which diagnosis?
I would sound a loud cautionary note at this point. By all means

let us welcome alternative therapists who are not quacks or charlatans. But some healers profess no interest in diagnosis at all, simply believing that they can cure the condition irrespective of its nature. I think this can be dangerous.

When we have had so many decades of scientific advance, I think we should guard zealously that which has been hard won by research and careful study. For me this is all part of God's goodness in his general providence and care. Like the rain, I think the benefits of medicine should be allowed to fall on the just and the unjust: they should be freely available to those who need them. But others, for many reasons, fight shy of science as if it were in itself against their faith. I have heard devout folk speak of the surgeon's knife as if it were never to be endured. Recall the earlier example, given in a previous chapter, of the lady with cancer of the larynx. She needed radiotherapy, but she took the view: 'either God must heal me or I will not be healed'. She died a painful, lingering death.

Such willful turning away from scientific and medical help in diagnosis and treatment is now rare, but it is tragic when it occurs.

A young woman had been treated for breast cancer. Now there was need for further treatment, but she was persuaded to adopt the macrobiotic approach and to shun doctors. She became emaciated and ill. Her family were able to intervene and at least get terminal care. A year later they are still rightly angry that proper care should have been denied her in the name of alternative therapy.

Whatever the failings of doctors, hospitals and the caring professions, it seems criminal that anyone in need should be denied modern help. Doctors still have a front-line role in helping with the strains of illness.

## How complementary is alternative therapy?
It is difficult to categorise the choices available. Some, such as

acupuncture, offer relief of symptoms in painful conditions, yet acupuncture is based on a systematic view of the body and of some 800 'points' where needles may be inserted. For millennia this practice has been used in China, where operations and childbirth may be painless with acupuncture used for anaesthetic purposes. Since 1950 acupuncture has been used in Europe. In many hospitals, including my own, anaesthetists trained in acupuncture techniques do good work in pain clinics. Other independent practitioners also use the technique.

Two questions arise regarding acupuncture. First, is the successful practice of acupuncture inseparable from the beliefs of those who invented it? Do we need to believe in invisible energy lines (meridians) in the body, and a special energy (chi), or the opposing principles of yin and yang? Is it a package deal? I believe most Westerners who try acupuncture do not know its theoretical basis. But patients undergoing surgery do not know too much about anaesthetics either.

Secondly, is the great effectiveness of acupuncture in China due to the general belief in the system, giving rise to great faith and trust in it – a kind of autosuggestion, as well as suggestion by powerful, experienced medical figures using it? If one is led from an early age to believe in a system of pain relief, then it will work more often.

We cannot answer such questions except by guesswork and analogy. We know that inert tablets, containing only sugar and coated red, work very well for many patients suffering from many conditions. Placebo tablets like that *may also produce side-effects*, certainly not because of their inert and ineffective content. 'Nothing is, but thinking makes it so.'

A scientific explanation starts with the fact that our own bodies will produce endorphins under certain kinds of stimulation. These morphine-like substances actually relieve the pain after the application of the needles, or of acupressure without needles. We cannot be certain of this explanation without a lot more research, but we must avoid any arrogant belief that only Western medicine is correct: it may be that ancient wisdom and experience can teach us a lot.

Personally I cannot see (as some maintain) that if 3,000 years ago in China the origin of acupuncture was linked to spirit worship then it must be an occult, forbidden area of treatment.

Homeopathy owes its origin to the work of Samuel Hahnemann whose book *Organ of the Art of Healing* was published in 1810. It came to England some thirty years later and has been very influential, partly because of the Royal Homeopathic Hospital and the support of generations of the British Royal Family. On the continent, pharmacies display the two words 'Allopathy' and 'Homeopathy' in their windows: this means they dispense for orthodox doctors (allopaths) as well as homeopaths.

*Homeo* means similar, and one of the many principles involved in homeopathy is that if a substance in large doses produces a toxic picture of a patient's symptoms similar to what the disease produces, then very small dilutions of the substance will cure the condition. In the words translated from Hahnemann: 'All homeopathic medicines cure illnesses the symptoms of which they most resemble.' He further taught that in the dilution and shaking of the solution (containing say one drop of the original in 1,000 or 10,000 drops of water), the water gets endowed with an 'immaterial, vital, dynamic energy'. This energy is seen as the effective cause of the cure.

One explanation introduces concepts from nuclear physics and biochemistry to suggest that free energy is in some way imprinted on the water and eventually in the homeopathic tablets that are taken. Again the question arises: do we have to believe the 'scientific' ideas of 1810 to accept that homeopathy may have a place in treatment? I doubt it. I certainly do not think, as some books allege, that homeopathy is evil simply because Hahnemann was a freemason and a hypnotist who may have had Hindu-like views.

The most difficult question is: what do we do when presented with a straight choice between well-proved orthodox medicine and homeopathy?

As a medical student in 1950 I went to a meeting where the President of the Homeopathic movement gave an outline of the case for homeopathy. At question time a Senior Registrar at the hospital asked him: 'If your daughter seemed to be dying of pneumonia and you knew as a doctor she had a penicillin-responsive organism and she could be cured by a few injections, would you choose penicillin or a homeopathic remedy?' We, as cynical students, waited while he equivocated. No clear answer was forthcoming.

If homeopathy supplements and fills the gaps in traditional medicine, all well and good. But I fear that some may lose the benefits they should have by turning exclusively to homeopathy.

These two examples may serve to show the problems that can arise. Reflexology is an example of how belief must be stretched to extreme credulity. The soles of the feet are deeply massaged because the therapist believes that the entire body, including its internal organs, is represented in the feet.

A patient of mine referred to her eminent reflexologist as 'Joe the Toe'. She believed implicitly that the massage of areas of the feet had helped the liver and so forth. Fortunately a surgeon had diagnosed how depressed she was and advised psychiatric help. After her depression was cured by orthodox means, she still diligently attended 'Joe the Toe'. Her faith was there, rather than in any of the customary forms of medical help.

It seems to me that we are called upon to be sceptical without being cynical. The New Testament advice of the Apostle Paul: 'Test everything. Hold on to the good' (1 Thess. 5:21) would seem to apply here. For instance, Reich's *Black Box* and orgone therapy can, it seems to me, be dismissed out of hand.

Chiropractic and osteopathy may both be helpful if they

involve skilled manipulation. My preference would be for proper medical diagnosis before manipulation.

This is based on an experience of four cases of 'slipped discs' where the prolapsed disc, causing a painful sciatica, was manipulated so effectively as to cause a threat of paralysis from the waist down, thus necessitating emergency operations. But many less severe cases may benefit from skilled care by well-trained osteopaths.

Again, strain causes so much muscular tension and pain that some find anything that helps with relaxation and improved posture to a be a boon. The Alexander technique is one such system which has helped many.

One can only select a few of the alternative therapies for comment. It may be evident to anyone reading about them that many owe their force and power to the present influence of Eastern religions in the West. They are part of a powerful world-view, and anyone attempting to benefit from them should perhaps take a careful look at any belief system attached to them. This is true of some kinds of yoga, and so-called 'easy ways of treating cancer' owe as much to Buddhism as anything else.

## Holistic healing

Therapists and practitioners of 'alternative' kinds often see themselves as true alternatives to doctors and do not like any idea of being simply complementary. When anyone of us becomes a patient we are aware of the professional jealousy which makes a practitioner speak of 'my patient' as if he owned exclusive rights. I believe the patient should have the full rights to decide about his own treatment and by whom it should be given. It would relieve much of the strain of many conditions if we could go to someone qualified in that sort of problem. But we live in a fallen, imperfect world and cannot often get the help we want in times of stress.

'What are we to make of holistic healing?' was the title of a first leading article in the *London Times* (1985) which described what is called 'whole person medicine'. It is a question we must ask ourselves too. Is it merely a new fad or fashion? Those who know the name of Dr Paul Tournier from his many books, may remember that he has long been associated with medicine for the whole person.

In Britain the formation of a *British Holistic Medicine Association* signals a recognition for the need to foster the practical growth of caring for the spiritual, psychological and social needs of men as much as the physical ones. But what is new in this? Very little, since the leaders by their own statements want to get back to what was known of old: we get ill from strain because a number of things in our whole lives can go wrong and lead to symptoms.

A good doctor should always try to listen patiently to the whole story that a patient has to tell him. The friend who really wants to help will do no less. We cannot fully understand the nature of the person's suffering without knowing something of his family, his background and his culture. It is a tall order to seek to do this.

Then comes the question of spiritual problems. What is the meaning and purpose of it all?

There are those for whom the first spiritual question is: why am I being punished like this? I think of the answer Jesus gave to those who asked him about the man born blind: 'Neither this man nor his parents sinned ... but this happened so that the work of God might be displayed in his life' (John 9:3).

We must do away with the idea that sin and diseases are always linked. Clearly they sometimes are. A Christian may justly feel that 'the Lord disciplines those he loves, and he punishes everyone he accepts as a son' (Heb. 12:6), and may include many kinds of suffering within this.

Each of us has to work out for ourselves the meaning of a time of strain as a kind of test. It would be a great help if we could talk about it in a counselling setting without being, as so often happens, preached at by the counsellor.

In good 'whole-person care' it has always been the case that the doctor, the counsellor or the minister gives himself in some way. One teacher used the memorable phrase: 'The drug most often prescribed is the doctor himself.' He argued that he should know himself sufficiently not to give an overdose of himself, overwhelming the patient; he should prescribe the correct dose of himself. All of us, when we try to help each other, need to know ourselves just well enough to be able to give sufficiently of ourselves to ease the strain of the person we are seeking to aid. We can all, in some sense, do our bit to put into practice the care of the whole person.

# 21

## CREATIVE ILLNESS:
## HOW TO UTILISE STRESS WELL

> But he said to me, 'My grace is sufficient for you, for
> my power is made perfect in weakness.' Therefore I
> will boast all the more gladly about my weaknesses,
> so that Christ's power may rest on me (2 Cor. 12:9).

How can a man who stammers with a speech impediment enjoy
making a difficult public speech? Why do we say: 'Give work
to a busy man'? He may be a workaholic, yet he will not only
cope with another task but will also enjoy it. Both men, one
with a handicap and the other addicted to working hard, will
rise to a challenge in spite of its stress factor.

To speak of the joys of stress may be excessive hyperbole,
but there are positive values in the pressures it brings. We must
therefore ask in what way tensions may become creative.
Christians, like everyone else, may suffer a creative illness. We
may have spiritual encounters in our lives today which resemble
those of Jacob. Something damaging and threatening, such as
that which left Jacob limping, may be creative too, as it was for
him.

## Compensating for our inferiorities

Most of us have reason to feel badly about some aspect of ourselves. Demosthenes, the famous Greek orator, began by going to the seashore, putting pebbles in his mouth, and declaiming his speeches to the waves. The same process of over-compensation made Winston Churchill and Aneurin Bevan outstanding orators, in spite of a speech impediment such as Demosthenes had. Both men could hold the attention of the House of Commons, and used their stammer skilfully.

In Christian history the principle is a firm one: God's power and grace is made perfect in our weakness, as the Apostle Paul put it. This is borne out in a more general way in Hebrews chapter 11 which lists the heroes of faith in the Old Testament. The writer says that through faith these men and women turned their weakness into strength (Heb. 11:34). Is it possible to understand this process?

Sometimes a person's physical constitution leads to a very strong personality development. We may think of many small, short people who fight aggressively to achieve. The history of Napoleon shows this well, and many others of similar build have been, in a lesser way, empire builders.

On a human level, and excluding for a moment the special activity of God's grace, the process of actually enjoying 'glorying in our infirmity' has been shown in our century by Alfred Adler. He was one of Freud's colleagues in Vienna who broke away from psychoanalysis to found a system of 'individual psychology' which has been very influential, particularly in American thinking. Many analysts agree that they borrow Adler's views without admitting it. One of the most magisterial accounts of the history of psychiatry, H. Ellenberger's book *The Discovery of the Unconscious* (London, Penguin, 1970), seeks to restore Adler to his rightful place as a doctor who helped many to understand how they might cope with inferiority feelings caused by some physical defect or disability.

Adler himself had rickets as a child and this may, because of the way it stunted his own growth, have given him special insight into the problem. Adler thought that any organ of our body may seem to be displeasing and unsatisfactory to the individual. Plastic surgeons know this and make much of their ability to alter noses which are too long or otherwise not the right shape; breasts, genitals and ears are frequently operated upon to help the person feel more 'normal' about their bodies. But Adler had a more profound understanding of such things, and would have realised why many people are unhappy even after surgery. He believed that much of our lives could be seen as an attempt to protest against our weak elements and turn them into strength. He called this 'the masculine protest', since in his days to be a man was seen as being strong.

I was talking to a pleasant and attractive woman who was eminently successful in her field. I asked her what had led her into her profession and driven her to achieve such distinction. She said: 'I was the ugliest girl in the class, so at school I decided I had to use my brains.' She had enjoyed the process, although she may have been exaggerating the description of her ugliness.

We do not hear so much today about having an inferiority complex, yet the vast majority of us have something to feel inferior about. It can be a great strain for the growing child to think of facing adult life with *anything* that marks him as less well endowed than he would like to be. If we feel rejected because of some part of ourselves, the consequences can be disastrous despair. Not every person is rejected as was Isaac Watts, the famous hymn writer. The woman to whom he proposed marriage rejected him with seventeenth-century politeness, saying: 'Dear Mr Watts, I admire the jewel but I cannot love the casket.'

A tragic result of rejection occurred in a local choir in London some years ago. A woman who was a successful nurse felt she would like to sing in the choir which was a friendly group that met weekly to practice for a concert at the end of each term. An audition was necessary, but was usually regarded as a formality. She failed the audition, and went home and killed herself. Perhaps there was some powerful depressive disorder driving her to suicide. We cannot be sure. What it does show is that an 'organ inferiority', such as a voice that is not good enough, can drive the person who feels that way about it to despair.

W. Somerset Maugham tells a story about a young man who wishes, above all else, to be a concert pianist. His elderly grandmother is asked to come and listen to his playing and pronounce her opinion. Is he talented enough to go on to the long training required? She listens, and then says no. The young man shoots himself.

## Creative illness

Many people who have enjoyed considerable success have had their achievements preceded by a period of illness due to special stresses and strains felt in their own minds.

In the history of the Christian church there are many such examples. One of my favourites is the life of John Bunyan, the English tinker who went on to write many books including the extremely influential *Pilgrim's Progress*. Bunyan went through a prolonged period of creative illness which he describes in his autobiography *Grace Abounding*. In one way we can read Bunyan as a typical Puritan going through an intensive period of feeling guilty for his sin, and finding forgiveness, new life in Christ, and a calling in the church as a preacher. We may add that it is his vivid imagination and his artistic gift of expressing complex ideas in simple, everyday English that has brought him lasting fame. Yet in another way we can regard him as suffering from depression and crippling, obsessional anxieties. Verses of Scripture would go round in his head and he would feel despair at the thought of being damned, or hope at the thought of salvation.

Bunyan's life, and many others, reflect that 'we have this

treasure in jars of clay' (2 Cor. 4:7). The treasure of Bunyan's spiritual experience of grace in Christ was received and held in a particular sort of vessel prone to cracks of a common kind. But as with most creative illnesses he did not actually break down, but emerged from his experiences as a robust person who lived a full and useful life as a Christian leader and endured two periods of imprisonment in Bedford gaol. Through his books, especially *Pilgrim's Progress*, Bunyan has exerted a very great influence not only on people of his own day but also on subsequent generations of Christians. The imagery and the teaching of Christian's pilgrimage has become part of popular thinking.

## Some modern examples

In the same way as Bunyan affected the thought of his own generation, so our day has been profoundly affected by the writings of Freud and Jung. Both these men had creative illnesses, well described by Ellenberger and others.

Freud suffered a great deal in his self-analysis (1894–1901), and emerged convinced of his mission to give the world the truth about the unconscious mind as he felt he had discovered it. For him the *Oedipus Complex* was a great truth, not, as many would see it, a concept that was only sometimes useful. While he was struggling with the ideas that made him famous, he felt isolated and suffered much painful distress of mind.

It is typical of creative illness that the person may function well at home and work while still going through much personal suffering in his private world. A similar illness happened in the life of Jung between 1913 and 1919, although he came much nearer madness and psychotic breakdown than Freud. Jung has been most influential among large numbers of people who, like himself, could not accept the importance of sexuality as Freud stated it. The discoveries he made in his period of illness were to be part of his great work until his death at the age of ninety-one.

Such creative illnesses may be compared with the way many healers, mystics and shamans of many traditions and religions come to be accepted as gifted and are given their exalted place in the society where they live. They emerge from their experiences of suffering invigorated and elated, with their personalities transformed. This can happen in the scientific world of physics and chemistry. Bunsen (of 'Bunsen burner' fame), after he discovered spectral analysis during years of painful isolation and distress, was so different a man that he was described as a 'king travelling incognito'.

Such apparent illnesses do not share the features of those artists and writers who have described how psychiatric disorders affect their creative lives. That is a different subject, and a great deal more is known about it than the more special form of creative illness which many biographers write about. All of us, however ordinary and remote from genius we may be, may go through periods of distress which lead to new discoveries and constructive changes.

## Creative encounters

In the biblical narratives no history is as interesting in this connection as that of Jacob, the father of the twelve sons who would in due course found the twelve tribes of Israel. Jacob's history, until he encountered the man who struggled with him in the night at the ford, was that of a cheat who had stolen his brother's birthright. After his wrestling he was given the new name 'Israel'.

> So Jacob was left alone, and a man wrestled with him till daybreak. When the man saw that he could not overpower him, he touched the socket of Jacob's hip so that his hip was wrenched as he wrestled with the man. Then the man said, 'Let me go, for it is daybreak.'

But Jacob replied, 'I will not let you go unless you bless me.'
The man asked him, 'What is your name?'
'Jacob,' he answered.
Then the man said, 'Your name will no longer be Jacob, but Israel, because you have struggled with God and with men and have overcome.'
Jacob said, 'Please tell me your name.'
But he replied, 'Why do you ask my name?' Then he blessed him there.
So Jacob called the place Peniel, saying, 'It is because I saw God face to face, and yet my life was spared.'
The sun rose above him as he passed Peniel, and he was limping because of his hip (Gen. 32:24-32).

Many Christians have had similar critical periods in their lives when they have recognised with hindsight that there has been a spiritual struggle with God. Commenting on this passage, John Calvin explains that it is God who providentially allows us to go through periods of struggle, and that it is with God himself that we wrestle, though we may not fully realise this at the time.

It is important to recognise that what may appear to others to be a time of illness does contain this spiritual encounter. This illness may be termed *creative* because the encounter makes an essential change in those who have lived through it. Jacob the cheat becomes Israel, a prince with God. The measure of the truth and depth of our spiritual struggles is the change they produce in our characters.

Charles Wesley provides a moving commentary on this passage of Scripture in his hymn, '*Come, O thou Traveller unknown*'. He sees it as an experience where the believer knows, more fully than Jacob could know, that at the end of the struggle, '*Thy Nature and Thy Name is Love*'. The point many cannot fit into their scheme of thing is that Jacob was also left with a damaged thigh and a permanent limp. What sort of healing was this? The character may be changed, but there is a permanent handicap

– in this case a physical one. I believe this story is true to life and that the finest, most experienced men of God have to live with a weakness which they accept as God-given.

## Honourable wounds

How is the story of an Old Testament patriarch's struggles relevant to our twentieth-century strains and stresses? Amy Carmichael was a remarkable leader in the Dohnavur Fellowship in South India. She has described the process of coping with stress in the Christian life in many books. In *Gold Cord* she gives an account of the formation of Dohnavur and some of their struggles. One of the poems from this book describes what I mean by honourable wounds in the Christian life:

> Hast thou no scar?
> No hidden scar on foot, or side, or hand?
> I hear thee sung as mighty in the land,
> I hear them hail thy bright ascendant star,
> Hast thou no scar?
>
> Hast thou no wound?
> Yet I was wounded by the archers, spent,
> Leaned Me against a tree to die; and rent
> By ravening beasts that compassed me, I swooned:
> Hast thou no wound?
>
> No wound? no scar?
> Yet, as the Master shall the servant be,
> And pierced are the feet that follow Me;
> But thine are whole: can he have followed far
> Who has nor wound nor scar?

The implication is clear: to follow Christ means suffering and scars. Even when 'worriers become warriors' and cope with the stresses of life well, such struggles usually result in honourable wounds.

Many limp from physical wounds they have sustained in fighting for their country. Every year we are reminded of the honourable wounds sustained by war veterans: those who fought in Word Wars I and II, or in Korea or the Falklands. They may wear medals which remind us of their bloody struggles. We see less of the emotional scars left by such wars, yet these may be more troublesome and lasting in the pain and disability they leave behind. We may recall the shell-shock after World War I or the drug problems after Vietnam. Many have written of the suffering in mental hospitals because of struggles involving not only bodily wounds but also psychological turmoil.

Private, personal and spiritual warfare goes on all the time – there are no Armistice Day reminders of it. Jacob's struggle in the night is repeated in the lives of many good people in our day who come to hospital with depressive breakdowns. Their illness is usually the result of struggling to cope with problems in their own personalities which conflict with the demands of their faith and obedience to God.

When a medical missionary comes home he may find himself profoundly depressed. The conflicting demands of his job in a needy country may have played their part in producing this state of mind. He may have gone out, as one such admirable doctor told me, feeling he could be a boy scout on a grand scale. There is nothing wrong with such a vision of wanting to offer aid to a desperately deprived area – where a mother might die in childbirth without the help that only he can offer. But the local population may have a different view of the mission that the helper from abroad has to fulfil. They may resent the attitudes of the doctor or missionary. Then the personal crises begin to mount with pressures on the marriage and the family. The depressive experience may lead such a doctor to a new view of himself and his work. When he has recovered he may find that his life or personality has been damaged in a definite way. His marriage may be affected. His children may not only resent having been a sacrifice on the altar of his ambition, but be cut off from him for good.

I have known all these things happen to patients who have gone through much spiritual wrestling, and in the fight have sustained honourable wounds. Such men and women recover, but they are left with a limp that may be a private, personal and painful loss of normal functioning in some part of their lives. In some senses, like Jacob, they have prevailed, survived and even succeeded. But there has been a price to pay, and the scars they hide point to their having come through a struggle which has ultimately been between themselves and God. John Bunyan called it 'the merciful kindness and working of God with my soul'. Or in C. S. Lewis' words, 'a severe mercy'.

## Creative tensions
We tend to think of all tensions as harmful and no possible source of good or enjoyment. But some tensions create the possibility of a new and valuable solution.

In the early growth period of childhood and adolescence, patterns of tensions are always being created between the demands of the child and the needs of society and the parents' attempts to meet those needs. Out of the tension comes growth and the gradual learning to adapt, so that aggressive and sexual impulses are controlled and channelled into suitable patterns of living.

Couples and families frequently experience the pull in opposite directions which produce these tensions. When I hear some brothers and sisters discussing in quarrelsome tone, I fear that murder may be done! Yet in such tense settings we learn how to handle feelings of aggression, anger, jealousy and envy. Where the tensions lead to this learning and development they produce a creative solution.

At work and in all professional relationships we cannot get away from conflicting demands, pressures and tensions. To learn to use them to make solutions easier to work out is part of the art of turning the strains into something that can be enjoyed. For many, these conflicts make for setting up intransigent positions where rights are fought for and no constructive resolution of the tensions involved is found.

Christians are called to help with reconciling those who are in conflict, to promote constructive solutions, and to help repair the damage done by demonstrating a loving and caring power. This may be done by listening and by understanding. Even in Christian circles, as Paul told his readers in Phillippi, it is important to agree with one another in the Lord, to be of one mind. How good that the Acts of the Apostles records disagreement and confrontation – this helps us not to despair when we see so much of it in our local Christian groups and churches. We can resolve the tensions creatively, just as such heroes as Simon Peter, Paul or Barnabas did. We must not think of the heroes of the faith as plaster saints but full-blooded men and women like ourselves.

'See how these Christians love one another!' has been turned into an ironic jest whenever deeply religious folk have quarrelled, fought and even killed each other in a 'holy war'. Small groups who share similar beliefs and ideals seem to split very easily: witness the parties in politics of the extreme right or left. To avoid such tendencies with their potential for destruction, isolation and death, we must recognise that the strong tensions that lead to conflict are in us all. The real test of whether our experience of grace works or not is to see if we can show the love and tolerant understanding which may lead to a new and viable solution which does not compromise the beliefs of those who are party to it. Such a struggle may be hard, but it has great potential for joyful achievement.

# 22

## Who Cares?

Teach us to care and not to care
Teach us to sit still
Even among these rocks
Our peace in His will

T. S. Eliot, Ash Wednesday

They made me a keeper of the vineyards, but
Mine own vineyard I have not kept

(Song of Songs 1:6 AV).

It has been said that a psychiatrist is a person with a question for every answer. So to be true to that statement, I conclude with a series of questions intended both to provoke and also to help us avoid Nelson's habit of putting his telescope to his blind eye and thus pretend that the problems did not exist. It is easy to say that stress is just a modern myth, instead of declaring as Christians that it is just another name for the pressures that the Bible refers to as afflictions and tribulations.

### How can I help myself?
I believe that self-help has a valid place in the care of the whole person. The writer of Proverbs tells us: 'Above all else, guard your heart, for it is the wellspring of life' (Prov. 4:23).

Heart in this sense refers to the essential person. In the Christian tradition I learn that to see myself in God's light is not, at first, a pleasant experience. It leads some, like Solomon to speak of 'the plague of his own heart' (1 Kgs. 8:38), or like Wesley, of 'the depths of inbred sin'. Before we meet the remedy in Christ, we have to recognise what is wrong – and this is inevitably painful. It is after the shock of recognising ourselves that we seek forgiveness and new life.

After receiving such knowledge and forgiveness, we come to learn the true meaning of looking after ourselves. We are not to become types or stereotypes, and we must not be brain-washed or steam-rollered. Think of the diverse characters in the New Testament: John, James, Peter and Paul. Their style is their own, for although they all show the hallmarks of holiness, they remain uniquely themselves. As we grow in grace we learn more about ourselves and come to accept more about ourselves. We learn how to apply our Christian faith in our lives and to work out our salvation. The Apostle Paul uses the image of the athlete to describe the process of working out and striving for goals in what can be the sometimes lonely life of the long-distance runner.

It is paradoxical that we have to care for ourselves as well as being willing to deny ourselves. We must take proper care of our whole selves as human beings. We must not neglect our minds and bodies, for they are part of the vessels which contain the treasure of our spiritual lives. Only through these bodies and minds, kept as fit and whole as possible, can our spiritual life find true expression.

## Am I my brother's keeper?
We cannot all love our neighbour in quite the same way. We are not all able to counsel. Our gifts of helping vary, both in the natural and spiritual spheres. But each one of us in some way or other may be called alongside to help someone who is under

strain and stress. One of the best ways we can do this is on a one-to-one basis. To offer friendly, personal help is a neglected duty. As one young woman said to me, describing her difficulties in getting help from her fellow Christians after tragically losing her husband in the first year of marriage, 'Why do my friends have to wear a mask of happiness, and not see me and help me just as a fellow human being?' I felt sad and ashamed, for I too had often looked on such a person as someone to be converted or spiritually edified, not just as a fellow human needing help and comfort first, and only then something more perhaps.

Of course, it may be necessary to rebuke or reproach someone, but never with any hint of threat or bullying, rather with gentleness and respect (1 Pet. 3:15). Even much-praised community care, with all the professional carers in the world, cannot be enough. The individual neighbour, as Luke 10:37 reminds us, is the one who shows mercy. Too often we are not like the good Samaritan, but like those who pass by on the other side. And too often that other side is the church or even the house group.

By learning more about how to help, most Christians will gain in understanding and lose the fear of talking with someone who is distressed. We can then be a source of consolation and support to the many individuals who, in my experience, are usually afraid to show us how anxious or depressed they are. I repeat that we do not always have to be skilled and experienced counsellors, but simply people who can offer some measure of sympathy and practical help.

### Can we care in God's family?

'Home is where the hurt is.' Whoever said that had the fact of many family quarrels to vouch for its truth. Does it go back to Cain and Abel? Rivalry and infighting has been present from the first Christian days, as we can see by reading about the disciples and the early church. When Christians quarrel it is as if they use megaphones in an echoing chamber. Fighting factions today are as much of a standing rebuke as the religious wars of bygone days. Just as bad is the whispering gallery of gossip which we, as Christians, frequently find ourselves trapped in.

To turn away from the fighting and the gossip takes a special grace, an absolute obedience to our call to show love and care to each other in the church. We need constantly to re-learn that we must accept rather than reject or judge someone who needs help or seems weak in various ways. The Apostle Paul is quite clear about this (Rom. 14). Bearing one another's burdens takes many forms: we must each find what we can do in helping the burdened.

We are called to share the freedom and love which Christ has brought to us, and to share it with those who often feel unloved and trapped in a prison of anxious misery. Instead, the church family often seems to be dominated by negative, destructive forces. One such bad influence is legalism. A leader or a group may produce a new code of rules and seek to impose it on others, telling them that unless they accept the new code they are second-class Christians. Where personal freedom to follow Christ is lost, the result is anxious, scrupulous and rather sad people. The experience described in Galatians, shows that this is a recurring problem. Such bondage, or loss of freedom, may be found in the most surprising settings. Being really free as Christians also means being free to care with a spontaneous, loving spirit.

### Is prevention better than cure?

It is fashionable to speak of being immunised against stress, i.e. learning how to deal with minor stresses so we are prepared for major ones. For instance, a child may be given a brief period away from his parents as preparation for longer separations such as going to school. The growing child learns to cope with separation anxiety, and may avoid becoming phobic or having panic attacks. That is one theory, and there is much to commend it.

Does the church have a role in preparing us for life's pressures, and does it offer a survival pack for coping with stress? I believe that many generations have found such a pack in the teachings of the Bible, and the descriptions of people's experiences of God's grace enshrined in many hymns and other accounts. I do not doubt the value of counselling and support: we need much more of it, at different levels of skill, and much more easily available.

I am also convinced that it is in the teaching and preaching function that we, as Christians, find the greatest help in preparing us for life's stresses. This point has been put very clearly by Dr Karl Menninger, an American psychiatrist reflecting on over fifty years of experience in the United States at the Menninger Clinic and elsewhere. In his book *Whatever Became of Sin* Menninger writes:

> Some clergymen prefer pastoral counselling of individuals to the pulpit function. But the latter is a greater opportunity to both heal and prevent. An ounce of prevention is worth a pound of cure, indeed, and there is much prevention to be done for large numbers of people who hunger and thirst after direction towards righteousness. Clergymen have a golden opportunity to prevent some of the accumulated misapprehensions, guilt, aggressive action and other roots of later mental suffering and mental disease.
> How? Preach! Tell it like it is. Say it from the pulpit.[1]

After half a century of work as a psychiatrist, perhaps Dr Menninger has a right to assume the prophet's mantle. I think he expresses a much neglected aspect of the problem.

The underlying theme in many of the chapters of this book has been that we all, as Christians, need to rediscover many

---

1. Karl Menninger, *Whatever Became of Sin?* (New York, Hawthorn, 1975).

neglected doctrines and teachings found in the Bible. Preaching has always been an important part of making these dynamic doctrines become powerful in our lives. The crucible of experience makes these teachings part of our lives. In the past, the informed and prepared Christian mind and the in-depth understanding which results from effective teaching, has helped many people under stress and strain to emerge more than conquerors.

# SUGGESTIONS FOR FURTHER READING

Adams, J. *Competent to Counsel.* Baker: USA, 1970

Balint, M. *The Doctor, His Patient and the Illness.* Pitman Medical: London, 1957 and Tavistock, 1976.

Bowlby, J. *Attachment and Loss 1: Attachment.* Hogarth Press: London 1969, and Penguin: 1971.

Bowlby, J. *Attachment and Loss 2: Separation: Anxiety and Anger,* Penguin: 1973.

Brown, G. W. and Harris, T. *Social Origins of Depression: A study of psychiatric disorder in women.* Tavistock: London 1979.

Cairns, W. T. *The Religion of Dr Johnson.* OUP: London, 1946.

Calvin, J. *The Institutes of the Christian Religion.* First edition 1536. Edited J. T. McNeil, translated by Ford Battles. SCM Press: London, 1961.

Caplan, G. *An Approach to Community Mental Health.* Tavistock: London, 1971.

Cecil, D. *The Stricken Deer: A Life of Cowper,* London, 1984.

Collier, C. *The Twentieth Century Plague.* Lion: Tring, 1987.

Court, J. H. *Pornography: A Christian Critique.* Paternoster: Exeter, 1980.

Dicks, H. V. *Marital Tensions.* Tavistock: 1970.

Dominian, J. *Marriage, Faith and Love.* Collins/Fount: London, 1984.

Edmunds, V. and Scorer, G. *Some Thoughts on Faith Healing.* Christian Medical Fellowship: London, 1979.

Edwards, J. *Religious Affections.* Reprinted by Banner of Truth: London, 1960.

Erikson, E. H. *Young Man Luther.* Faber: London, 1958.

Field, D. *The Homosexual Way: A Christian Option?* Grove Press: Nottingham, 1976.

Foyle, M. F. *Honourably Wounded: Stress Among Christian Workers.* MARC Europe: 1987.

Freud, S. *The Future of an Illusion*: Compete works standard edition, volume XXI. Hogarth Press: London, 1961.

Gilbert, P. *Depression: From Psychology to Brain State.* Lawrence Erlbaum Associates: London, 1984.

Gillett, R. *Overcoming Depression. A Self-Help Guide.* Dorling Kindersley: 1987.

Hallesby, O. *Conscience.* IVP: London, 1950.

Hurding, R. *Roots and Shoots.* Hodder: London, 1986.

Jung, C. G. *Psychological Types.* Routledge Kegan Paul: London, 1924.

La Haye, T. and B. *Act of Marriage.* Marshall Pickering: London, 1984.

Lange, A. and Jakuowski, P. *Responsible Assertive Behaviour.* Research Press: USA, 1979.

Lazarus, R. and Folkman, J. *Stress: Appraisal and Coping.* Springer: London, 1984.

Leech, K. *Soul Friend.* Sheldon Press: London, 1979.

Lloyd-Jones, D. M.
>*Healing and Medicine.* Kingsway Publications: Eastbourne, 1987.
>*Conversions: Psychological and Spiritual.* IVP: 1960.

Maddocks, M. *The Christian Healing Ministry.* SPCK: 1981.

Parkes, C. M. *Bereavement.* Penguin: 1974.

Pierce, C. A. *Conscience in the New Testament.* SCM Press: London, 1955.

Price, V. A. *Type A Behaviour Patterns.* Academic Press: London, 1982.

Sargant, W.
>*Battle for the Mind.* Heinemann: London, 1957.
>*The Mind Possessed.* Heinemann: London, 1973.
>*The Unquiet Mind.* Pan: London, 1971.

Scougal, H. *The Life of God in the Soul of Man.* Christian Heritage: Ross-shire 1996.

Seyle, H. *Stress and Distress.* Pan: London, 1981.

Smedes, L. *Sex in the Real World.* Second Edition. Lion: Tring, 1983.

Stanway, A. *Overcoming Depression: Sympathetic Advice for Sufferers and Their Families.* Arrow: London, 1981.

Tyrer, P. *Stress: Why it Happens and How to Overcome It.* Sheldon Press: London,1980.

Wagner, G. *Barnardo.* Eyre and Spottiswoode: London, 1980.

White, J. *The Masks of Melancholy, A Christian Psychiatrist Look at Depression and Suicide.* IVP: London, 1982.

Wing, J. K. *Reasoning about Madness,* OUP: London, 1978.